MW00768735

TRIUMPHANT WOMANHOOD

Jennifer
Henliken

TRIUMPHANT WOMANHOOD

GOD'S NEVER "WHATEVER"

Jennifer Houlihan

Triumphant Womanhood: God's Never "Whatever"

Copyright © 2015 Jennifer Houlihan

All rights reserved.

ISBN: 1508521212
ISBN 13: 9781508521211
Library of Congress Control Number: 2015902581
CreateSpace Independent Publishing Platform
North Charleston, South Carolina

Extracts from the Authorized Version of the Bible (The King James Bible), the rights in which are vested in the Crown, are reproduced by permission of the Crown's Patentee, Cambridge University Press.

Printed in the United States of America.

"The word of God is quick, and powerful, and sharper than any two-edged sword."

Hebrews 4:12

For Elizabeth, Claire, Maggie and Rebecca
and also for Patrick

TABLE OF CONTENTS

PREFACE

———⌘———

We live in a Biblically illiterate society. This is very dangerous. The Bible addresses every issue that humanity will ever face. But we overlook the Bible and believe it is outdated and completely irrelevant to our modern lives. If we notice the Bible at all, we consider it to be merely a touchy feely emotional thing (pat the sweet, faithful people on the head).

As I recently walked through the streets of Rome, Italy, I was witnessing our nation's past and its possible future. America and all of Western Civilization began in ancient Rome. Christianity spread through ancient Rome. I have written this book with the hope that, in some small way, it might help to prevent our great and powerful nation from being reduced, as was Rome, to one city full of ruins.

The strength of a society hinges in large part upon the degree to which each woman personally understands God. This book was written with affectionate adoration for every woman and girl who is seeking Him. In the first parts of the book, I am talking and God's word is backing me up. The last part is God's word and I am backing Him up.

This is not a parenting or child training book. Many good ones are already out there. When I address the issue of children — and every topic, including beauty — it is ultimately from the standpoint of spiritual warfare. C.S. Lewis said that one of our enemy's ploys is that people will go along with anything if only he can make them laugh.

Right back atcha.

I believe this book contains an Answer to the question everyone today seems to be asking: What can be done for our culture?

Jennifer Houlihan

Part I. Who's Your Daddy?

———✦———

Women can try to be the moon.

Or, we can be the thing that holds the moon in the sky.

CHAPTER 1

MY PARENTS NEVER FIGHT

—— ✦ ——

"Come and see my free car," my friend's boss said with a big smile on his face. At least three guys followed him out the front door. My husband was one of them.

Our family was at my friend Kim's house, celebrating her job promotion. Her boss loves to tell folks about his free car. It's a little electric car, one of those newfangled funky things that runs on a battery charge rather than using any gasoline. They're expensive, but if you lease one and factor in the tax break the government was giving out at the time, and the savings in gas, her boss was just about breaking even with driving this car.

Thanks a lot, Kim.

The day before her party, my husband had been looking at BMWs. He had test driven a brand new BMW. He had been e-mailing me pictures of luxury cars, asking what I thought about the colors. Our oldest child had just turned 16 so we wanted another car. No, our son doesn't get a beamer. He would drive our older truck, and my husband would buy something luxurious and sporty for himself.

Yah baby. Take me out in that Jaguar or Lexus. That's what I'm *talking* about. Visualize my teenage son and me doing a little cabbage patch dance followed by a secret hand shake, then a chest bump with a happy war cry. We were pleased. My husband and I have been driving family truckster kiddie cars our entire married life. With Cheerios scattered on the floor. And a diaper bag plunked down in the back seat. We have been practical and functional about cars and most everything else for nearly 20 years. We needed a midlife crisis car. We deserved a midlife crisis car. I was totally up for the sports car. My husband told me I'd make that black Lexus look good. I agreed.

But ... we've got five children to put through college and some weddings to pay for someday. So just like that, at Kim's party, poof, the sports car idea was gone into thin air like the hard earned money you pay for a gallon of gas, and now we're looking at goofy electric cars. Boxy little futuristic things.

For a little while there, a few days there, my son and I exchanged sympathetic glares with each other, as well as comments under our breath in private moments about the sports car dream's having just been shattered. The cool factor was way gone now for a 16 year old, if we ended up with some squatty ol' electric car. "I was already the homeschooled guy," was his sentiment. "Now I'm the homeschooled electric car guy." I felt his pain, as images of my hair flying in the wind in the silver Mercedes lingered in my mind, my stud husband in his sunglasses taking me somewhere romantic and fun, with the sun setting and jazz music playing. We don't know anyone else who drives some bizarre battery lil golf cart thing. The idea of an electric car was foreign to me and not glamorous. And you cannot find the words Nissan Leaf anywhere in the Bible.

But guess what? The Bible says for wives to follow their husbands in all things. That includes car purchases. I realized I was not following my husband on this issue and, even though I had not said anything to him, I had been crying out for a Lexus on the inside.

So I decided to get on board with the electric car.

I knew that's what I had to do. I was glad that I had not brought my husband down, created stress for him, lessened his enthusiasm or made him question his leadership. I was glad that I had not made a fuss over it. I realized that this very well could have turned into a big ol' argument. Or a lot of little arguments, like a continual dripping of water.

A few years ago, our children were playing with some other children who said something about an argument their parents had. I was stunned and grateful when I overheard my daughter say, "Really? My parents never fight." Wow. I would like to keep that track record. (My husband and I have had our share of tense conflicts that I regret, lest you think we are perfect.)

Whatever ideas or plans our husbands have, those need to become our ideas and plans. That's our job as Godly women. We wives need to mold ourselves to our husbands, we need to follow along behind our men, on every issue, like a family of ducks happily walking along in line. Not because we're weak or can't think for ourselves, but the opposite. We are strong and smart enough to do it God's way. It takes wisdom and strength not to pout or squawk about getting your own way.

Arguing is weakness, because it's easy.

Following is strength, because it's hard.

What a silly thing like a car to become an area of contention in my marriage anyway. It's a big hunk of metal that transports you around. Who really cares? I decided that I'm all about this electric car now. I'm excited. We went and looked at one and they're cute. They're actually really nice. Prepare yourselves ladies: they have a heated steering wheel. That's right, you heard me. We're going to close the deal on one soon. It's brilliant not to have to spend money on gas. With a car like that, we can scoot out and buy one banana if we feel like it. Then laugh, high five and drive back to the store to buy another banana, just for fun.

The electric cars are comfortable, and my husband is very smart to get one. I love him more for it. He is putting his family and our future before his own pleasure or ego. If he were single he could probably have two flashy sports cars and a boat by now. But he's a devoted family man. I would not stop loving him if we bought a shiny new BMW. I would be on board with that too. But I love that we're getting an electric car. I love it all day long.

WHERE'S THE SPORTS CAR?

Well now wait just a second there, missy.

Hold up.

To say something on the cover of a book about triumphant? And then this crazy lady is writing some chapter about how awesome it was not to get her way. Smiling about some dorky car she didn't even want. At least the "whatever" part on the cover is right. Where's the part about getting the luxury car after all? Where's that chapter? That's not a happy ending.

I hear you. We'll get back to womanly joy and how that's working for us but for now, here is what drives me not to care what I drive.

Adam and Eve ruined it for all of us the way it works on a sports team. If the quarterback and the linebackers and the kicker all give it their best and play with perfect precision in a game, but the punkleguards mess it up then the whole team loses. Sorry, I ran out of positions, and I am proud to announce that I finally understand what a first down is, after five years of explaining from the men in my life. Girls? "Downs" means "chances."

So, the way it works in a football game is each player doesn't get his own score. The whole team wins or loses. Same thing with the fall of man in the Garden of Eden. All of humanity became unworthy to live eternally when Adam and Eve disobeyed. Actually it was Adam who disobeyed, while Eve was off the deep end about some fruit and knowledge tangent. Adam is to blame. One man.

We get to go to heaven if we believe that Jesus came down here to Earth and took the punishment for our personal sins. He came to clean up Adam's mess. Again, it's a collective thing. One man can fix it. He came for everyone, but we each have to put our trust in it. We have to receive it individually. We each have to respond actively and personally to His coming, by acknowledging that we are sinful and in need of a savior. That's how we get our salvation. His leaving heaven, which is paradise beyond what we can begin to imagine, to come down here to deal with us would be like our choosing to skip out on a free, seven-day cruise with our man to go to work scrubbing bathrooms for less than minimum wage instead.

Nothing wrong with that job, mind you. I'm proud of ladies who aren't afraid to work hard to pay the bills. I actually did that job when I was a lifeguard back in the teeny bopper day. I was ready to twirl my whistle around, chew gum and sit on the lifeguard stand wearing sunglasses. On the first day of work, the boss lady started showing me around the bathrooms and telling me how to clean them. "Excuse maaay?" I thought to myself. "I'm the lifeguard, not the, like, bathroom cleanahhh."

I did that job because I had to – and I do that job now in my own home, out of love for my family. Christ chose to humble Himself. God came here in the flesh as Jesus Christ to come deal with us and what a mess we all are because He loves us so much, just as we love our children enough to get up from a romantic dinner to tend to the baby. Mothers don't have that hard a time getting this concept of how much God loves us once we relate it to our own children and then instantly understand the fierce adoration and genuine sacrifice. It's a universal mom thing. All women have within us this mothering instinct, which, if we don't have children we bestow on that precious niece or nephew, or on that sweet kitty or dog. So, all women, children or not, get what I'm saying. Someone is our baby.

We're God's baby. His son Jesus came to Earth and then willingly died for our sins, having no sin Himself, when He allowed himself to be crucified on the cross. I'm not even that willing to take some other driver's speeding ticket that he deserves, much less die for him. But that's how much He loves us.

Outside in the yard one day, I was staring at fire ants crawling around in the dirt. They scurry around busily and, buddy, watch out if you get too close because it feels like 450 sticks of dynamite are exploding on your foot if a few of those little suckers bite you. Just think what they could do to you if you became their size. As I was watching them march around doing their ant thing, and trying not to make them mad or let them notice me, I thought of our savior Jesus Christ and how He in His greatness became as a tiny ant, placing Himself among terrifying, mean little predators who He knew would eventually hang Him on a cross. He did this for you and me.

We are all sinful and deserving of punishment. I sure do wish we were always sweet and good, but it's just not so. Deep down everyone possesses quite the yuck. It's okay to realize this about ourselves, because we don't have to fix it. Christ bore the punishment that we deserve. The only way to get to heaven is to get that. Not merely to believe it because, I mean even a villain can believe it, but to trust your life with it.

CHAPTER 2

PURPOSE

———— ∞ ————

It's not that Christians are judgmental about other religions. It's just that we see the futility in them. I don't hate anyone who tries to put his house key into his car ignition. I simply see that it is not going to work. No other religion besides Christianity is going to get you to heaven, later. No other religion is going to give you the joy you're looking for in this life, now. It's not narrow-minded. It's just true.

How can we trust Christianity over other religions? Second Corinthians 5:5 says that God *"hath given us the earnest of the Spirit."* When you buy a house, if you don't pay cash for it, then you give a down payment. This passage is telling us that the Holy Spirit is our down payment from God, it is our guarantee, our earnest that we have eternal life. It's our promise.

I believe that the Book, the Bible, is the divinely inspired word of God. So if Paul wrote it, that's God writing it. If the prophet Isaiah or Daniel said it, God said it.

Can we prove that the Bible is the divinely inspired word of God? No, we really can't. We weren't there when it was written so we don't know. Even if we were there, we could never be sure those writer guys with their scrolls and togas weren't just wackos, scribbling out maps for missile launches off the coast of Crete in Hebrew code. But in 2 Timothy 3 the Bible claims to be the inspired word of God, and so we have a choice. We can believe what the Bible says about itself is true, or we can believe what the Bible claims is false. And so it is a matter of faith, a matter of belief, and a matter of logic in that, which is more likely? That the Bible contains lies or truth? If we haven't read the Bible all the way through, then we can't make an educated decision on that — it's nothing but a *Green Eggs and Ham* opinion. I've read it, and I'm going with truth.

In the year 1811, a father wrote this in a letter to his son: "No book in the world deserves to be so unceasingly studied, and so profoundly meditated upon as the Bible." For example, this father said, "the book of Ecclesiasticus contains more wisdom than all the sayings of the seven Grecian sages." This father, like us, believed that it is difficult to prove that the Bible is the divinely inspired word of God. But he said strong evidence is that the truth contained in the Bible has remained to this day as the rules of faith of every enlightened nation. How is that possible? He said this of the scriptures: "it is their intrinsic excellence which has preserved them." [1]

The father who wrote those words was John Quincy Adams, sixth president of the United States of America and son of John and Abigail Adams.

Jesus said, *"Ego sum via et veritas et vita,"* meaning, *"I am the way and the truth and the life,"* John 14:6. He then said that no one can come to God except through Him. He's the way. In Latin, "via" means "road" or "way." Jesus is the via. He's the path to heaven, y'all. My husband gets to work via I-85. We get to heaven via Jesus. He is also the truth. Ancient philosophers like Plato and Socrates were all about finding the truth. They were almost there. So close. Bless their hearts. They sometimes even said things like: We are beginning to believe there must be one all good, powerful and unchanging being that's holding everything together. Those guys did acknowledge a God and so I think if they had had access to a Bible they would have loved it. Scripture would have blown their minds. It would have fit in all the missing pieces of the jigsaw puzzle of truth they'd been working on their whole lives. We have the truth; we have access to it in the Bible. We have what the ancient smartie britches philosophers didn't have. If we are wise we will read it.

So Jesus is the way, He is the truth, and that last part about His being the life is way cool because, how it is written in Latin can be thought of like this: Jesus is where we find our life. Jesus = life. Or, we can sigh happily as if floating sleepily on a soft raft in a blue ocean while saying, "Man, this Christianity thing is the life."

That's why I don't really care if I ever have a fancy sports car. Christ is the joy in my life. Everywhere we look, we see all around us people who are seeking to find their *way*, they might be resisting the *truth*, but it's the only way to *life*. That sentence is sounding a little Joel Osteen, but there it is.

TAKING THE BIBLE LITERALLY

A common objection to taking the Bible seriously goes something like this: "The Bible is ridiculous nonsense. It's full of peculiar stuff like fire on altars, floods, burning bushes and sacrificed goats. Only an idiot would apply that to daily life."

I agree with that last sentence.

Let's compare the Bible to a favorite cookbook. The author tells us that at age 8 she came to love cooking as she stood beside her sweet and kind grandmother, who smiled and let the author chop cucumbers. Along with recipes, the author explains her favorite methods, what she's learned as she has traveled to different countries and how she keeps her kitchen stocked. She tells some fascinating stories about utensils and ingredients. She might, for example, tell us that basil was first used possibly 4,000 years ago in Egypt for embalming. Ew. Later, after gladiators did their gladiator fighty-killing thing, it is believed that basil would appear. In medieval times, people thought basil was so sacred that they placed it around temples.[55]

That is all very interesting. Name one person who would throw that cookbook down and say: "This cookbook is absurd. If I'm going to make her basil focaccia bread, I'm going to have to embalm somebody with basil and then kill someone in a gladiator ring before I go to Greece and smear some basil leaves on a temple. This book is cuh-razy."

No one says that. Why? It's because we universally understand that a cookbook contains two categories:

1. History
2. Instructions

So does the Bible. I take the Bible literally. I literally believe that some mighty bizarre stuff went down. I also literally believe that sometimes the Bible is instructing us personally on how we ought to live. Cookbooks very clearly separate the history from the instructions. The Bible tends to mix the two together. The fascinating challenge, especially for anyone who enjoys a good puzzle or riddle, is to study the Bible for a lifetime and gradually decipher the difference.

A DECISION

If we believe all this Bible talk about Christ and savior action is more than just historical fact and that it has meaningful value for us personally, then we have a decision to make. Throughout all of history, after the fall of man, all people have been faced with the question of whether they are perfectly complete and without need of God just as they are, or whether deep down they know all is not quite right without Him. The decision is whether they want to continue being on the throne of their lives, or if they see that it would be better for Jesus Christ to be on the throne. It's the decision Saint Augustine came to understand as he poured out his *Confessions* around 400 AD. It looks something like this.[52]

Wretchedness of Self   Life in Christ

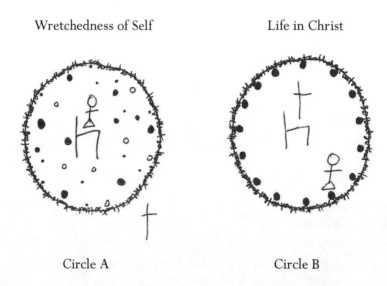

Circle A   Circle B

It's very simple but very important. We all start out being born into circle A. This is not our fault. We were stuck in there at birth. The dots represent every relationship, issue, challenge or problem in our lives. The dots could be given names such as money, beauty, marriage, drugs, sensuality, bullying, divorce, children, weight, painful relationships, and strife. Well look-ey there. Those are the names of the chapters in this book.

When we are sitting on the throne of our lives, all of that is a big jumbled up, chaotic mess. It takes a while to realize that our being in the wretched circle is the problem. We think the confusion and chaos have some other explanation for a while, but we eventually must realize the problem is that we're in charge of our lives and ought to give up control to the Lord Jesus Christ.

When we decide that we want Christ to be on the throne, we release all authority to Him and are only too happy to have Him wrestle with all those miserable dots that have been causing us to be weary and troubled for so long. We are prompted by the Holy Spirit to see all of this clearly for the first time. That's our born again experience because, having been born into circle A, we ask to start all over again with circle B. God's like, word up sistah, welcome aboard. I was almost 30 years old before I was able to admit that I needed God to be on the throne of my life. That's okay. He is ready and waiting.

It's not necessarily a big dramatic, loud thing where the Praise Jesus choir is singing in the background while thunder and hail rain down upon us. Nothing spectacular like that needs to happen. More like: mascara running down into our cup of coffee. Exhaustion from being trapped in wretchedness brings us to the point where we look at the circle with Jesus Christ on the throne and we say, "I want that one."

Someone simply needs to say quietly in her heart, "I don't want to do it by myself any more, God. I need You to be in charge of my life." At that very moment, her name is then written in the book of life and she gets to go to heaven when she dies. It would be lovely for us all to do exactly as we please, keep ourselves on the throne, be a nice person, have interesting opinions that are contrary to scripture and still go to heaven and also have true joy in this life. But that isn't the way it works. So you say, "I want that one." And it's yours.

———⊶⊷———

LIFELONG VICTORY: HINDUISM AND YOGA?

We don't eat one meal and for the next 75 years say, "No thanks, I'm good." The same is true for a life in Christ. After the moment of salvation, we are prone to wander, as the sweet old hymn goes.

Nothing can ever send us back to that wretched first circle.

I can't emphasize that enough. Ladies, we are forever in the other circle, safe and sound with Christ on the throne.[44] We get to go to heaven and that's that. But it's those pesky dots inside the circle that can bring us down. Those dots are the reason why some people who claim to be Christians are mean as snakes. They asked to switch circles and then went back to living in their own strength. And they aren't paying any attention to their manual, the Bible. Just as we don't put gas in our car one time and keep going forever, or for us fashionably modern electric drivers, the battery charge doesn't last forever, we have to refuel or recharge. In the same way, we must continually release control to God on a daily basis. If we are going to do this successfully, we have to understand why we are even alive.

Jesus said whoever chooses to lose his life will actually find it (Luke 17:33). People do not always stop and evaluate what their purpose in life is. Well, other than mischievous philosophy professors who love to stir us all up. Except for those guys. We all walk around with a list of assumptions in our minds. If people stopped and thought about it a while, they might say something like: "I want to be a good person. I want to enjoy happy relationships and be successful in worldly pursuits. I want a happy family. I want a happy life."

We can say all of that, but it won't ever fully satisfy if it is outside of the Biblical context. The only thing that satisfies in the full sense is to surrender our lives to the Lord Jesus Christ, and once that has been done, to honor Him by living within the plan He lays out for us.

Now we need to know the real God because people throw around the word "God" a lot. Hinduism, for example, is an eastern religion that talks about "God." Its teachings are arguably quite peaceful, and yet, with all respect, those who practice Hinduism are still ultimately without hope because they are without Christ. The goal of Hinduism is self-realization.[37] To that I say: observe any 18-month-old child. Pretty sure we are each highly accomplished in the self-realized category at birth. Christianity, on the other hand, says our goal in life is to glorify God and seek to know – to realize – Him instead. Hinduism says the way to get to heaven is through sacrifice. Christianity says that the way to heaven is through Jesus Christ, who quoted the Old Testament when He said, *"Go and find out what this means: 'I desire mercy rather than sacrifice.'"* Matthew 9:13.

Hinduism says the enemy is wrath. Christianity says that the real, true God becomes rightly full of wrath at His stubborn, rebellious children and that the enemy is evil. Hinduism says that the world contains demi-gods. Christianity says that we all have equally fallen short of the glory of God. Hinduism says all of this and then claims to be about "God" and "the Lord." It even refers to itself as "scripture."[37] That is a lot like handing someone a rotten banana and calling it candy. It is not candy just because you say the word candy.

Many people are being confused and led astray – and possibly led to roll a joint – by the Hindu religion, even heavy hitting writers such as Henry David Thoreau, whose work has influenced Western education. This eastern belief system is also the basis for the popular stretchy-exercise yoga, which is influencing women all over our nation. The word "yoga" comes from Sanskrit and means "to join," or "to yoke," as in, joining mind, body and spirit in harmony together. Well, what do you know? Jesus talked about some yoke Himself when He said in Matthew 11:29, *"Take my yoke upon you,"* because His burden is easy.

He is telling us the truth which is that His yoke, His way is the only path to joy and happiness. Cain't no stretchy-fying and breathing deeply give us none-o-that. The concept that yoga could be relaxing is not necessarily a huge threat to humanity though. When someone enjoys a cup of coffee with a friend, or goes fishing, or takes a bubble bath, we don't all panic and shout: It wasn't Jesus, it wasn't Jesus, can't be relaxing.

Still, we have to address the eastern influence of yoga. We Christians were supposed to have abandoned all that when Western Civilization was established in ancient Rome. In 2 Kings, God really does become quite wroth when we burn incense and pay homage to funky statues and images. Moses's brother Aaron did respectfully burn incense to the real God and that was cool. But in later Old Testament times in Judah and Israel (and that's what you might call The East), a God-fearing king would come along, and the first thing he would do was to get rid of all that incense and statue nonsense that was for pretend gods. Then the next wicked king brought the incense and statues back. The next, even more wicked king would burn even more incense and put up even more wacky statues, then the next good king would honor God and get rid of it all. Back and forth it went.

We can take all of that to mean that, when it comes to incense and statues? God doesn't play.

Albert Mohler, president of The Southern Baptist Theological Seminary, said that "yoga begins and ends with an understanding of the body that is, to say the very least, at odds with the Christian understanding."[50] Only if you want it to, sir. Only if you want it to. King David from the Bible danced with all his might before the Lord after all, and he wasn't going zen on anybody.

I think what Dr. Mohler means is that the concept of mind, body and spirit are the right equation, but the eastern religiously influenced yoga people are plugging the wrong values into their variables. We have three forces working together here, "tri" meaning "three," where we get the word Trinity. God is the mind (Creator and Father) + Son is the body (Jesus said, *"this is my body broken for you"*) + Holy Spirit (um, that's the spirit.) So the yoga people are on the right track actually, but they are confused because they don't know the Bible. If we don't know the Bible, we won't fully understand why we are alive.

----- ∞ -----

WHY WE ARE ALIVE

We know that other things in the world have a purpose to fulfill. We can say easily enough that a fireplace is for fires, a flute is to make music, and fried okra is for people who aren't me to eat. It's crazy talk for any of those objects to try and switch jobs with the others. Let's apply that principle to women and what do we get? Something that we misunderstand and therefore reject. All through-out the Bible, we see that our purpose in life is to bring glory to God. That's true for everyone, ladies and gents. The way that God has specifically planned for women to bring Him glory is in a supporting role. In Genesis, God said that He made people to be distinctly male and female, and that He created a woman to be a helper to a man.

Somewhere along the way, the next few verses in the Bible actually, which is to say from the beginning of time, women decided this purpose was not their idea of fun and have been striving against it ever since. The supporting actress Oscar award isn't what we had in mind. Instead of giving a gracious and endearing thank-you speech, we toss the Oscar trophy into the trash and say, "I wanted the lead."

Many men who want to be uber cool and modern have, from the beginning of time, said that it is sewwwwww old fashioned for a woman to be a helper. When men say this, they are only as cutting edge as the very first man because it's what Adam said when he gave in to Eve. She brought him the forbidden fruit, told him she figured out some stuff that God didn't know and Adam said: Mmkay.

When we speak of a support or help role, this is not an insult. It is not treachery. It is an admirable, urgent job.

A helper:

- Lends strength
- Relieves
- Changes for the better
- Cures
- Gives aid
- Contributes to a cause
- Delivers from difficulty or distress
- Advances a greater purpose
- Supplies something that is needed

When we take on a role of support, we are:

- Upholding
- Sustaining
- Keeping something from falling
- Becoming a foundation
- Maintaining another
- Preserving from sinking or falling
- Keeping something from languishing or failing
- Becoming a pillar, a comforter, an advocate and a defender who helps another to carry on

Anyone who finds those breathtakingly inspirational descriptions of "helper" and "supporter"[47] to be a downer, must dislike within them the idea of anyone's being involved but one's own self. If we find the idea of helping someone else humiliating or beneath us, then we are apt to say that helping is weakness or inferiority. But that is the opposite of the truth. In fact, it is in the absence of help where we find inability, the state of being destitute like a newborn baby, without strength. Indeed one is, in fact, helpless.

Women misunderstand this and try to trade in their support job for leadership instead. Have we even thought through this objection? Is leadership more worthy than supporting? God said we are to be a helper and that is good enough reason, but let's think about the alternative.

Here is leadership:

- To go first and show the way
- To conduct and guide
- To exercise dominion
- To have precedence
- To direct

That's some pretty cool sounding stuff. I guess. But the job of leadership does not contain more power than the jobs of helping and supporting. If it is power we are after then the job of supporter contains about four gallons of it compared to the teaspoon of power in our description of leadership. Within the definition of leadership is also the necessity of living for someone besides one's own self. So there's no more selflessness to be found in either job.

If it isn't actually great power we are after, then women at least ought to clamor for equality, the thinking goes. What's that all about? Equality means being the same, having the same magnitude or proportion, we think it means having the same value, it certainly means having the same qualities and conditions. We are asking for justice, similar rights and advantages. We think equality will give us the same terms or benefits. We think equality will make us achieve being adequate and will show that we are competent. We'll have dignity because the scales will be even.

But God just told us in Genesis that men and women are not the same. He did not say, "male and male He created them." Or, if we try to even things out by emasculating men, we notice He did not say, "female and female He created them." And so, in trying to even the scales, women are grasping at something that can never be reached. We cannot successfully defy this absence of sameness any more than we can defy God's physical laws such as gravity. Seeking dignity and value is understandable and right. Our omniscient Heavenly Father lays out in scripture for us how to attain these things. Going around Him to get there is insanity.

Then it must come to the part about not being first that makes us suspicious. The idea of dominion or rank becomes, well, rank to us. It troubles us to have something or someone to follow. Should women then spend our energy and our very lives elbowing our way to the front of the water fountain line? Is fighting to be first in line really what we want? Whom have we beaten down and destroyed as we plow past and trample everyone, and what does it even matter if we ever got to the front of the line? It all amounts to exalting ourselves higher than God intends for us to be.

This is a lot like a ladybug fluttering her wings menacingly at a tiger. It's a lifetime of unsuccessfully fighting to move around the chaotic dots of our wretched circle and insisting that we can do it ourselves. All that is needed is to give up the throne of our lives to Christ and then trust that He knows very well how to make every dot fall into place. God's purpose for women is to glorify Him in the role of supporter. To defy God's plan is to defy God. As long as women ignore Him while seeking sameness or superiority, we have abandoned our purpose in life and are doing nothing but beating the air.

BUT WAIT

"Are you saying a woman's only purpose in life is a husband?" You might ask. What if a wife has a job or hobby that she loves? She can't sit around and gaze at her husband all day long. What if she pours her heart into a ministry or volunteer work? Is there no purpose in that because it's not wife-ish? Is that of no use to God? Yeah and while we're at it, what if someone isn't married? She can't exactly propose to herself. Does this mean she's an outcast among the Bible chicks? What if her dear husband has died? Can't be in the God club anymore? What if her marriage ended painfully in divorce? What then? She has no purpose in life?

The short answer is: y'all sure do ask some good questions. The long answer is: please think of a delicious soup. My mind would wander to a warm Thai coconut soup that has green onions and mushrooms floating around in it. I love this simple but tasty soup. It makes me happy. All your interests, hobbies and work that have nothing to do with a husband represent the soup. Now what is the one thing we take for granted but is necessary to enjoying this soup?

The bowl. Your husband is the bowl, ladies. Everything a wife does and is, must be kept in the strong safety of the husband framework, in order for her life to serve its true purpose. Without the bowl, all our efforts and striving will eventually amount to a great big useless mess. For ladies who are not married, Isaiah 54:5 gives us the answer when it says, *"God is thy husband."*

For girls, God tells children very clearly in the Bible to be obedient to their parents. So God will guide unmarried ladies into the area where He desires their help.

The world screams at us every day to follow our own desires without stopping to ask what our leadership thinks. A certain unattractive arrogance is within that outlook. I am whispering quite the opposite to you. It might sound like way too much trouble to take God, parents or a husband into consideration. But women and girls would be wise to take to heart this passage[30] in Isaiah 47, which says, *"Your wisdom and knowledge mislead you when you say to yourself, 'I am, and there is none besides me.'"* To carry out our own interests independently of our husbands and against their wishes, or for single ladies without acknowledging God, is about as smart as ordering our favorite soup at a restaurant and then saying to the waiter, "Sir, I don't need a bowl."

CHAPTER 3

FEAR AND TRUST: ISLAM VS. CHRISTIANITY

People get a little squirmy when you throw out the "S" word, as in Satan. Say that slowly with a really deep voice. Say-tannn. So stick with me. Roll with me and let's agree that forces of evil are out there. Jesus is the good guy, so there must be a bad guy.

When I rise each day I try to remember to say something like this to my Father in heaven: "My life is yours, God. I'm up for anything You have for me." I'm not getting sappy on you now. This is for real. This is not, oh the sky is so pretty and the butterflies are landing on the flowers today. I'm seriously telling you that when we trust God with each hour, that turns into trusting God with our day, and that turns into trusting Him with our life.

In summer of 2014, our nation first began to fight the violent, merciless Islamic State terrorist group known as ISIS. Of course, we know from the book of Genesis that the religion of Islam is not new and, in fact, originated with Abraham's son Ishmael whose name means "he will hear God." The Judeo-Christian religion came from Abraham's other son Isaac, whose name means "he laughs." Which one sounds like the obedient child who is happy? Yes, the Bible says God ordained Isaac, not Ishmael, to be the father of His anointed people. Isaac's son was Jacob and was later called Israel. As in, the nation of Israel. The tension and strife between Ishmael's and Isaac's religious groups are as old as the Bible. Ishmael's descendants are now the basis of Arabian culture, and Isaac's descendants are the foundation of the

Judeo-Christian belief system found in Western cultures such as the United States. Isaac and his son Israel are direct ancestors of Jesus Christ.

This is not my interesting little theory. It's all in the fourth chapter of Galatians, in which the apostle Paul (he's a post-Jesus guy) writes about *"two covenants"* from Abraham's two sons, the one from Hagar and Arabia *"gendereth to bondage"* and *"answereth to Jerusalem."* The terms Islam and Christianity are not in the Bible – they came later – but what Paul means by Ishmael's answering to Jerusalem is that Islam will have to answer to Christianity because Jesus was crucified there, just outside the city walls. I like the sound of not being on Hagar's and Ishmael's team. Paul agrees when he says, *"We, brethren, as Isaac was, are the children of the promise,"* once we have yielded our lives to Christ. *"We are not children of the bondwoman, but of the free."*

Why do we care about all of that? Well, we are being given a compelling reason to be glad we are adopted into Isaac's lineage (born into it if Jewish) when we embrace Christianity instead of other religions that are in extreme contradiction to the Bible. The Islamic State is one of the most horrifying religious sects in all of history. At the time of this writing there are approximately two million refugees in the Middle East because of ISIS.[46]

When I read the Koran, which is the teaching of Islam, here is my first thought: "There, there. Someone needs a hug." This book is one very long rant. The Koran is so vastly different from the Bible that I hardly know where to begin. It is believed to have been written by Ishmael's descendant Muhammad a couple hundred years after the Bible was completed. Well, to be more accurate, the words were said out loud by Muhammad and someone else wrote them down for him because he did not know how to read or write. This means he had never read the Bible. He might have liked it.

The Koran speaks of the "superiority of men" over women. The Bible, on the other hand, says that everyone is equally flawed, that God is our authority, and that *"no one can serve two masters"* Matthew 6:24. A man, then, is not seen by Christians as his wife's authority, only as his family's leader.

More disturbing is Islam's hatred toward "infidels." That would be me. Anyone who is not a Muslim, especially Jews and Christians, is called an ungrateful infidel. Personally, if I had written the Koran I would chill on the exclamation points. The shrill hysteria really comes through. Don't take my word for it. Decide for yourself. Here are some excerpts from the Koran. "God loveth no infidel, or evil person." Well now, that group contains all of us including Muhammad, unless we have some sort of a savior, and God loves us all enough to have sent us One. But the Koran gets pretty bent out of shape about anyone trusting in "Jesus, the son of Mary," as it is careful to call Him, not the son of God.

The Koran says, "And they say, 'God hath a son.' No!"

Anyone who disagrees with them really has it coming. "Infidels shall suffer a grievous punishment!" the Koran says, "a cruel chastisement," and "O believers! retaliation for bloodshedding is prescribed to you." Here is the reward for infidels: "Kill them wherever ye shall find them." The Koran actually says don't kill anyone whom God tells you not to kill, "unless for a just cause." In which case, let that person "taste the torment." Jesus says the opposite in Matthew 5:44: *"Love your enemies, bless them that curse you."* As for "hypocrites" and "men of tainted heart," the Koran says, "cursed wherever they are found; they shall be seized and slain with slaughter!" The Koran says their faces shall be "rolled in the Fire," "we could sink them into that earth," "if We please, we drown them," and "no helper shall they find!" It just does not stop, the entire book talks junk about the infidels: "On their necks have We placed chains," and "Couldst thou see how they shall tremble and find no escape?"[24] I could not bear to put in print some of the more savage examples. This punishment of infidels is not merely an unfortunate attribute of Islam. It is Islam.

One of the creepiest aspects of the Koran is that sprinkled throughout all of its unstable threats toward the people who "await but a single blast," is the promise that whoever obeys "indulgent, merciful God! with great bliss shall he be blessed." And, "One blast shall there be, and lo! ... Joyous on that day shall be the inmates of Paradise."

Am I the only one who thought of the September 11, 2001 terrorist attacks in New York just then? I'd say ISIS comes as no surprise.

There is plenty of violence in the Bible, yes, in the Old Testament. But in the Bible, the bad guys are the ones doing everything the Koran suggests will please God – actually Allah. No idea who that is. In the Bible, the good guys do often fight back, but the comfort is always that God – the real God – is ultimately in charge of any avenging and He is quite grieved about it. In the Koran, the Muslims do the punishing for Him. And they seem rather to enjoy it.

The Koran calls Islam "the Baptism of God." The most crucial difference between the Bible and the Koran is the crucifixion of Jesus in the New Testament and foretold in the Old Testament because through that event, God provided us a way out, an Answer, an end to any need for the chastisement that Islam so deliciously craves. They want every last one of us and that is not paranoia, it is straight out of the Koran: "Lord, leave not one single family of infidels on the earth."

The Islamic State is highly motivated by the chilling, twisted belief that through its barbaric actions it will bring about the apocalypse.[46] My, that is some goal. No wonder ISIS is going all black-ops on us as if there is no tomorrow. The Bible, in contrast, teaches that the end times will happen when we least expect it, that no one can know when that will be and our job is to sit tight and glorify God while we wait.

Because I know the Bible, I am not afraid of ISIS. If we want to know what will eventually happen to the world, it is all right there in the book of Revelation. The very idea that mankind is able to do anything to hasten an apocalypse is amusing. *"Hast thou an arm like God? Or canst thou thunder with a voice like him?"* God says in Job 40. *"Where wast thou when I laid the foundations of the earth?"* He asks. *"Hast thou commanded the morning?"* and *"Gavest thou the goodly wings unto the peacocks?"* or *"Hast thou given the horse his strength?"* and *"Doth the eagle mount up at thy command?"* or *"Wilt thou disannul my judgment? Wilt thou condemn me, that thou mayest be righteous?"* and *"Have the gates of death been opened unto thee?"*

God has quite a sense of humor, and He asks us in Job 41: Will a massive sea creature *"make a covenant with thee? Wilt thou play with him as with a bird?"* There is nothing to say in reply to these questions that go on for three solid chapters of the Bible except that a group such as ISIS cannot prevail.

Now I understand not everyone in the faith of Islam is devoted to beheadings, bombings and forced slavery. Many Muslims are kindhearted, productive citizens who practice Islam peacefully. But the Koran is still their book.

Whether they personally carry out grievous punishments of infidels or not, when they profess to be a Muslim, they are saying all of that is okay. They don't have to. No one can stop a Muslim or anyone else from silently choosing instead to become a follower of Jesus Christ. At that moment, he or she is no longer a Muslim and will have been grafted into Isaac's family where grace and love and truth and beauty and life will be found.

We go there with Islam vs. Christianity to demonstrate that Abraham's and Sarah's lineage is a powerful example of what happens when we give in to fear and stop trusting God's plan.

Abraham's wife Sarah had had all she could take of sitting around waiting for this special descendant whom God had promised years earlier. They were growing old and had never been able to have any children. Sarah got good and fed up and stopped trusting God. She began to despair that she and Abraham would ever have this baby, so she got an idea that is way beyond my personal comfort zone. Sarah was all: Hey Abraham, here is my handmaid Hagar. You can go get cozy with her in one of those tents over there, and she will then have this alleged special baby of yours that we are never going to have if we keep surrendering this situation to God. Apparently Abraham said yes dear to Sarah and hey baby to Hagar – I find that very weasly – because nine months later, Hagar bore Abraham a son. Who was that fellow? It was Ishmael, the father of the Islamic faith and ancestor of Muhammad.

Here is Sarah's hit the forehead moment. A few years after Ishmael was born, God did what He promised He would do all along, and Sarah conceived a baby of her own with Abraham. Who was that child? He was Isaac, the father of the Judeo-Christian faith and ancestor of Jesus.

These are the two legacies left behind by Abraham and Sarah. When we ladies, like Sarah and Eve before her, take charge in our personal lives and try to go around God? And our husbands display a wimpy lack of leadership in response? We end up with disastrous circumstances that, in Ishmael's case, have created ripples of violence and unrest throughout history and we are still suffering those consequences today.

I am not suggesting that all married couples must sit in rocking chairs and stare at each other until they are in their 90s, wishing and hoping for a baby and not doing anything to make that happen. I am pointing out, rather, that Abraham and Sarah specifically defied God's very clear plan for them by not sitting tight and waiting for Him to act.

Sarah did so well with trusting God when she was younger, as we will hear later. We can truly admire her womanly example in many ways. But as she grew older, she became fearful. She began to grow weary of her once bright-eyed, trusting nature. Ladies, we don't get to graduate from child-like trust in God. Eventually Sarah did return to acting on faith though because the book of Hebrews says through her faith Isaac was conceived. So Ishmael was a lapse of trust. One trickle-down effect from him created my own lesson in fear and trust this past summer.

In a recent go-round, Isaac's team, Christian Kurds in Northern Iraq, had been driven from their homes by Ishmael's team, ISIS, into the hills of Sinjar Mountain while my husband was deployed to the Middle East for our nation's military in the summer of 2014. The United States Air Force sent cargo planes to fly over Iraq and drop supplies to the Kurdish people. The following is what I wrote while he was away.

My husband is flying a humanitarian airdrop mission into Iraq right now. The bottled water and food from his C-130 crew are the answer to prayer for hungry and thirsty Christians driven from their homes by ISIS. I wonder if the bad guys in Iraq will try to stop him.

I sit on my front porch in Georgia watching neighborhood traffic and I wish all the cars would stop driving back and forth as if everything is normal. I want to shout at them but it comes out as a whisper.

My 5-year-old daughter likes it when I read a book to her from when I was a little girl. It's titled *The Daddy Book* and it's out of print now. When I have finished reading, I close the book and she says, "I used to have a daddy. But he's lost." That is my worry. Some things are worse than death. I know that my husband has been highly trained to meet the enemy face to face, though he doesn't talk to me about that. I tell him that I am waiting for him. I need him to know that

I.
Am.
Waiting.

I sit in church on Sunday mornings while he is deployed and I sing words like "God is perfect and great." If something happened to my husband, I wonder if I would still sing those words? Would I sing them then? Would I? I've decided that I would, because I already am.

We have a choice, each of us. We can wallow in our circumstances or embrace them. We can choose fear or courage. When we look for God's blessings, it's a treasure chest. I can prove it to you. I show people my husband's picture, wherever I go. I say, "Isn't he good looking?" My picture is what keeps him going most days. We have been married almost 20 years and here we are gazing at each other's pictures. I don't need to quibble, criticize, argue or work anything out in my marriage. Tomorrow, all I need as a wife is to hear six words: "We're done flying and I'm okay."

The sick feeling in my stomach is exactly the same as it was 20 years ago. If you asked me, hey there Jennifer the self-proclaimed triumphant woman, what is your least favorite thing in the entire world? It would be a tie between deployments and pregnancy.

But I am so very proud of my husband's honorable military service. I'm honored to be his wife. He is someone's lifeline right now. I sometimes feel that I am his lifeline. What an honor. I realize how fortunate I am to go about my ordinary life of laundry, scrubbing, organizing and child raising while the stranded Christians my husband is helping wait for food and water to fall to them from the sky.

My husband took a picture at sunrise from the control tower of his not-so-luxurious base at Qatar, when he was pulling an overnight shift on July 4. It was 115 degrees that day. Nary a blade of grass could be seen by the human eye, only dust. My husband saw past the dry desert and thought the sunrise was beautiful. We can become strong during our weakness. We can look for the good hidden in the loneliness. The exhaustion. The danger. God wants to show us a sunrise in the dry desert.

My husband came back home safely a month later. He found out when he got back that his military unit is being deployed to Africa, to assist with the fight against the deadly, contagious Ebola virus. We don't know yet if my husband will have to go or not. If he does, we will trust God.

The Apostle Paul wrote those Bible passages we mentioned before in his letters to the Galatians and Hebrews. Paul was a Roman citizen who once perse-cuted Christians. He was the guy who stood there and held people's coats while they stoned Christians to death. When Paul was converted to Christianity, God spoke to him in such a bright light that he was blinded for a while. He did not know if that was to be forever or not. Even so, Paul was completely up for serv-ing God with his life. God did send Paul a guy to fix his vision soon enough. It was merciful of God to do that. You know for a little while though, Paul might have thought that was it, that the world would forever be complete blackness for him. As far as I can tell from reading the book of Acts, Paul was good with that.

The Bible says that Satan is like a roaring lion, ready to devour whomever he will. The Bible also says that light wins over darkness, somehow, some way. Islam will have to answer to Jerusalem. We cannot give in to fear. If we trust the Lord Jesus Christ with every detail of our lives, every moment of every day, then the enemy has nowhere to go.

———— ∞∞∞ ————

ABRAHAM'S AND SARAH'S TWO LEGACIES

Fear (Islam)	Trust (Christianity)

Sarah says here's my handmaid

Should have waited on God

Abraham says giddy-up

Again with the waiting

Ishmael is born to Hagar

Isaac is born to Sarah later, his son is Israel

A people in bondage

A free people

Arabia *"answers to Jerusalem"*

Judeo-Christian faith is *"of the promise"*

Prophet Muhammad

Jesus Christ the Son of God

The Koran

The Bible

Cruel punishment of infidels

Christ bore the punishment

Fear-based salvation

Grace-based salvation

Try to earn paradise through actions

Heaven is a gift from Christ

Create the apocalypse

Glorify God until Jesus returns

ISIS attacks Christians summer of 2014

Christians flee, the U.S. sends aid

Satan is sipping a chocolate latte

Satan's like "Wait, what?"

PART II. WOMANHOOD

—◦◦◦—

"Beautiful is the woman
who has learned to value her own
happiness and self-esteem.
Beautiful is the woman who
lives by the authority of her own soul."

A popular philanthropist who
claims strong faith in God,
summer 2014

Stop. Stop. Stop.
Those statements are in such powerful contradiction to the Bible
that they deserve their own spin-off show, *What Not to Say*.

CHAPTER 4

SELF

———— ∞∞∞ ————

If you think you are the ugliest girl in your school? I want you to multiply that by about 73 and you've got what I looked like when I was 14. I had to wear a back brace to correct scoliosis. I wore glasses. I had some serious acne. I had not yet cracked the code on what to do with my wild, bushy hair. Not a lot of fashion sense going on back then either, but cut me some slack: it was the 1980s. I wasn't overweight, but size was an issue because I was a foot taller than all the boys. Not cool tall, not play basketball tall or runway model tall because I was very unathletic and awkward – I'm the girl who got tangled up in helium balloons on stage during a ballet recital. Just ugly tall.

The back brace was the thing that mortified me the most. I went to public school so that was going to be super not fun, quenching the flaming darts of being ridiculed. I dreaded it. I beat the bullies to the punch though by making fun of myself before anyone else could. That removed most of the fun for the mean people. Sorry, back brace humor's taken, not an enjoyable topic, let's move on.

When people did make fun of me, I waited until everyone was almost finished laughing and then I said something even funnier about the back brace. I out-humored them. And sometimes, if the people who had been making fun of me seemed perplexed enough by that, I would go over to them quietly and say, "Would you like to see my back brace?" And I lifted up the lower part of my shirt and showed them. I let them knock on it with their fists, and we'd tell knock-knock jokes. Then I changed the subject. It was Proverbs 15 *"a soft answer turns away wrath"* in the truest sense.

I have not mastered anything great or worthy of admiration, but God has. As a girl I didn't talk to Him the way I do now, but in His endless mercy He put some good stuff about the self on my heart at an early age, out of kindness for a girl who wore a back brace.

God showed me that if I was going to survive this unattractive back brace experience, I would have to stop thinking about myself. Or I would go crazy. I made it my habit for the several years that I wore the brace, that every time I walked into a room full of people, every single time, every day, I would look around, evaluate everyone's facial expressions and body language, and see who needed encouraging. I'd go sit by that person and hang out and laugh together. Gradually other people would come and join us. I did that every day for several years. I still do it now to a lesser degree, but in those days it was life or death. (Ladies, if these tactics do not put a stop to agonizing bullying, please see chapter 17, Painful Relationships.)

One summer I went to a church youth camp and had to get someone to help with the brace for showering. I could not really participate in all the activities, especially outdoor ones. But I kept up my go-find-someone-who-needs-encouraging ways. At the end of the camp, the leaders asked everyone to vote for the most likeable, enjoyable person there. I won. I wasn't winning any beauty contests, but I was fun to be around because I chose to focus on other people, rather than on myself.

Ephesians 2:9 says everything we have is a gift from God, "*lest any man should boast himself.*" Having to wear the brace taught me not to think about myself. What a gift that was for me.

I could have turned reclusive and self destructive and gone into a little shell, but I didn't do it. I could have escaped with drugs or harmed myself. I could have been too consumed with self loathing and self pity to attend that summer camp at all. I could have gone into self preservation mode and lashed out at other people to boost my self confidence and self interest. I could have gone to a counselor to raise my self esteem. But I didn't.

I took my focus off of myself.

God was at work in my heart even then and He's still teaching me now. Our Lord knows that focusing on self creates complete misery. No surprise to Him.

He tells us as much in the Bible. John 5:30 says we really have nothing to offer apart from what God has empowered us to do: *"I can do nothing of mine own self."* Who knows the purposes God has for each of us? As C.S. Lewis said, in not looking for joy, that's where you find it.

Try as I might, every time my birthday rolls around, I'm having to call on Jesus to keep from being a big ol' grouch. "Seems like somebody else could throw this trash away, here it is my birthday," tired sigh. "Scrubbing these dirty pots and pans right here on my birthday," huff then grunt. All day I'm thinking something else should be happening. Normal, routine things become a source of grouchiness for me. I'm focused on myself and thinking I deserve more.

Terrifying thought for us: what would happen if we focused on ourselves like this for 365 days a year? Misery. Treachery. Thinking we deserve better. Jealousy. Resentment. Wishing we had more. Wishing things were different. That's what would happen. And that explains why people are so wretchedly miserable. Thinkin' bout themselves.

Fast Forward

I was 24, lived on the East Coast and traveled to a San Diego conference for my public relations job. I came down the stairs in the hotel to meet my peeps to go out to dinner one evening. A tiny woman saw me, rushed up to me and asked me if I would model for her agency. I said, "Sorry, I can't," because I was about to get married in two months and not only that, ma'am I don't live around these parts. This lady was very artsy with black clothes and a chic hair cut. "You've got to model for me dahling," she said. "Your look just works, here's my card." I never called her but it was nice of her to ask.

And so the moral of the story is: things like that really do happen in California.

The other moral of the story is that the humble will be exalted. *"For whosoever exalteth himself, shall be brought low, and he that humbleth himself, shall be exalted."* Luke 15:11. I would not have believed you if you had told me when I was 14, ugly, and spending all my time building up other people in order to avoid self destructing, "Hey Jennifer, just wanted to give you a head's up that in 10 years?

You're going to be turning down a modeling agent to go marry a handsome Air Force pilot because you two are crazy in love. Then 20 years later, you will write a book about that and other stuff."

My daughter has to wear a back brace now, and I wonder if God wanted me to endure the back brace for her sake. In the Old Testament, Queen Esther was told she came to the kingdom *"for a time such as this."* For my daughter, the brace has just been no big deal. It hasn't caused all this despair and anxiety for her that it did for me. She has to wear hers only at night so that's a plus. But also, she knew that her mother wore one, and she doesn't mind as much going through something that I did.

I'm glad that I wore a back brace if one of God's purposes was to have paved the way for my child to accept hers a little more easily. And then write about it to you.

❦

Social Media Popularity

"Mommy, how's your blob?" one of my children asked me.

My "blob" is pretty good, meaning my website blog, now that I finally started to trust God with the results of my writing. I was so off the deep end at first about my writing that I even thought about The Prayer of Jabez, which is a bit silly. It's this tiny little obscure passage in the Old Testament where some random guy you never hear about again and who isn't in the lineage of Christ asked God to increase his land territory. A serious book was written about it a while back and this movement got started and probably little Bible studies sprang up about it and coffee mugs and everything else. I thought they blew the whole Jabez thing slightly out of proportion although it's always good to consider God's word. I stooped to praying The Prayer of Jabez over my blog: Lord increase my virtual internet territory.

The whole thing was robbing me of peace and keeping me distracted from devotion to my family. My husband told me to throttle back. He shrugged his shoulders while we talked it over at a Mexican restaurant and he finished his steak fajita. "Just do one blog a week," he said. Don't make me choke on my shrimp quesadilla. Frown. I see now that he's right, as usual, but at the time I thought if I posted only once a week, the blog would be lame and pointless and all four of the people reading it would run away including my Mom.

I asked one of my teenagers about it and got the bitter truth. "Mom, there are a million apps and blogs. They all want big numbers. Like three of them ever get that." Another frown from me. I know that's true, but like every other tool out there, I thought my blog was special.

The Bible does not say a word about Facebook. However, the Bible addresses every issue known to man before any of us ever thought of it. It's hard not to care how many Facebook likes, Instagram followers or Twitter re-tweets we get. I'm going for a couple hundred a day myself. Here's what the Bible says about that: *"For we dare not make ourselves of the number, or compare ourselves with some that commend themselves: but they measuring themselves by themselves, and comparing themselves among themselves, are not wise."* 2 Corinthians 10:12.

I take it back. My 26 followers are the bomb. I'm not making myself be "of the number." That's a possessive phrase that means we belong to the number. It owns us. If a biggest number exists, then I'm sure our God knows what that is.[17] As far as our human brains are able to understand them, though, numbers are seemingly infinite. So they can never satisfy. There's no Z. Whether we are talking about website popularity, financial numbers, sales, customers, clients, Instagram likes or perhaps the number of cubits the Tower of Babel people were striving for, whichever number we reach, we can always go higher.

My Dad told me he recently read about some mathematician who announced he had discovered the largest possible number. Dad and I got a chuckle out of that when we said to each other: well, whatever number that genius found, we can always add one. Then square that and add six more. There's always a bigger number. We can't allow ourselves to be enslaved to numbers. Or get giddy about our popularity demonstrated by numbers. Our lives are but a shadow, and none of us wants to become "a poor player who struts and frets his hour upon the stage," as our man Shakespeare puts it.

I asked God to rescue me from myself. Gradually He brought me back to normal after I had gone zany zealous and turned myself into a blog blob. And

I forgive the Instagram penguin with the red scarf and sunglasses for getting 12,000 likes.

I needed God to get me to a place where I realized that ultimately my goal needs to be honoring and obeying Him, not impressing, pleasing or even helping people through a blog, a book, Facebook drama or anything else. If God wants to help someone through me then that's great, but it isn't my goal because that way He gets the glory. The scriptures tell us we cannot add one iota of time to our lives by fretting and striving. We also can't add one likey person. God gets to decide the popularity scale. Grand or small. Numbers can drive one mad, even to the point of suicide especially from once-famous people who basked in the numbers when they were large. When those numbers started to dwindle, those people saw their human worth fading away. There was no longer a reason to live. We can have wisdom by not giving popularity numbers that sort of power.

Ladies, our God knew there would someday be Instagram and this is what Galatians 1:10 says about it: *"Do I seek to please men? for if I yet pleased men, I should not be the servant of Christ."* My pastor said in a recent sermon that he loves his small church, and he wards off wishing his numbers were bigger by staying grateful and realizing that his message probably would not appeal to the masses anyway. He goes verse by verse through the Bible. Nothing flashy. No Easter bunny jumping out of a helicopter.

I have always felt rather perplexed, and then inadequate, and then ashamed of myself when Daniel helps King Nebuchadnezzar's son by interpreting a creepy message from God. The new king is throwing a big party with his friends one night. He gets an alarming message that he doesn't understand, calls Daniel in and says something along the lines of: Hey Daniel, I have heard about you. You're one of those God freaks. You know stuff. Help me out with this message and I'll clothe you with scarlet, put a chain of gold around your neck, and you'll be third in command in the whole kingdom.

If that had been me, I would have been like, "Thank you king, it's about time I had me some bling, yo? Zing. Dog, you gave me 8K on the follow. All in one day, yo? Chur-ching." But that is not what Daniel says. Daniel says, *"Let thy gifts be to thyself, and give thy rewards to another; yet I will read the writing unto the king and make known to him the interpretation."* Daniel 5:17. Keep your gifts, Daniel says. He meant it too. That passage has always blown me away. That's some selfless Mother Teresa level junk right there. (The message was that because God found the king lacking, he would die and lose his kingdom. Pretty much happened right then.)

All I can figure out is that Daniel knew and loved God enough to understand that adulation from man eventually brings humiliation from man. He would rather have nothing to do with it.

BEAUTY AND AGING

It happened.

An old man asked me the other day if my toddler was my granddaughter. I'm all right, no thank you, I don't need the box of tissues, very kind of you to offer. Thank you girls. Group hug. It's going to be fine. It just means we get to turn it into a section in the book. The Bible says to be thankful in all circumstances, so let's give that one a go. The man didn't ask me if she was my great-granddaughter? Hmm. A little comforting. No one has asked me if I would like the senior citizen's discount at the grocery store yet? Everyone looks the same age when you're 115 years old like that guy was, much like the way I'm scared to ask a young person how junior high school's going because I'm afraid he'll remind me he's actually in med school. We can explain it away and make ourselves feel better all we want, from a logical perspective. Here's the deal. We have a spiritual enemy and this is what God tells us about Thay-tun in the book of Ezekiel:

"Thine heart was lifted up because of thy beauty." Ezekiel 28:13-19.

Ooo, shiver. It startles me to think that the initial reason for Say-Say's downfall was because of being lifted up about his beauty. God could have finished that sentence so many different ways. So many things could have been Satan's first weakness: greed, slothfulness, lust, anger. So many things.

But it was beauty.

In an effort to feed us a lie, all culture has defined one aspect of beauty as being youthful. Satan, the extremely annoying enemy of our hearts, uses this weakness to play around with us ladies. If only we are young and beautiful, then everything will be perfect, the enemy tells us. What a dismal outlook, if part of beauty is youth, as time keeps right on ticking and that age number can only get higher. He tries to get us to keep our hearts lifted up as if we are the grandest tiger in the jungle when we are feeling lovely and beautiful, and then he tries to get us to despair when we are feeling so not. Such as this morning when I did not agree with the accuracy of the number on my bathroom scale. "Maybe it's broken," my Mom said.

God gets a little forceful with proud Satan-poo in this passage and goes on to tell him what's about to go down because of his heart that's lifted up about his beauty:

"Thou hast corrupted thy wisdom by reason of thy brightness: I will cast thee to the ground, I will lay thee before kings, that they may behold thee (and that's not in a good way, y'all). *Thou hast defiled thy sanctuaries by the multitude of thine iniquities, by the iniquity of thy traffick; therefore will I bring forth a fire from the midst of thee, it shall devour thee, and I will bring thee to ashes upon the earth in the sight of all them that behold thee. All they that know thee among the people shall be astonished at thee, thou shalt be a terror, and never shalt thou be any more."* Ezekiel 28:13-19.

Not that nice of a feel-good passage there from our buddy Zeekie. God's basically telling us the opposite of what the world tells us. Loving our beauty doesn't bring happiness. Rather, loving our beauty to the point where it crashes us around emotionally like a tidal wave leads to destruction. The Bible says to fear God alone. We can't let fear of aging and of looking older grip us to the point where it destroys our joy. As author Debi Pearl says, our husbands think we are absolutely gorgeous if we will only smile lovingly and contentedly at them.[34] That's the truth and will be the truth, in youth and when we are great-grandmothers. We have nothing to fear. And hey, people are taking so long to grow up nowadays, that 60 is the new 40.

God created us females to be beautiful. True beauty is an attribute of God Himself after all, and we are created in His image: *"One thing have I desired of the Lord, that will I seek after; that I may dwell in the house of the Lord all the days of my life, to behold the beauty of the Lord and to enquire of his temple,"* Psalm 27:4.

Of course we want to look nice, and we want to be attractive. For example, when I do nothing to my hair, I look like Moses. I highly respect Moses. I just don't want to look like him. So I keep my hair fixed all the time. What was the secret to Samson's strength? His hair. Just saying. Fixed hair is to female attractiveness as a made bed is to a bedroom, and as wiped counters are to a kitchen. That sentence is so profound it should be on the SAT.

We have to be really careful, though, that our attractiveness doesn't control whether our hearts are lifted up or whether our hearts are broken. Beauty can't be the barometer of our hearts, the way it was for Satan.

But yes, just so you know, I smiled graciously at the elderly gentleman who apparently is in need of new glasses, and I said, "Noooo, she's my daughter," and we both stood there smiling at my little girl, both completely delighted with her, agreeing how cute she is, and watching her prance and twirl around without out a care in the world.

WEIGHT

I have almost become the evil witch in the Snow White story, rejecting the way I look and obsessing over someone else's being more attractive than I am. God yanked me out of that destructive mindset. Just claim it: "This is my body, how dare I hate it?" Once we are Christians then we are told that our bodies are the holy temple of God because the Holy Spirit indwells in us.

The first thing to do in the area of struggling with weight is to accept your body type. It's really hard to do this. The way to accept your body type is to see it as a matter of obedience to God when He says that you are *"fearfully and wonderfully made."* Psalm 139:14. We don't get to argue with the Almighty Creator of the universe about the way He designed us. As long as you fight your body type, you are robbing yourself of joy and are going to feel defeated in this area. Personally I would have given myself a little more curve and maybe darker, more exotic looking skin, and better-behaved teeth, if I had designed myself. But who am I to question? We also have to be honest with ourselves about our optimum weight and size. If you set your size and weight goals to an unrealistic level, then you are going to do nothing at all because you have just sabotaged yourself.

Have you ever thought maybe God has a greater purpose for the specific body type He gave you? Now that gets exciting. If you struggle with weight and your own self image because of it, think how many other women are feeling the same way. People are watching you. They might be consumed with despair. If you surrender this issue to God, then they will see you and think, "Wow look at her. Look how content and confident she is. I want that." And then when they ask you what has given you victory, you can point them to God. This could be a ministry that is more effective, one lady at a time, than any big flashy high dollar organization. And you're the CEO. It won't be on the six o'clock news, but your God will see what you're doing and that's all that matters.

Something very wrong is happening to many of us with our thyroid. No matter what you do, you can't take off the weight. My teenage daughter's thyroid is not cooperating. After three years of trying many different remedies, we have discovered a new plan for her that involves resetting her body's basal temperature. This in turn psyches out her thyroid and tells it to get a grip. It's called the Wilson thyroid protocol. We are very thankful that this seems to be God's answer for our daughter. She has lost 20 pounds and looks and feels like her old self. If you have low thyroid symptoms, but your numbers keep coming up normal, the Wilson protocol could help. I hope this is not just one more thing to let you down. God might have a different solution for you. Just ask Him.

My thyroid is all right, but I struggled with my weight years ago around the time my younger brother was getting married. I had recently had my third baby but more than that, I was dealing with a crisis: my husband had lost his job. I was eating a big gigantic bowl of ice cream every single night as my reward for buoying my husband up all day and caring for three little children under a lot of stress and strain. This was a dark time that God used in mighty ways. I would not give up that time of adversity for anything in the world, for the spiritual growth it gave me. But derriere growth? We've got problems. I didn't really think about my weight during the time my husband was out of work. I thought I looked fine. Scoop me another one of those mint chocolate chip flavors. Squirt some chocolate syrup on that too. Yay-yuh. You know what, just give me the whole container and a spoon.

It was time for my brother's wedding and time to give his lovely bride my measurements for my bridesmaid's dress. I did not pay any attention to those numbers, wrote them down, then ate one of those nice Everything Bagels lightly toasted to perfection and about a half a pound of cream cheese slathered on there. Let's wash that down with a big vat of extreme moose tracks double fudge chunk. When the dress arrived weeks later, based on my measurements, the dress people sent me a dress three times larger than my normal size. Whah? There must be some mistake. I tried on the dress and it fit. Again, whah?

Here is what I did after the wedding. I prayed. I said to God, "Could I please be this certain size, Father?" I knew what size I would be happy with as a mother whose hips are never going back down to a certain measurement. I know what size and weight are attainable, realistic goals for my body type. I didn't ask to be a size 2 okay.

Then I went on the offensive and stopped eating foods like ice cream and bagels with cream cheese all the time because those sorts of foods were keeping me ballooned out. Food had become an escape rather than just a re-fuel thing, in the midst of a crisis. Our Lord can fill any void in our hearts if we will just go to Him for comfort rather than to food. I also increased my physical activity, by going on brisk walks on a regular basis. I was the size I wanted to be within a year.

EXERCISE

At first glance (can one glance at a 1000-page book?), it seems that the Bible doesn't have much to say about exercise. It does tell us in 1 Timothy 4:8 that *"bodily exercise profiteth little"* as compared to godliness. Paul says in Hebrews 12:1 for us to *"run with patience the race that is set before us,"* and tells us, *"I have fought a good fight, I have finished my course,"* but what he meant by that is that he had *"kept the faith,"* 2 Timothy 4.

If that's all we can squeak out of the Bible about exercise, then we might conclude that it is not all that important to God. Certainly the ancient Greeks were a little off the mark with their extreme athletic competitiveness and their near worship of the body. Oh my goodness, such show-off divas. And the Hindu-influenced yoga exercise has a religious component that does not quite line up with scripture, as we saw in chapter two. Something like Pilates could be a better alternative to yoga.

We must look past the words in the Bible for a moment and listen to the actions in the Bible. Jesus and His buddies walked or rowed boats everywhere they went. Many of them were fishermen. Pulling up fish into boats from nets is very physically demanding, I would imagine. Many of the people in the Bible were farmers, and my Dad can tell you that is extremely hard work. Ruth gathered grain that was left over in a field, and her humble heart was irresistible to God. She must have been rather achy after that. The women in the Bible did not have modern appliances as they held babies and kept house, and God tells us that an honorable woman will work hard with her hands. The Bible says an idle, lazy person is not reflecting God's character.

And so what is happening in the Bible is that, as people go about their days honoring Him, they are physically active and hard working. Physical exercise is built into their lives. Today we have people who hire a lawn or cleaning service to maintain their homes while they go to the gym. One option is to mow your own yard, right? Just clean your house.

Unless someone has a job that is physically demanding, it might be good with God for us to supplement working hard at home with some exercise. Compared to what the God-fearing people in the Bible were doing, it might be necessary for us to view regular exercise today as manufacturing what people's bodies were once required to do but no longer must because of modern convenience. Exercise might even be essential today because of Adam's disobedience in Genesis. God says Adam's consequence was that he would have to till the ground *"in the sweat of thy face."*

It is possible that, as part of the consequence of the fall of man, physical exercise is now necessary to maintain our imperfect bodies and their cardiovascular systems, neurological health, muscle tone and joint strength. Note to self: Wouldn't life have been easier if Adam had never disobeyed? We have to keep exercise in proper perspective, which is that it will profiteth little compared to what's going on in our hearts.

There's my Bible schpeal, and here's how I rock my exercise swag. I never think about exercising. Instead, I tell myself to put on my exercise clothes. I'm not going running. I'm just changing clothes. That much I can do. Then I tell myself to go downstairs and get the dog. I obey myself. Then I turn on some killer worship music and start running outside. When I need some motivation to exercise, I ask my teenager for some good Christian music to add to my player. My favorite song right now is *Afterlife* by Switchfoot. Girl you could totally work out to this song. Moms, it is too gritty for young children. But your teenagers will love it. They will see that you understand them.

I've worked up to a two-mile morning run. I go really slowly at first and then get a faster sassy trot going the second mile to where I might even start looking a little *Chariots of Fire* toward the end. Every single time I make myself exercise, I'm always glad I did. I feel like I am dancing to God. I think, "This is so uplifting. Why did I not want to do this?" After running, I stretch on my back porch where I won't frighten the neighbors.

Puh-lease don't compare yourself to anyone else. I can't go running with my husband. He can run a mile in seven minutes. Leaves this white girl in the dust. I'm slow, but I don't realize I'm slow if no one else is along or telling me her stats. Now my friend Rhonda loves exercising with her husband. It's like date night to them. Whether someone is an exercise loner or wants an exercise buddy, we can always look at it this way: whatever we are doing is more than nothing.

FOOD

Our unfortunate reality is that we need to eat only when we are hungry. The rest of the time, if I think I am hungry but I'm not, I drink a big gigantic glass of water all throughout the day instead. Our input (food) needs to be less than or the same as our output (physical exertion). It's a simple logarithm. Or maybe it's a function. Somebody figure that out for me.

A strict, self-inflicted "what in the world are you putting in your mouth all day?" awareness program is helpful. If it doesn't go in the shopping cart, it won't go in your mouth. Pretend the naughty aisles at the grocery store aren't there. If your family loves ice cream, but so do you, then ask them to buy the flavors they like but you don't. That way, the ice cream cannot harm you. Unless you have a sensitivity to them, try to gravitate toward foods like cashews or pecans, fresh fruits and veggies, protein shakes or cheese because they are our friends. I have written out a precise, skimpy list of exactly what I will allow myself to eat every day and I try to stick to that. I do eat a little bowl of dark chocolate chips after dinner and I am not giving that up, you can't make me.

In the first chapter of Daniel, the non-God people ate a lot of rich food. Daniel and his buddies have been captured and taken into Babylon, and they respectfully ask if, instead of eating the king's meat, could they please have vegetables and water instead? That word "meat" is thought to mean something like rich delicacies. Elsewhere in the Bible, God provides meat and is cool with meat plenty of times, so we are not theologically knocking meat. After avoiding the king's rich food, Daniel and his posse ended up with countenances much more healthy than everyone else's. And Daniel was quite the preferred, respected fellow.

As the author of *French Women Don't Get Fat* says, no one is making you eat fast food or brownies. Tell yourself that unhealthy and highly processed foods do not exist and are not an option, no matter how compelling the advertising. I truly understand the temptation to run by and pick up burgers and fries when you are exhausted. But look at it like this: in the 20 minutes it takes to get fast food, we could just as well have browned some ground beef and thrown together some spaghetti sauce in the crock pot that morning. Or, make the spaghetti sauce before you go to bed and then fire it up the next morning.

The money spent on fast food could buy a fancy schmancy pre-made chicken pie if you have a grocery store that carries something like that. It takes about seven minutes to dump a bag of lettuce into a bowl, throw some stuff on it like sunflower seeds or pecans, a sliced avocado, dried cranberries and smoked salmon and call it a salad. Healthy eating doesn't have to take a lot of time – just some advanced planning. If I am forced to eat at a fast food restaurant on a road trip a couple of times a year, then I get a salad and water.

Following a strict, Daniel-esque eating lifestyle takes some self-discipline. It's a choice we are making. Do we want to curl up on the couch and chow down the better part of a bag of cape cod potato chips with ranch dip and a nice cold soda with a bag of candy afterward? Or do we not want to have a muffin top later when we try to button our jeans? Aristotle said this about self-discipline. "Moral virtues come from habit ... whatever we learn to do, we learn by actually doing it ... by doing self-controlled acts, we become self-controlled."[2]

Don't you love that women can talk about Aristotle and muffin tops in the same paragraph? We can enjoy food. But we have to be deliberate about enjoying small amounts of smart food.

Just Say No

If someone's life is going at such a frantic pace that she does not have the time or energy to exercise or eat right, then maybe she never consulted God.

When we say yes to everything that moves, we are saying no to our own family and our own health. We might even be saying no to God. If we've truly given our lives to God, then it's not our time to give. It's not our call, it's His. All the interesting activities our colleagues and our children present to us as urgent emergencies ("Mom, I have to take voice lessons or I will die") generally amount to fun. How much fun do we want other people to have while we run ourselves ragged to make it happen?

We must get on our knees and ask God: "What do you want my life to look like? What specific commitments do You want me to make?" And then we wait and listen for His still, small voice. The Bible says that a virtuous woman is compassionate toward the poor and will generously help others. If we are tight with God, this will happen in a way that will not come at the expense of our own families and our own health. Other people will keep you hopping with busywork your entire life if you let them. Children are very good at this. Some ladies speak wearily of their exhausting lives as if none of it was their choice.

Tell the precious ones no. My friend Pam asks her children, on a scale of 1 to 10, how badly they want to participate in something. Until they can drive themselves, the children in my family are allowed one major activity such as a sport or a musical instrument. If the children sign up for the traveling softball team, you've just signed up for a traveling softball team. Do not let your children's fun activities run your life. God runs your life.

Valiant leaders of a worthy cause might approach you for help and might have exciting ideas and sincere motives. But they also might never have once prayed about beginning that ministry, developing that ministry, or dragging you in on that ministry. Some erroneous theology is there: the idea that people can solve the grand scale problems of the world, apart from God. Instead, we listen to and obey His voice, not necessarily an inspirational speaker's.

People rarely ask me to help with anything because I'm just not giving off that bake sale vibe. Especially while my children are little, I am fiercely guarding my time. Six people in this world desperately need me. Well-meaning, passionate Christians will sometimes show us heart breaking pictures and videos of world tragedies and then use enticing words that holler at us to "do something for God."

I have a family.

I am doing something for God.

Eli was a big shot priest but it was one juicy failburger when he neglected his own sons, who turned out to be *"vile and he restrained them not."* 1 Samuel 3:13. If someone asks us to get involved in their cause, all we have to say is, "Oh that sounds wonderful. Let me think about it (or even pray about it, if you will truly do that) and get back to you." Then later, unless God tells you otherwise, you say you're so sorry but you can't. And you can't, because you are going to be listening out for God's will for you and spending that rare, precious extra time and energy exercising and eating well.

CHAPTER 5

HOMOSEXUALITY

———◦≈∘———

I want to give three things to women who are in a same sex relationship and are seeking God: An apology, two requests and an invitation. Well wait, that was four things. And not necessarily in that order.

THE APOLOGY

A family member of mine worked for a client who swindled him something fierce. I mean really took him. He's still picking up the pieces from it. My family member had trusted this client, in large part, because the client proclaimed the name of the Lord Jesus Christ. This client is a wealthy professional, and his Twitter account profile even proclaims the name of the Lord Jesus Christ. He might have at one time loved the things of God, but we can gather that this man is nothing but a big crook. It really chafes me because he is making all Christians look bad.

I tell you about that because I am deeply sorry if anyone has mistreated you or condemned you publicly or personally in a mean-spirited way and then claimed the name of the Lord Jesus Christ. Perhaps they forgot they weren't talking about their rival sports team and were talking about actual people. If it makes you feel any better, the bully Christians are mean to everyone. And the logic scholar people say that when your attacker begins calling you names, you know you've just won. Your opponent has resorted to name-calling when he has nothing of substance left to say. [8]

Sometimes the pain that stings the most is from the people closest to us. Jesus Himself said a prophet is appreciated everywhere except by his own people. He understands. We're not perfect like Jesus. But we catch His drift.

A Request

My dog Sawyer is about as cool a dog as you can find, really sweet and laid back. He's a golden retriever, so there you go. As long as he gets a walk, he's extremely chill. He weighs 100 pounds and is the size of a small pony, but he doesn't know he weighs 100 pounds. He thinks he's a tiny lap dog. He loves it when I sit in the floor and let him put his head in my lap. On our morning run he always likes to stop at certain spots and inspect every blade of grass – wait we missed a couple blades, go back – so I linger and give him

that because I figure, hey this walk is all the guy's got in life. The rest of his time is spent stalking my every move or sleeping.

Our pets are so predictable right? We know them so intimately. Well one day Sawyer was pacing by the back door, suspicious about something in the woods beyond our back yard. "It's the deer again," I thought without paying any attention. I went over and let him out, and he'd stand there in the back yard looking out toward the woods, very agitated. Ears perked up and everything. Nose just a-twitching. He would come back in and do the same thing off and on. In and out. He'd pace around, then stare down those deer. Frozen cold stare. Frigid. This went on for the better part of a morning and I finally got to thinking, Sawyer is more annoyed than usual. I finally looked out at the woods.

A plastic grocery bag was stuck to a bush.

No deer were in the yard at all. That ferocious Sawyer had been protecting our home from a menacing plastic bag all that time. I went outside and got rid of the bag to relieve him from his torment. Sawyer one point, the plastic bag zero. I think he high fived me with his paw when I came back inside. The bag lost and he could finally relax and catch up on the four naps he'd missed that morning.

And so class? The lesson we take from this story is: You just never know what's going to go flying out of the recycling bin into the yard.

That and, if you ever hear or read something about homosexuality, I would ask you not to assume the dog is agitated at the deer necessarily. There could be a plastic bag, people. If you stop and listen and truly pay attention to their message, they might have something to say and it might not be what you thought it was. I might have something interesting to say in a few moments here.

⁓

THE INVITATION

My invitation is that you would get to know God better. Get to know the scriptures better. That is exactly the same thing I'm saying to everyone including myself. If you are seeking God's direction in the area of your sexuality, a very good book from two Christian women who aren't mean is *Intimate Issues*, by Linda Dillow and Lorraine Pintus. The authors talk in one chapter about what God does and does not ordain in sexual relationships. Mostly it is a book for married male and female couples. But I think you will appreciate their discussions of womanhood and our sexual identities in a way that is Biblical and kind hearted.

Christian-ish books or not, including this one you are very kindly holding right now, forget everything you think you know about the Bible and God, and get to know Him better. The real God, the God of the Bible. Once you know Him, your life can't help but reflect Him. I don't think there is a way to know Him without reading His book. We know pets by their affection and neuroses perhaps. We know God by His words.

We might get stubborn and can't get very tight with God if another Christian has hurt us, especially a family member or someone we needed to be there for us. They let us down and so we can start thinking God's like that. We can start thinking that God is a certain person or group but He's not. As long you believe that, then those people are in control of your life.

And so an invitation within the invitation is that you would free yourself by choosing to forgive any people who have wronged you, strangers or those close to you, as a matter of a decision and not an emotion. The only way I know how to forgive is to make a decision to forgive, as a matter of the will, and then ask God to get my feelings to catch up with that.

Jesus Himself said as He was hanging from the cross, *"Forgive them Father, for they know not what they do."* Of course He was sinless and we are not, but that's the kind of mercy we can extend to people who are cluelessly brutal. It's very hard to show compassion to someone who's not showing it to you but that's what I'm asking you to do. You are pulling an awesome Ephesians 4:31-32 when you do this. If our actions today are even in small part based on the previous or current incompetence of other people, then we haven't forgiven. Don't give them that. They are not the boss of you.

⸺ ❧ ⸺

A FINAL REQUEST

My last request is: let's talk Bible. I want to go in order chronologically and consider Genesis 1:27 which says *"male and female He created them."* The Bible says this before God had even made the first woman, Eve. I don't know why we care about that, but I'm just saying. He had set up the world to have distinctly male and female people, is what we get from that.

Then in Genesis 2:22 God takes a rib from Adam and *"made he a woman, and brought her unto the man. And Adam said, 'This is now bone of my bones, and flesh of my flesh: she shall be called Woman, because she was taken out of man.' Therefore shall a man leave his father and his mother, and shall cleave unto his wife: and they shall be one flesh."*

So God is saying here, almost on the very first page of the Bible, that this is His plan for us. God doesn't change, so we'll see throughout the Bible that it doesn't go well for people when they try something contrary to His order or plan.

Then that whole Eve serpent confusion thing went down, and we talk about that more in the first chapter in marriage. It's fascinating. For now we'll just say that the bad guy knew the way to get to Eve was to tell her that usurping authority and questioning God were the ways to become wise. Which was a big fat lie.

Now we get to Genesis 19 where God destroys the city of Sodom and Gomorrah and this was not done delicately, as God was rather wroth. The reason for their destruction was because the men were all about homosexuality and we know this specifically because they said to Abraham's nephew Lot, *"Where are the men which came in to thee this night? bring them out unto us, that we may know them."* Scholar people who study Hebrew assure us this *"know them"* here is not talking about finding out what toppings they like on their salad. It's sexual without a doubt.

For you and me, this passage is not extremely helpful because it really doesn't say anything about women other than Lot's wife who loved the city and God smote her for that. Mostly though, we are told it is the men who are behaving *"wickedly."* For us to talk about female same sex relationships in light of that passage is a little bit like when you get in trouble for something your brother or sister did, when all you were doing was standing in the same room. But the passage about this city does reveal God's plans for sexuality and we can't ignore it. We are seeing throughout the Bible that God's plan for sexuality is consistent. We are also seeing that defying that plan angers God.

We have in Leviticus some rather strong and clear verbage regarding man not lying with man in 18:22 and 20:13. But again, this is men, and when it comes to Leviticus, it's hard for me to tell the history from the doctrine sometimes, with all those offerings and skin regimens. So Leviticus is not doing much for me. Not really feeling it.

Exit the Bible for a moment and let's consider the fact that all of those passages were written a couple thousand years before the time of the Greeks. When Sapphro wrote her beautiful poetry on the Greek island of Lesbos a few hundred years before the birth of Christ, God had already established all of His plans for men and women. Not a new idea to Him. He had already dealt with people who strayed from that plan. When we read Sapphro's poetry, we realize she is delighting in other women, enjoying other women, she even says "how I have worshiped you" to a woman.[42]

In thinking about that, let's see what our buddy Paul has to say in the book of Romans, which was written a few hundred years after Sapphro's poetry. Paul was a well educated Roman citizen himself, so he must have been familiar with her poetry. He quotes other Greek poets several times in his New Testament letters.

I really encourage you to read the entire first chapter of Romans sometime, especially the King James Version because the new versions ruin everything. They put the scriptures in baby talk and remove much of the beauty and meaning.

The verse we'll focus on is Romans 1:26 which says, *"for even their women did change the natural use into that which is against nature."* Here we see the Bible addressing women in relationships with women and we already know from the rest of the Bible that this is not what God desires for us. And notice the Bible says, *"even their women"* implying: listen up, we know things have gotten to a certain extent when even the women are doing this. It is a compliment to women because God understands that we women have a great capacity for spiritual things. As in the Spirit, the Holy Spirit. He expects us women to want to understand and know Him.

What we care about the most here is the "why." We'll back up a few verses and see how we get to this point where women are in sexual relationships with other women. Buckle up. She's a real doozy:

"Because that, when they knew not God, they glorified him not as God, neither were thankful: but became vain in their imaginations, and their foolish heart was darkened. Professing themselves to be wise, they became fools."

That is Romans 1:21-22 and it is very hard for me to hear these things about myself. But we have to understand what will begin to happen when we don't know God. To all of us. You and me, everyone. Paul goes on to say this of them, *"who changed the truth of God into a lie, and worshipped and served the creature more than the Creator, who is blessed for ever."* That's Romans 1:24-25 and it really does capture what is happening in Sapphro's poetry, when she desires other women. She has forgotten all about God, and that is not necessarily her fault, having lived in a polytheistic society. Instead of letting this admiration and discovery of the beauty of women make her marvel at her Creator and be thankful to her Creator, she began to worship the creature instead.

When we hear an exquisite piece of music, or see a magnificent garden, what's the first thing we want to know? Yes, we want to know who composed it. We want to know who the master gardener is. We want to know more about that person. We read about her. We tell everyone about her. We give her glory. Same thing with our God. His creation should make us want to find out all we can about Him and glorify Him.

The way never to get to the point we are warned about in Romans, is to do the opposite of what the passage says can happen.

GOD'S WAY	NOT GOD'S WAY (ROMANS 1)
Know God	Do not know God
Glorify Him	Do not glorify Him
Thankful to Him	Not thankful to Him
Realistic purpose	Vain imaginations
A heart that understands truth	A heart that does not understand
In the light	In darkness
See only God as wise	Profess themselves wise
Believe God's truth	Change God's truth into a lie
Worship the Creator	Worship the creature
RESULT: RELATIONSHIPS AS GOD PLANS	RELATIONSHIPS OUTSIDE GOD'S PLAN

We have to take this seriously because in 1 Corinthians 6:9 Paul says, *"Know ye not that the unrighteous shall not inherit the kingdom of God? Be not deceived."* He goes on to say in verse 11 that, *"And such were some of you, but ye are washed, but ye are sanctified, but ye are justified in the name of the Lord Jesus, and by the Spirit of our God."*

He said, *"were."* Past tense. That's what we were. But once we accept Christ as the boss of our life he talks about what we *"are."* Right now. Regardless of re- lationships that previously have not been righteous in God's eyes, His salvation is open to us all right now.

What we see before us is the choice that everyone is given. Many people rely on their own insight and wisdom, and they stray from God's plan as the list on the right side showed. It starts with not knowing God and goes downhill from there. If we deny all of this and roll with ourselves the way we are naturally, without considering the truth in scripture, we ultimately end up with relation- ships that are out of sync with God's plan.

For example, when Sapphro speaks of "O weak and fitful woman bending the knee before any man," she completely misunderstands God. She fails to see that one woman placing herself under one man is not weakness but rather is her beautiful purpose in marriage. It's much easier not to do it, and so it takes strength to do it. I can't sew to save my life, and you really don't want to be anywhere nearby when I ride a bicycle. Those things do not come naturally to me but they're not important to God. It doesn't matter if I ever learn to sew or ride a bike. Male-female relationships are important to Him.

What about Jesus? He doesn't have anything to say about homosexuality, right? No. That isn't true. Jesus says that homosexuality is outside of God's plan for us. Here, I will show you. Jesus and the Father are one, so if God says it then Jesus says it. John 1:1 says *"in the beginning was the Word,"* and it's talking about Jesus. He is the Word so if it's in the word of God then He said it. That means all the other passages we've looked at regarding homosexuality were Jesus say- ing them too. Jesus was born into a family with one father and one mother. John the Baptist, who prepared the way for Jesus, was the child of one father and one mother. Every time Jesus speaks of marriage, He always refers to one man and one woman.

That is interesting, sort of. Zzzzzz. Sorry, I made myself doze off just then with that paragraph. It isn't enough. We need something more. I used to think that Jesus was Santa-Claus-cutesy-love-everybody. He's got the beard, He smiles, children gather around Him, and so He must love everyone just the way they are, right? This simply isn't true. He does love us, but I cannot read Matthew chapter 12 for example without realizing that He socks it to us and verbally corrects us all. How is this consistent with a loving God?

Here is my answer. Jesus is a very good teacher. Does an excellent teacher sit on the floor smiling, hold her arms out to her students and hug them, then accept incomplete assignments by saying, "Lovely, everything was lovely." No, that is a very nice teacher. But that is not a very good teacher. Her students see through the niceness and know that her class is meaningless.

A good teacher corrects sharply but with kindness. She has high standards for herself and her class. She requires excellence, not to be mean spirited, but because she loves her students and wants them to thrive. She is tough because she wants them to achieve greatness. The students understand that. They might groan a little, but they love her. She is one of the most influential people they will remember and adore their whole lives.

That's our Lord. Thinking of Jesus in that way, let's see what He says about homosexuality. In Matthew 19:4 and 5 He specifically talks about people's be-ing created as male and female and keeps that in the context of male-female marriage. More interestingly though, in three of the four gospels – Matthew, Mark and Luke – when Jesus wants to illustrate that someone is at the highest height of going against God, He refers to Sodom. He says, *"it would be better for Sodom"* than for the people He is correcting. We know why Jesus disapproved of Sodom was not because of overdue library books. It was homosexuality.

And so now we come to the point where we say, "This author is telling me what God's plan is. I don't fit into that. He must not be my God." Oh, my friend. That is exactly where the enemy of our hearts would like to keep us. Our spiritual enemy wants us to believe the lie that you are a man trapped in a woman's body. That isn't true. You are a beautiful woman.

I want to tell you something intense but simple. I want to tell you about a person in the Bible named Naaman. He was suffering and wanted God's help to change. God told him to go wash in the Jordan River seven times. That answer, understandably, really infuriated Naaman. He was insulted by it. It was a ran-dom and bizarre request that seemed to have nothing to do with his situation.

The Bible says Naaman was wroth. He stormed away *"in a rage"* and must have thought: you people have no idea. But his friends said: Wait, Naaman. If God, *"had bid thee do some great thing, wouldest thou not have done it?"* 2 Kings 5. Naaman saw the wisdom in that question and decided to try washing in the Jordan seven times. It worked. He reached his goal.

I'd like to be your friend who says to you that, if you are seeking God in no longer desiring a homosexual relationship, the answer is to ask God to change your mind. Don't pull a Naaman and scoff at that, when you haven't even tried it. If I asked you to do some great thing, would you not eagerly do that? Ask God to change your way of viewing women and men. Ask Him this continually and gradually, and then wait. Ask again continually and gradually, then wait some more.

As you do this, through the hours, days and weeks, I ask you to consider the following question, and I hope your answer is "no." In Jeremiah 32:27 God says, *"Behold, I am the Lord, the God of all flesh. Is anything too hard for me?"*

CHAPTER 6
SENSUALITY AS A CAREER

———— ⚬⚬⚬ ————

Sensuality is not inherently good or bad, any more than water is inherently good or bad. Water to drink in a hot and dry desert? Good. Water flooding the carpet of your living room? Bad. It's all in how we use the thing. Sensuality within the sanctity of marriage is the cool drink of water in a hot, dry desert. We'll talk about that in a different chapter. Sensuality outside of marriage is the water disaster that ruins someone's entire home. We're fixing to talk about that right now.

If you are getting paid for showing or giving away your body, I really appreciate that you are reading. I'm talking to exotic dancers, models and actresses in the sex industry, sensuous waitresses, escorts. I'm proud of you because you are drawn to the things of God. Your teachable heart is very beautiful.

Another loveable thing about you is that you have sometimes wondered whether you should be doing what you are doing. It is a very wise thought and one that ancient philosophers used to have as well. "Age quod agis" is Latin for "do what you're doing." The smartie pants guys in the old days would say that to encourage one another to be deliberate about making sure they wanted to be doing what they were doing.[27]

We might be tempted to dismiss the thought and tell ourselves, "Hey, a lot of lonely single guys and unhappily married men are out there. I'm just showing them a good time." I need to ask a hard question. Could we flip the thing around and ask if you could be the cause of that? Could you be the reason they are single and lonely, or unhappily married?

Stick with me here: When we ladies work in jobs like yours, we are giving guys the benefits of marriage with none of the work. We're giving him the fun part. Then he faces his wife (or future wife if he's single) and something more is required of him than tipping big, buying drinks or paying for a magazine. Or barely lifting a finger, literally, on his computer mouse or phone to find you on social media. He goes home to a real life family atmosphere where toilets break and babies cry. So you've just stolen your own thunder, sistah. Once you're a guy's wife, you alone are supposed to be his gorgeous haven of sensuality. But a husband isn't in the mood for homemade lasagna (you as his wife) after he's been getting hits of heroin (the pretend you).

I say the pretend you because you're not even you when you do your job anyway, if we think about it. The guys enjoying your body don't ever see you pitch a hissy fit or pick out a big chunk of salad stuck between your front teeth. The only difference between us as a wife and us at these jobs is reality. The picture of you on social media is not real life, for the men or for us. God created our glorious sexuality to take out on one guy in private, a husband. Not the whole world.

This is why you keep going through broken relationship after broken relationship. The guys you know have an appetite only for the pretend you. But no one can sustain that. Real life women, the full package, all of us, you and me, take effort and are not merely pleasure removed from reality. It's why men get addicted to porn. In person or images. A wife is a sensual haven for her husband and this is as it ought to be, but you're giving men more than a haven: you're giving them an escape from reality. That's the definition of a drug.

Friend, we have so much power over guys with our sexuality that it is as if we are leading an ox to the slaughter. Those aren't my fierce words. They come from Proverbs 7 which goes on to warn men to stay away from a stranger's flirting and flattery, not to lie with her on her perfumed bed – virtually or in person – because *"many strong men have been slain by her."*

Why would any of us girls do this to guys? It is not because we are so terribly naughty, any more than anyone else. It is because something is not quite right in our hearts. Are we big enough to admit this? I think we are.

For some of us girls, their daddy should have told them they were pretty and paid more attention to them. He should have but he didn't. And so we keep searching to meet that need from men. There's a surge of pleasure to know men like the way we look and are enjoying us. The surge goes away though. It's only temporary. We're looking to the wrong guys to meet this need when we do this. The pain from a distant, uncaring or painful daddy can't be fixed by looking to aroused strangers out in the world. Until we are married, we ought to be looking to Jesus. He's the Guy.

A good friend of mine was in pain because of her daddy. He just wasn't loving her or treating her the way she wished he would. She told me she prayed about it and here is what the Lord said to her: "How many perfect Fathers do you need?"

Jump back.

God reminded her that He is the perfect Father. He's the One who can meet this need for adoration, attention and affection. We can forgive our earthly parents and let God take control of our lives with or without them. Your social media followers or your boss might seem like a caring father figure, but no good daddy pimps out his daughter. Maybe some of these people do truly care in some ways. But when it comes down to it, our bodies are essentially a commodity and they are making money from it. We're the drug, they're the pusher. We're already so gorgeous, we don't have to keep proving that at work to take away the pain from our daddy or other men who've done us wrong. Because if we are, then the pain from them is still in charge. The pain from them does not have to be in charge for the rest of our lives.

"Well," you might say, "you wrote this stinkin' book to make money." Maybe I did, maybe I didn't. Fist bump because now you are thinking like someone who is not going to allow herself to be used by anyone. She is questioning what she sees, hears and reads. I like it.

Perhaps you're living your lifestyle because it's familiar. Evaluate your life. Evaluate your friends and your surroundings and ask if your life is bringing glory to God. There is more to you than this.

God is ready for you to come to Him right now with an open heart. In the Old Testament, Rahab was a lady who had provided sex to men as her job but something in her heart was drawn to God. She helped God's people take down this big evil city, Jericho. She was on the side of the good guys, and one of the good guys married her. God didn't care what her past had been. He saw her heart. He honored her and did mighty things through her. She is named in the Bible as one of the ancestors of Jesus Christ. This is what God says about her, *"By faith the harlot Rahab perished not with them that believed not."* Hebrews 11:31. So I say, better to have some faith and perish not.

And listen, God always gives us a way out of a bad situation if we ask Him. First Corinthians 10:13 says, *"But God is faithful…will also make a way to escape, that ye may be able to bear it."* You could do a total 180 on the thing and say, "I'm not posting these pictures or working in this job anymore because I'm creating a lot of unhappily married men out there." Or future unhappy men, including your own, because they'll be comparing their future wife to the pretend you. Or an even better reason: "I'm not working this job anymore because it's dishonoring to God."

Wow.

Think of all the people who know you and would be blown away by that powerful statement, by that powerful decision and by the trust that it would display that your Heavenly Father would somehow provide another way. All I can do is yammer away in a book but child you know people. You've got some power. Probably a fourth of them will follow you. And a fourth of the people who know those people will follow them and on and on. Boom, you've just changed the world.

They'll just find someone else if you quit, right? Yeah exactly. Let some other sucker put herself out there and you keep your dignity. God's favor will be upon you, not them, from the moment you turn to Him and it's about to hit it when that happens. Your life will never be the same.

King David was *"a man after the Lord's own heart"* and he was constantly asking God what to do: Should our army approach the enemy now? Should we go into this land? Should we leave today? Do you want me to go here, do you want me to go there? Your God knows that you need a job and someone to love you. He knows that you are beautiful and hard working. If you say to the Lord, "Where do you want me to work, God, where should I go?" Then your heart is as mighty and beautiful as David's. If you start applying before you quit then you might be amazed at how God truly is there for you with another job.

You might think: "Look lady, not everybody has a sugar daddy pilot husband, and my job pays really well." I hear you. God understands. That's what the Israelites said when faced with having to wander in the wilderness after getting away from being slaves in Egypt. They even said sometimes in complete frustration: maybe it would have been better if we had stayed captives in Egypt where at least we had good food, than to come out here in this wilderness and starve to death. So it was hard for them right at first. But God is always faithful and promised to prosper them in a new land. And He did.

So it comes down to: do we trust God to provide for us? If we honor Him with our life, He promises to take care of us. Seriously listen to what this passage says, after the Israelites had been wandering in the wilderness for 40 years after they left Egypt, "waxen" just means "become." Here it is: *"And I have led you forty years in the wilderness: your clothes are not waxen old upon you, and thy shoe is not waxen old upon thy foot."* Deuteronomy 29:5. If anyone else had worn the same clothes and shoes for 40 years they would be looking plenty raggedy. That's the kind of miraculous thing God loves to do for those who are faithful to Him and trust Him.

When I was younger and living a lifestyle apart from God, I surrounded myself with other people who were doing the same things so that my life seemed normal. Change your scenery. Go to a Bible teaching church. I've got a secret for you. Everybody in that church is a sinner, same as you and me. Some are saved, some not. If anybody at church looks down on you, that's their problem because they've forgotten that without God they are nothing. They're the fool and you are wise.

Many of the guys at church are very nice and gentlemanly. Sometimes evening services or groups are less formal and more friendly. You will probably really like church; the worship music is really rockin' these days in a lot of churches. Don't laugh, I'm serious. We used to have only organ music and Amy Grant when I was a young lassie. Google the song *Unbreakable* by Fireflight and you'll see what I mean.

But you don't have to wait until Sunday. I want you to do something you've never done before and then I promise to get out of your face. Go into your bedroom by yourself and close the door. Download the song *Hallelujah* by Heather

Williams. Play that and dance to God in front of the mirror. I'll be your backup singer. Your heart will burst. Then listen to Natalie Grant's *Your Great Name*.

Talk with God. Give Him your life. Ask Him what His will is for you. Ask Him to show you the way. He's waiting. Your Heavenly Father misses you.

CHAPTER 7

Purity and Modesty

—◦◦◦◦—

My 17-year-old son messed up his wrist after dunking a basketball in our drive-way. My son's friends said he broke the concrete when he landed. That was almost the truth. His sister saw it happen and thought he was dead. To that our Russian pediatrician – we'll hear more about him later – said, "Why are you dunking these ball? You not gething paid. The guys gething paid? They can dunk ball. You no need to *reeeeesk* your *life* to dunk ball."

Harlotry is nothing new. The Bible has examples of women who sold them-selves out and dressed a certain way to advertise it. What is new is that your average girl these days is not getting paid for it. That was cold. But if I'm writing a book, I'm not wasting your time and my pages lying to you. Because I mean is that smart? To show the world your stuff for free, and give your body to a guy for free when you're not married (or to another girl, see Chapter 5)? Or let him see sexy pictures of you? I don't think so.

If you get sexual with a guy and you're not married, he's getting something for nothing. God created sex for marriage. He made us ladies to look very at-tractive and inviting so guys would want to marry us and make babies. Duh, right?

We need to wait until we're married. You're good at waiting. You wait all the time. I know you can do this. You wait for school to be over. You wait for Christmas and your birthday. You wait for summer break to come. You or someone who annoys you waits for Justin Bieber to post something on Instagram.

But why? What's our true motivation for waiting to get physically intimate with someone? What if the guy isn't perfect after the wedding? Well, unless you run into Jesus Christ or Mr. Darcy from *Pride & Prejudice* some time soon, that's pretty much everyone. No guy is perfect. Jane Austen was a brilliant writer, but she had it completely backwards when it came to Mr. Darcy and Mr. Collins. She sure did enjoy kicking around the clergy. But where's Mr. Collins now? Where's Mr. Elden now? Nowhere baby. This is our book and we say: no guy is perfect and Christian boys are cool. Even so, we aren't saving ourselves only for him.

Let's think it through. What a crushing blow and not that fun a start to marriage, if you saved yourself for him. "I saved myself all that time and now you're falling asleep while I'm talking to you about curling my hair." Or, "I saved myself all that time and you forgot to take out the trash and now you've gone and lost your job." It sets the bar pritttt-tee high for the guy.

Or, worst nightmare, you saved yourself for him but he didn't save himself for you. Or, even worse worst nightmare, you saved yourself for him and he messes up and commits adultery or struggles with pornography after you are married. And you would need to forgive him for that. But we've got a rotten recipe for never forgiving him right there. Saving yourself for your future husband forever sets the tone of superiority of the perfect wife over the doofus guy the entire marriage. Which might not last very long. The marriage, that is. Think I'm exaggerating? Wait till we get to the marriage chapters. Big ol' mess. And I'm sure you've heard many wives talk down to their husbands haven't you. But precious child of God, you can get a head start on all that good wife stuff right now. We accomplish this by realizing our reason for waiting ultimately has to be for God.

I'm going to hit you with a bunch of Psalms that are going to make you think God is talking directly to you about waiting in your relationships with guys. We'll look at these passages and then chat again after that.

Ready? Let's rock.

Psalm 37:7 *"Wait patiently upon the Lord, and hope in him: fret not thyself for him which prospereth in his way, nor for the man that bringeth his enterprises to pass."*

Psalm 37:9 *"For evildoers shall be cut off, and they that wait upon the Lord, they shall inherit the land."*

Psalm 37:34 *"Wait thou on the Lord, and keep his way, and he shall exalt thee, that thou shalt inherit the land: when the wicked men shall perish, thou shalt see. I have seen the wicked strong, and spreading."*

Psalm 40:1 *"I waited patiently for the Lord, and he inclined unto me, and heard my cry. He brought me also out of the horrible pit."*

Psalm 42:5 *"Why art thou cast down, my soul, and unquiet within me? Wait on God: for I will yet give him thanks for the help of his presence. My God, my soul is cast down within."*
God understands that waiting is hard.

Psalm 69:3 *"I am weary of crying: my throat is dry: mine eyes fail, while I wait for my God."*
As that vintage Sheryl Crow song says: I can't cry anymore.

Psalm 129: 5-8 *"I have waited on the Lord: my soul hath waited, and I have trusted in his word. My soul waiteth on the Lord more than the morning watch watcheth for the morning. Let Israel wait on the Lord: for with the Lord is mercy, and with him is great redemption. And he shall redeem Israel from all his iniquities."*

Kind of makes you want to wait for the Lord, reading all that. Besides all those Psalms, here are a few more passages for you. Who is it that will mount up with wings like eagles? Who is going to run and not be weary? Somethin somethin? Ahhh, people who wait on the Lord. That's who. Check it out:

Isaiah 40:31 *"But they that wait upon the Lord, shall renew their strength: they shall lift up the wings, as the eagles: they shall run, and not be weary, and they shall walk and not faint."*

Micah 7:7 *"Therefore I will look unto the Lord: I will wait for God my Savior: my God will hear me."*

Zephaniah 3:8 *"Therefore wait ye upon me, saith the Lord."*

Well okay we know we should wait, and we know our motivation should be to honor God rather than honoring our future husbands. But how? Joshua Harris in *I Kissed Dating Good-Bye* points out that the only way King David committed adultery with Bathsheba was for him to do the very first thing he should not have done. He should have been off at war with the other whoop-up-on-bad-guys warrior types but he wasn't. Home skillet was trynna laze around at his crib. That was the first thing. He wasn't where he should have been. Then he saw hot Bathsheba and they got busy. It was very tragic the way that whole thing ended and I'll tell you more about that in the chapter on painful relationships. The point is, David did not wake up one day and say, "It's a nice sunny day outside. I think I'll go get sexual with someone who isn't my wife."

We have to be intentional about not doing the very first thing that could possibly lead to giving up our purity. The first thing is: don't let yourself be alone with a boy or a man. Boom, we've just taken care of the problem right there.

"Okay you seem really nice and all but aren't you like 40 years old or something?" You might be asking. Yeah I'm some mom, but listen. I'm still a flesh and blood chick. My husband gets deployed for the military for months at a time. I go to parties or activities where it seems everyone else has their man with them and it's just me without a guy. No one hugging me or whispering to me that I'm pretty, never alone with my man's arms around me. It's very solitary. It's lonely.

Sheesh, that was a downer. What were we talking about again? Oh I know, I was telling you that I can do lonely. It's really hard for me but I do it. If I can do it, you can do it. And if my husband goes to be with the Lord in heaven before I do, I'll be holding myself to the same standard of purity as I am asking of you. Oh it'll be a problem too because I'm fixing to be a babe when I'm 86 years old. They'll be standing in line to cozy up to me and my blue hair, you just wait and see. I'll pop the rude ones upside the head with my phone too if they try to get flirty with me. I'm not taking a selfie with any one of those geezers till there's a ring on my well seasoned finger either.

Whether 16 years old or 86, we girls really can live without affection or intimacy with a guy until we're married and I'll tell you how. Trust your God.

This often means listening to your parents. Or whoever looks out for you on God's behalf. They can pick up on stuff that we don't always see. They are so in between you and your fun, right. I know this. But look. Until you're married, your parents are on your side. They're the good guys. When we resist the authority of our parents it's not that genius of us to do this. It's like a squirrel spending his whole life trying to prove, "I can be a lizard if you'd only let me!" I know they've got that Geico guy, but just embrace your squirrelness, little man. Enjoy your acorns. You've got tree branches to jump around on. You get to raid my bird feeder before the birds ever knew I'd filled it. It's a great life. Being a lizard might not be all you think it is. If we spend our whole lives trying to be someone that our parents won't let us be, then we are wasting all our energy and efforts striving against God. As far as I can tell, throughout all of history, striving against Him has never been successful.

So we need to see our parents as protecting us. Yes, they can be annoying, imperfect, they don't understand you all the time, but we still need their protection and I'm preaching to myself as I preach to you because I respect the leadership of my husband. Amazing discovery: I honor my leader and he didn't lock me in a closet and not let me have any fun. If your parents and other family members are looking out for you and won't let you do certain things with certain people, then you are very blessed. You might even begin to feel sorry for the girls who get to do and say whatever they want.

We have an interesting story in Genesis where a girl named Dinah goes and has sex with a prince of another kingdom. Her brothers go ballistic. I mean they kill the prince and his whole family. I thought that was really sad actually because the prince was sweet to Dinah and truly loved her. He asked her daddy if he could marry her afterward and everything. But her brothers were not having their sister's purity taken that way before marriage. They were like, Bro, do you really think we're going to let you treat our sister like a harlot?

I wish we all had someone who would fiercely defend our honor like that. They don't need to go slaughtering everyone, and Dinah's father was very dismayed at what the brothers had done. But at least give the guy a hard time if he touches us. Anyone who messed with Dinah had to answer to someone. It was honorable of her brothers to defend her.

Some of us girls feel like we don't have anyone truly looking out for us. The "adults" that God has entrusted to look out for us are too wrapped up in themselves and are busy acting like children. They have no time for us. They just yell at us for their own convenience and aren't even thinking about what's best for us.

God understands. And I'll be honest with you, I have to ask those brothers of Dinah's: hey guys, where were you when Dinah first met Mister Prince? Yah, where were you then? Sometimes when I read the passage it sounds as if the brothers were thinking about their own reputation, not hers. I can't really tell. The Bible does say she went out to see the other maidens of the land and apparently none of her brothers or anyone else was along with her.

That's like, Oh I think I'll go down to Daytona Beach by myself to see the other maidens of the land. See? She crossed our purity plan guideline: never put yourself in a situation where you could be alone with a guy. She could have asked a friend to go along but then that's two cute chicks alone at Daytona Beach. Not much better than one. She probably just should not have gone. Which means not getting her way. And that's the way we Godly girls roll.

If Dinah had a phone you know she would have been texting that prince and snap chatting every night till 1:00 in the morning. Not cool. Dinah would have had to ask herself on a daily basis: Am I texting with him like any other friend? Or am I acting like we are a thing. Because if we're a thing, and he can't give me a ring, then eventually I'm going to feel some sting.

Let's state the obvious: the guy isn't the one who can get pregnant. Have you ever talked with someone who has had an abortion? She will tell you that the unbearable grief that haunts her is something you never want to experience. Do not be deceived. Abortion is not a quick fix. And sexually transmitted diseases are a horrifying reality, a grave consequence to defying God's plan for intimacy between one man and his wife. It's challenging but we have to yield our will to God's so we will never get to that point. Dinah could have asked her family to invite the princely people over or something. Have some family time. See him and his family in, like, person. Do it right, be friends, grill some burgers, hang with the family rather than one-on-one. The prince proposes and thennnnn you can text all you want and get physical. No one would've gotten slaughtered, happy ending, but Dinah and the prince did it all backwards.

God's our Father, He just truly is, open almost any chapter of the Bible, that's what it's going to say. He provides the affection, attention, comfort, love and intimacy we ever thought about needing and then some. He's our overflowing supply of that. You read some tricky stuff for school, so if you can survive all that then I know you would love reading the whole Bible. Don't rely on people like me to explain the Bible to you because a lot of them have never even read the whole thing themselves. If you read the whole Bible then you have more knowledge of God than 85 percent of pastors. I made up that number. But it's got to be really high.

I know you can wait on the Lord. I know you can ask God to tell you where to go, whom to hang out with and how much to text with someone. If you've already messed up with a guy or guys, Satan-pants wants to have a big party with that and tell you that you can't ever be pure. It's such a lie. David would never have written all those Psalms we just read if that was true. Don't be listening to that loser Say-Tee because God's word says He makes all things new. Yes He sometimes allows tough consequences when we fail, but when we come to Him, "here is my heart, I'm yours Lord," we are cleansed by the blood of Christ. We are made pure spiritually that very moment.

Right now, today, commit to purity from now on as expressing your devotion to waiting on God. Commit to believing the authority of your parents is good, and ultimately report directly to your Heavenly Father whether your parents are there for you or not. Commit never to let yourself be alone with a guy or get sexy with a guy. Commit to honor God, and you've got the Creator of the universe on your side.

MODESTY

My Mom was talking to a friend about how difficult it is to place one's life continuously in surrender to God. Her friend said, "Yeah, like you might have to go to a third world country to be a missionary."

My Mom said, "No, like I might not get to wear pretty clothes."

There's just no telling what the Lord might ask us to do. We are talking huge sacrifices here people. But once we've committed to honoring God with our life, we are going to want to display this on the outside. We have got to be modest in the way we dress. My Mom is very stylin' in her 70s and I dare say like-mother-like-daughter on that one. Modesty takes a little effort. God's worth it.

Deep down inside of us all is a naughty little girl but, as the authors of *It's (Not That) Complicated* say, if we're serious about honoring God, then we'll want to control our inner vamp.

Packaging and titles are not impressive. We can make up our own. Food companies that sell mischievous treats try to pass them off as worthy for consumption by calling them "snacks." When really, we all know that those fluffy desserts are 500 percent sugar, 300 percent lard and one molecule away from plastic. The same concept goes for clothing. These days the clothing manufacturer people say something is a dress when it is barely a shirt. I have turned many a tiny "dress" into a tunic worn over jeans to spare other people's husbands and sons from being assaulted by my legs and almost my hynie.

I mourned the loss of this one purple dress I dearly loved. It was so pretty. It was too low-cut in the chest though, and there was nothing I could do about it. It wasn't sew-able or, more my speed, safety pin-able. And it wouldn't look right with a camisole under it. It had to go back. I loved this dress. I'd try it on and say to my daughters, "I'll try it on again tomorrow. Maybe it will grow tonight?" They would laugh and say, Mom it's not going to grow.

Alas, they were right and we mailed it back. On the order form, the store asks for a reason code such as too short, too wide, did not like fabric or did not like style. I checked "other" and wrote "shows cleavage." My daughters thought that was hilarious. I mean there was no "shows cleavage" option. I had to provide that information and help these people see that not everybody wants to walk around looking like that.

After I first became a serious God-fearing Christian, I went through a potato sack phase for a while there and wore clothes with zero personality whatsoever. I didn't feel beautiful for my husband though. So I went back to more stylish clothes, but I know modesty when I see it. Summertime is hot but a modest alternative to shorts is, brain cell: the same thing ladies have done all throughout history. Skirts. Long, straight maxi skirts? Totally haute couture these days.

I did go through a brief rebellious moment a couple of years ago when I was sick and tired of everyone else walking around looking sexy. And meanwhile I'm some church lady. Humph. I told my children that you can watch any 1980s movie that has prostitutes in it and spot those immediately. The prostitutes are the ones dressed the way everyone looks at Six Flags today. Sick and tired of being a good girl.

So I bought a smokin' hot red dress one day. And I could rock the red dress let me tell you because sister I am fit and svelte. But guess what? My husband very gently and sweetly told me he didn't like that dress. Wow. Guy travels the world and what he wants in the love of his life is for me to honor God with the way I dress in public. In private? Don't use your imagination. My husband thinks my modesty in public is beautiful and attractive. He loves having a God-fearing wife who looks like one. I never wore the hot red dress again.

The Bible says, *"In like manner also, that women adorn themselves in modest apparel."* 1 Timothy 2:9. We aren't given a lot of specifics about that in the Bible, but we can figure it out. The idea is not to accentuate your particular attractive features for anyone except in private for your husband. As opposed to accentuating them in front of, say, my husband. Or my teenage son for that matter.

It's the heart behind the thing that matters. Our standard should not merely be: look a little less smarmy than the rest of the world. That is not hard at all to do. Our standard should be:

- Does this article of clothing honor God with the way it looks on me?
- Will people know that I'm a Christian when I wear this piece of clothing?
- Could they believe anything I say about God while I am wearing this?
- Or are they too busy thinking about my lovely figure? If I'm not blushing, something is wrong.

Men are not going to speak up about this issue, even pastors. It's very awkward for them. They basically would have to admit that they find us all very provocative. Then they'd feel like a dweeb and unworthy even to say the word church. We girls have to hold one other accountable and set a good example for one another. Save the sexiness for your husband in the bedroom, y'all. There was a reason for those choir robes back in the day. Don't make me buy you a potato sack now.

PART III. MARRIAGE

―⸻―

"When I go home, I put away that person who's in control and demanding and let him be in control … I don't want to grow old by myself, and I don't want to be a single mom."

Celebrity chef Giada De Laurentiis, *Parade Magazine*, July 13, 2014

CHAPTER 8

JOY AND POWER

—⚬⚬⚬—

Oh wow, that was awesome. We nailed it just then in that last part didn't we? We explained so beautifully to our girls how urgent it is for them to respect their parents and not try to be like the rest of the world. To honor God inside and out, and to care only what He thinks. Hoo. That was exhilarating. I think they totally listened.

Um, but there's this scripture God keeps sticking in my head and here she is: *"Thou therefore that teachest another, teachest thou not thyself?"* Romans 2:21. Sewwww, that just put the screech on the mama party for me right there. Ladies? God has entrusted us wives with a big job.

Men have God as their authority. Men answer to their boss like we do if we work, but ultimately in every aspect of their lives men answer to God. Whether a man recognizes and respects this or not, it's true. Boom, pretty simple. But women? God realizes women can multi-task and He has given us two jobs. They are:

- Loving God's authority over us and seeing it as good.
- Loving our husbands' leadership and seeing it as good.

Big job realizing this. Massive. It's where women find joy and power. We ladies misunderstand "leader" and think it means "better" and so we try over and over our whole lives to prove that we are as good as men. We're just as smart, we can achieve as much. Of course we are and of course we can. But all that amounts to is pleading and striving that, "I'm a juicy hamburger too."

If every Fortune 500 company was led by a woman, we'd still never quite feel that we had reached the point where we were a juicy hamburger. Because really, God doesn't want us to compete to be a hamburger at all. As long as we keep doing that, we'll never get to see that He wants us to be filet mignon with lobster bisque. Vegetarian version: sautéed asparagus crepes with hollandaise sauce. Gluten/dairy free version: Hummus soufflé with avocado salad. Whatever. Man, you girls are so picky.

Let the guys be the burger and let's move on.

We tell girls to respect their parents' leadership, and we can truly show them by doing it ourselves in our own marriages. What are we teaching girls if we override our husbands' decisions or speak to them disrespectfully? We are teaching girls that we don't believe what we are telling them to believe. We're teaching them to care what people think. We need to teach them to care only what God thinks. I've lost track at this point who is the lizard and who is the burger. Can I be the ice cream? But the message is the same. We cannot afford to waste our lives trying to prove we're someone we were not designed to be. Our girls are watching us.

Try getting professional literary worker people to take a book seriously when it has the word "homemaker" on the back cover and "Whatever" on the front cover. Try that for like 30 minutes. It's the opposite of fun. I could have named it *Powerful Females of Global Dominion Who Must Acquiesce to the Almighty with Their Womanhood in Order to Sweep the Nation Before It Crumbles into the Abyss*. That title rolls off the tongue very nicely. Especially followed by an evil cackle. Why didn't you girls tell me I could name it that? Well, it's okay because I decided something important a long time ago: I can't take myself too seriously.

I just can't find anything in the Bible that says women need to show the world that we deserve equal treatment to men. Can't find it. So it must not be important to God. If it's not important to God, then it shouldn't be important to us. In fact, if the spiritual enemy, silly ol' Satan, can keep us busy shooting for an unreachable goal, then we'll never experience the fulfilling life God has for us. What the Bible does say is that if anyone would boast of anything at all, it would be that she knows and loves the Lord Jesus Christ. Do we take Him at His word?

Whether they stay home or work – or a combination of the two – women are the heart of their homes and the heart of our nation. If the women do not understand the goodness of God's authority and the goodness their husbands' leadership, then they are robbing themselves of joy, power, love and protection. Our women are brokenhearted because of it. Men are the head of the home and the head of the nation, and their wives have great power over them. With a land full of brokenhearted women, our country has lost its head.

OLDEST ONE IN THE BOOK

Something that holds women back from embracing their husbands' leadership is the very sensible and right objection to the insane concept that all men have authority over all women. All men do not have dominion over all women. That is abusive, in any society. All God asks is that each wife place herself under the leadership of one man, her own husband. We do not obey the delivery man or the church pastor – or our own parents once we are grown. Scripture says for `chil-drennnnn`, not grown-ups, to obey their parents. Women can be kind and respectful toward their parents, but once we are married, mommy and daddy no longer have a say. Y'all remind me I said that when I have four sons-in-law.

In rightly aiming to avoid abuse of power, our society has now stripped men of almost all power in marriage. We have swung wildly in the opposite direction away from abuse with no regard for God's order. Have you noticed the men in our nation behaving more and more like little boys? Our culture has removed from them any expectation of their having leadership in their families for so long that they think they do not need to take responsibility.

One aspect of womanhood is that a wife has astonishing power over her husband, either to support his leadership or tear it down. Our buddy Job is about the only guy in the Bible who overcame a negative, discouraging wife. And Satan specifically went on the attack against Job. He must have seen him as an exceptional challenge and threat.

Wives are their husbands' weak spot. It's not our fault or our idea. I didn't decide it would be this way. God decided it. We can demonstrate that easily enough. Three words: Fall of man. Eve totally got to Adam in the Garden of Eden because she was his weak point. That naughty snake knew Eve had this power; why else would he have gone to her? Consider Delilah's power over Samson, the strongest man who ever lived. Scripture says she pressed him daily to give up the secret to his strength and *"vexed him unto death"* with her words. If another man had tried to bring Samson down the way Delilah messed with his mind, it never would have worked. Samson would have been like, "Dude."

Here is what God has for us. And it's rather incredible. The wife, not the husband, has the power to decide if her family is going to follow chart #1, which is God's order laid out for us in 1 Corinthians 11:3, which says *"... the head of every man is Christ, and the head of the woman is the man, and the head of Christ is God."* Or, the wife can decide to go with chart #2, which is complete chaos. When God says to us, *"Let the wife see that she reverence her husband,"* He is explaining that the guy can't force us.

Wife's Choice #1:   Wife's Choice #2:

God's Way in 1 Corinthians 11:3   Misunderstanding leadership

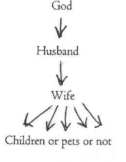

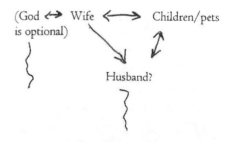

The husband in this chaos doesn't know which way is up in his own family.

Spooky version? Apply these charts in a collective sense to the entire world. Explains a lot, huh. Look at any newspaper or turn on the television for six minutes and shudder at the immoral, violent mess out there.

In 150-ish B.C. the Roman official Cato implored men to be stronger leaders in their homes. He was warning the men what would happen to their society if Rome continued going in the direction of chart number two.[42] Unfortunately, he was talking to the guys. Our man Cato could only get so far because all of that is up to the wife. Rome collapsed not too long after that.

My handy charts are new, but the concept behind them has been an area of tension since the beginning of time. So why even try? Because I believe that our nation has a crucial, urgent opportunity right now not to go the way of Rome. Of course people disagree and debate about the complexities of why the Roman Empire fell. But one thing is clear: when individual families misunderstand God, then a whole nation dishonors God, and we see throughout the Bible and all of history that He's not having that go on indefinitely.

Women need to see that God has given us a double buffer of love and protection. God and our husbands stand between danger and us. Why would we not welcome this? Why would we say, "No thank you, I don't want two air bags in my bulletproof van before I get hit by this 18-wheeler. I'd much rather flip a convertible over with nothing in between the pavement and me." Why do we do this? It's because we have a spiritual enemy who has been feeding us a lie since the beginning of time.

The lie is that a husband's leadership is bad. And also that there is no danger. It seems to be working pretty well. I would not have bothered writing this book if I didn't think we are smarter than that.

Satan got Eve to be stupid two ways. He questioned God's words. It worked. In Genesis, Satan said to Eve: Did God really say not to eat the fruit? Are you sure about that? He made Eve question God's words. Women can be smarter than Eve and ignore this outrageous lie by reading and loving God's word our entire lives. We can believe what it says, believe it is true. Then Satan contradicted her husband. See, God never told Eve the deal about the fruit in the first place. God told Adam, and then Adam briefed Eve. Power point presentation or whatever they used to do back then. After that, Satan said to Eve: Sweety, doing what your husband said to do is holding you back girl, it's so yesterday to listen to your husband. Just think of all the good and knowledge that would open up to you if you took charge and branched out with this fruit thing.

Ladies, we can be smarter than Eve and ignore this ridiculous nonsense by gladly following our husbands and refusing to contradict them.

The "why" Satan gave Eve was pretty sly. He didn't say: Look the Braves will get six homeruns every game from now on if you disobey God and your husband. Men insert your team. Sir, I told you in the preface that I'm talking to my girlfriends. Satan didn't say: Check it out Eve, you'll never have to sharpen or charge your cordless power saw again. You can sleep late every morning and still get a paycheck.

No. He told her she would be wise.

I've got to hand it to Satan. That was pretty savvy. He really knows how to play us ladies. He knows women want to be respected as being smart, to be seen as having great faculties of knowledge and sound judgment, we love brilliant ideas, we love to discover the truth. All of which is to say, women love wisdom. The enemy knows that wisdom is what women are seeking. He wants us not to find it. He sends us in the opposite direction of where we will find it. He knows women have great potential in this area. He knows much of the power of our entire culture depends on women's not finding true wisdom.

Say-Say says that the way to find wisdom is by defying God and your husband. But this is the very opposite of what the Bible says. The Bible says that the fear of the Lord is the beginning of wisdom and that a wise woman builds up her household. We will find wisdom in knowing and trusting God's word, loving and trusting God's authority and loving and trusting our husbands' leadership. We've never even found the clue bulb, much less turned the lamp on, when we think ignoring God is going to get us anywhere.

We as a nation don't know the scriptures, and so we don't know our God or understand that His authority and ways are perfect. In the rest of our discussions about marriage, we will see how wives need to grasp that God's order for our marriages is good. "Following" doesn't mean "loser." Only when women act like women, are men free to act like men.

There was a reason God begins the Bible with this scenario between Adam, Eve and the enemy with wisdom at stake. We need to pay attention to it. God did not begin the fall of man with two gladiator type guys duking it out to win the affection of a lady. He did not begin the Bible with a fable describing a struggle between a lion and a mouse over cleverness and safety. He did not begin the Bible with two nations warring over land and wealth. No, the war of humanity originated in a struggle for leadership among one man, his wife and the enemy, over wisdom. And silly Satan's been doing his best to keep the flames of rebellion going in the hearts of us wives ever since then. Puh-lease. If we start being tempted to question God's word or contradict our husbands' leadership, we can remind ourselves: Well pooh. That's the oldest one in The Book.

QUEEN OR CO-WORKER

If you're a curious, lively lady like I am, then you love to be in charge of something. And you love a challenge. The following Bible passage gives us both. *"And if a house be divided against itself, that house cannot stand,"* Jesus said in Mark 3:23.

If we trust God's order of things in our family, then we cheerfully give up the job of head honcho to our man. He's the king. This means we get to be the sweet helper wearing a tiara. I like that job but it hasn't come naturally, because I'm naturally opinionated and bossy. One way God helped me was to convince me that if the husband is in charge, then the way for a household to be divided against itself?

You got it. The wife.

Under normal circumstances, we're the ones who can do the dividing. Quite a responsibility for us ladies not to do that, eh? And a challenging one because, at first anyway until it becomes a part of us, it's a daily thing that basically goes against every selfish thought or desire we ever have.

Let's look at that word "against," in *"divided against itself"* because there's our bad guy. Our goal is not to go against our husbands. In Latin, the preposition "against" is "contra." From that we get the English word "contradict," the "dict" part meaning "speak." The English adjective "contrary" is derived from this too. That "contra" is not a sleepy sort of "against," such as leaning against the door frame while you file your fingernails. It's a very active sort of "against" that expresses motion or movement,[27] such as a train wreck. Which we are trying to avoid in our marriages. Add all that together, stir it up in a bowl and lick the spoon. What do we get? A big ol' Don't Be Contradicting Your Husband Pie, fresh out of the oven.

This is easy when he does what we want him to do. You would probably agree with me that this is easier before we have children. We really don't care all that much about the color of the new roof. But that's my baby he's messing with. That's some serious passion right there. Mama lion kicks in and God created us to protect our children so giddy-up with that. The problem is, women misapply this intuition of protection and take it out on the good guy. We take it out on the baby's daddy. If we step back and think about it, we've up and gone a little cuckoo if we try to protect a child from his own father, except in extreme cases. I'm talking about day to day normal issues:

- Small (goldfish crackers aren't organic)
- Medium sized (daughter's eye appointment)
- And large (buying a house)

Children or not, what would God have us do rather than contradict our husbands? The Bible says for wives to *"submit to their own husbands."* Ephesians 4:22. Let's think about that word "submit" because it is more shocking than Lady Gaga's new outfit. Is "submitting" some kind of wacky third world uneducated turban abusive situation repression imprisonment thing happening? No. The Latin preposition for "under" or "below" is "sub." As in subway, below the ground transportation. As in, *"wives, subject yourselves to your husbands."* Do we have enough love and fear of God in our hearts to believe Him when He asks us to place ourselves below our husbands? We must, or we wouldn't be into a sassy-chic book that quotes scripture.

Submission doesn't mean we have no value, no brain, no worth. Just the opposite. Submitting to our husbands is where we find great value and worth. It's a big thing to do in a world screaming at us not to do it. It is feminine and lovely to look up adoringly at our husbands. The only way to do that is to consider ourselves below them.[34] This concept of submission is not insulting if a wife can picture herself below her husband in the same way Superman was below a bus when he miraculously lifted it off the ground. Your husband needs you. The word for "I lifted up" in Latin is sustuli. Another form of that same word is sublatus which means lifted. We see "sust" and "sub" there, and this reveals to us that when you **sub**mit to your husband, you are lifting him up and **sust**aining him. When you sustain him, you sustain your marriage.

If a wife is not placing herself under her husband, then she is placing her husband beside herself as a co-worker. Which, on many issues, means she will be resisting his leadership, so she is actually placing him under herself. This pretty much means she has become his mommy. And that's weird.

Not too long before Christ was born, the historian Livy reported that a Roman wrote the following to husbands about their wives: "The moment they begin to be your equals, they will be your superiors."[42]

A couple of thoughts. One, that guy plagiarized me. But also, his statement demonstrates that this issue of wives resisting God's plan for submission is nothing new. The struggle is real. It doesn't have to be. You don't have to wait for your husband to deserve submission from you. You'll be waiting a long time because he's only human. Rather, ask God to give you a submissive wife's heart. And sustaining your husband through submission will be what flows out of you.

If you run all this by your husband and ask him if he would like for you to be submissive to his leadership, then you might be hoping he will let you off the hook by saying, "Submission? Who me? Oh no, never dear. This is America." He might very well say that but we can't believe him. One, he's thinking it's a trick question and he's better off playing it safe or he'll pay later. Two, he's gotten so used to being not in charge that he doesn't even know what that would be like.

My Granny felt sorry for an indoor, caged, pet bunny rabbit who, when let out of the cage for short times, didn't know how to hop around quickly or even perk up his ears, which lay limp and drooping around his head. "Bless its little hearrrrrt," she'd say. "It doesn't even know what it is anymorrrre." The world has been telling our men for so long that they aren't to lead, that they are selfish and bad to try to lead or expect a wife and children to follow. That they are incapable of doing it. That the very idea is for uneducated losers, and that smart, successful men are progressive enough to defy something as irrelevant and outdated as the Bible. This is all a lie. Men don't even know what they are anymore because of it.

A wife asking her husband out of nowhere if he would like to be a real man is going to be disorienting to him at first. Most husbands never considered that as a happy option. The need for leadership is so intense for a man that the only way he might be able to express verbally the agony of doing without it is through humor. "I don't need Google," the husband joke goes. "I have my wife."

I'm not laughing. A wife can love viewing her husband as the king of their little kingdom because if he's the king, then she gets to be the queen. Being a queen is a lot more fun and romantic than the world's way. It sounds awfully dreary to consider ourselves co-workers. Blech. To make co-decisions after co-deliberating sounds like a sterile conference room arrangement to me. To view marriage as an equal partnership? Boring. Not romantic.

Keep your equal partnership and give me back my tiara.

Queen Esther, who quite arguably was the bomb, understood that she was risking her life to go and humbly ask her husband to reconsider his decision to wipe out the nation of Israel. That would be in the "large" category of importance. And yet she was really humble and gracious about it. She went to talk to him with fear and trembling. It had to have been the first time she ever bothered him like that. He hadn't been enduring 65 contrary opinions every day for years from her about the dishwasher or the kitchen trash. She approached him with beautiful queenly humility and a submissive heart. How irresistible. That king was loving that. He ordered a new decree that would defend the Jews. Through Esther's humble, submissive spirit, God saved the nation of Israel.

Slap chat that.

I don't know what that means but we're saying it. There's nothing interesting, radical or progressive about a wife taking the lead over her husband. It doesn't take any brains or strength. It's what everyone else is doing. It's nothing new. Eve did it, Delilah did it, Jezebel did it. Defy the world instead by giving up selfish contradicting and embrace queenly submitting. Do that, and girl it's on.

———

NOT A DOOR MAT

People who do not fully understand the nature of Godly womanhood will object to wifely submission. They are concerned about its turning the wife into nothing but a door mat. They fear the husband is skipping along happily while playing his wife for a fool. I hear you. I see that. It's a concern. But it isn't. Many of us have read and heard lots of brainy experts citing "research" about the pursuit of happiness in marriage. These people truly care about marriage and think they will help marriages by empowering women to stand up for themselves and demand an equal partnership. They are sending wives in the opposite direction of where they will find joy. Their goal is all wrong.

Some of the Important New Research includes studies about women who are facing divorce after becoming harsh, demanding wives.[49] One reason they became that way was because they had grown up seeing a woman they loved being mistreated by her husband. They saw their own mother or their own grandmother wait on the guy hand and foot and he treated her like dirt. Or they saw movies, books, everywhere they looked actually, shouting at them their whole lives the message that, when a wife is humble, she is miserable and mistreated. A girl might grow up clinging tightly to that belief. Stuck in her head and embedded in her very soul is the thought: "submission equals misery." As a child, that little girl formed the following thought process:

Humble-acting wife? —→ Mean Husband —→ Unhappy Marriage (Wrong)

And so she resolves to become an outspoken, take-charge wife in order to break this perceived cycle of unhappy marriage. She believes that a wife must speak up and take leadership. She wants a happy marriage. She sees the pain from her own childhood and a lifetime of unBiblical literature and warped entertainment and she thinks she can fix it in her own life by doing the following. But it won't work:

Take-charge wife ⟶ Whipped husband ⟶ Happy marriage? (Also wrong)

Let's take apart all that incorrect arrow flow in a couple of ways.

First, the humble-acting wife. In a joyless marriage, I severely question whether a wife is truly humble in the first place. She's simply acting humble on the outside. Children are very perceptive but they do not see the layers of junk going on in marriage. It is possible that the mother or grandmother who seemed to wait on her husband hand and foot was, in reality, playing the martyr in front of the family. In private she might very well have been cutting him to shreds with criticism verbally and nonverbally, and withholding physical affection. Guy hasn't had any action in the bedroom for 45 years. No wonder he's cranky. Men don't play along with the subtle female neuroses and so, to everyone watching, the misery seems one-sided. He doesn't pull power plays, he's just plain old grouchy for all the world to see.

A truly humble wife in the Biblical sense, a wife who is genuinely making it her goal to shower love and honor on her husband in every way, as unto the Lord, is very unlikely to endure a lifetime of being treated badly by her husband. It's just not in the nature of your average man to keep up that kind of evil scoundrel personality in the face of that much Godly sweetness.[34] He'd melt in a heartbeat. So I question the presence of wifely humility in a joyless marriage and call it all a charade. What a little girl doesn't realize is actually going on is this:

Cold frosty wife ⇆ Deeply hurt, aloof husband ⟶ Unhappy marriage

In this more realistic scenario, the arrows go back and forth between husband and wife because it's a sad cycle in which no one is honoring God at all. The more frosty the wife, the more deeply hurt the husband is, the more he detaches and the worse he treats her. The more dramatic show she makes of bringing him his coffee and newspaper so all the family can see how wonderful she is and how terrible he is and on we go. And it is an unhappy marriage indeed. But it is not caused by a truly humble wife. That's not humility. That's something else. Use your own modern words to describe it, pouty passive aggressive. The wife is exalting herself over her husband. The important thing to see is that God is nowhere in this picture at all.

Now what about those wacky arrows showing the take-charge wife and the whipped husband? Jezebel and Ahab from the Bible can explain how that works. Ahab was a very incompetent, girly fellow. I started laughing out loud once when I read in the book of 1 Kings where he doesn't get his way about some vineyard he wanted, and he goes and sits on his bed and looks at the wall. He won't eat anything. Sounds like my 2-year-old daughter. This is not mature behavior. Well, Jezebel was quite the forceful wife. We don't really know which came first, but her assertiveness never made the guy more manly, only less so. We end up in this story with the very violent destruction of them both.

Let's say circumstances really do create a scenario where a wife is truly living out all God requires of her nearly every single day and she is mistreated for half a century. Our husbands are only human so all of us are going to feel this way at times. That's just life. But for the entire marriage? A husband could have an overpowering addiction that is making him behave so. He could have serious spiritual struggles that are bigger than his marriage. That is, he is not fully walking with God.

Abigail from the Bible completely understands. Her husband Nabal's name actually means "fool." This guy was a sinister, heavy-drinking grouch and the Bible says he was *"churlish and evil in his doings."* 1 Samuel 25. Abigail had to tiptoe around him and could not even tell him about some major, important stuff happening until he was in the right mood. He was such a grump that *"a man cannot speak to him."* 25:17. You can't even talk to the guy, he's so touchy and mean. And so dumb that he did David and his men very wrong which, sorry but I'm not crossing King David. He and his posse are fixing to slaughter Nabal's entire town because of Nabal's selfish, shortsighted foolishness and God would not like that.

Abigail saves the day. How does she do it? Does she sit Nabal down and tell him off? Does she whine about him at support groups? Does she call home and cry to mama? Does she read books containing lists of ways to make her husband change and improve? Does she get a divorce and tell everybody what a punk her husband was? No. Abigail the sweet wife makes haste and rides out to meet David. She falls on her face and takes all the men food and says I'm so sorry, blame me, please don't be angry. Sounding pretty humble to me. Sounding pretty "humble wife —→ mean husband" to me.

She has bowed to the ground and is at the eye level of, say, a door mat. She cleans up her husband's mess with grace and lowliness. David immediately softens and thanks God for sending Abigail. *"I have hearkened to your voice,"* David said to her in verse 35. One of the greatest men who ever lived was grateful to humble Abigail. He listened to her. He changed the course of his actions because of her and did not go slaughtering anybody. She reversed Nabal's clueless folly, appeased David's rage and saved many people's lives. This is heroic womanhood.

God's truth always comes out. God's ways are never wrong. We can always rely on His justice and here it is. Ten days later, God smote Nabal. Struck him dead. And David loved and married Abigail. True story, not psychobabble research, true story.

And so here are the facts from the Bible regarding being a so-called door mat wife. This could be you, but you playin:

Truly humble, Godly wife + Mean or nice husband —→ God will provide wife's joy

It might not end up that a happy marriage is what comes from a humble, submissive wife. I wish that were always so but it's not a promise we are given in God's word. But that's okay because it's not our goal. We can't manipulate our marriages. Anyone who tells you to manipulate your marriage hasn't read six pages of the Bible. Any six. Our goal is to glorify and honor God in our marriages, and the results are up to Him. Many authors, including well meaning Christian ones, will tell you that they have answers that will create a happy marriage. I'm not promising you that. I'm feeling a little Paul-esque right now when he says, *"Am I therefore become your enemy, because I tell you the truth?"* Galatians 4:16.

Anyone who views wifely humility as the weak root of a bad marriage, please consider this. Yes, the marriage in that passage in the Bible was an absolute disaster. Everyone watching Abigail and Nabal must have seen a submissive wife being treated gruffly by her husband. Her humility did not create a happy marriage. But she ultimately had joy, while her husband did not. And so we have to ask who in the story is the fool? And who is the wise?

CHAPTER 9

KEEPING YOUR MARRIAGE STRONG

———— ✴ ————

When we ladies think of keeping our marriages strong, what do we think? Romance, dates, weekend getaways, spending time together. Making time for a husband, talking with him, keeping some energy left over for him rather than using it all up on the children. Taking a walk together and holding hands. Those things are all right. Um ... especially if sex is eventually involved, from the guy's point of view. A man wants his lady's companionship. Genesis says that it is not good for a man to be alone. But I've got news for you. Those are the things that *we* like. Those are the things that are important to *females*. Those are the things that keep the marriage strong for *us*. Given the choice between those things and what I'm about to sock you with, our husbands could do without another date night for the rest of their lives.

What keeps the marriage strong from the husband's point of view? Here she is: Husbands really want us to go along with whatever they say. They want us to smile approvingly and adoringly of every decision they make. Every time. They really want us to look at them with warmth and respect in our eyes, all the time. Even if they turn out to be wrong later. Especially if they turn out to be wrong later. They want us not to be contentious with them and then justify it by telling ourselves we're just having discussions.

"Therefore as the church is subject unto Christ, so let the wives be to their own husbands in every thing." Ephesians 5:24.

It's not fun for husbands to go on a date on Friday night with someone who has been tearing them down the rest of the week and making them fight to feel like a man. It feels dishonest to them to get dressed up and do something special with someone who has essentially decided to be their enemy.

We have to get this right, ladies. Proverbs says there's nothing worse for a man than a contentious wife. A frown counts as contentious. A calm, quiet, intellectual discussion that shoots down his views counts as contentious. Cold tone of voice is contentious. Disapproving looks are contentious. Loud sighing. With a frosty matching facial expression. Hostile eyebrow activity. Unhappy body language. Pointing out all the ways he might be wrong, is contentious. Pointing out all the ways we might be right, is contentious, and that includes the footnotes and bibliographies of all our brilliant research. This is so destructive to our families that we should commit ourselves never to do it. The only genuine way to avoid a disapproving exterior is actually not to be disapproving on the inside. Try as we might, sooner or later we're going to slip up and say or do something that displays to all the family that we are looking down on our husbands. You can't be an orange tree that grows pears.

My man Noah Webster wrote the real deal dictionary in the year 1828 and I've got a copy of that bad boy sitting right here on my lap, open to the page with the word "contentious." He knew the Bible, his definitions are all Biblically sound. His name is Noah so hey. Thumb's up for this guy, we don't know what all those other modern dictionary versions are about. I don't mean this in a bad way, but sometimes when I cannot fall asleep, I will read portions of Noah Webster's 50 page introduction and I am out cold in no time. It's actually very fascinating once you get past the nearly microscopic font size. This guy doesn't mess around when it comes to words or the Bible. In his preface he applauds our "constitutions of free government" and refers to "that best gift of God to man, the christian religion."

Here are the words our beloved Mr. Webster says have to do with "contentious." You might be a contentious wife if ... you recognize any of this in yourself toward your husband:

- To strive against
- To struggle in opposition (Mr. Webster quotes Deuteronomy here, as in don't contend with the pesky Moabites)
- To use earnest efforts to obtain
- To defend
- To strive in debate (here he quotes the book of Acts and all the debating those early Christian fellows had to endure)
- To reprove sharply
- To chide
- To strive to convince and reclaim (he quotes the book of Nehemiah as he defended rebuilding the wall)
- To quarrel
- To dispute fiercely
- To wrangle as in two competitors

Not that smart to be doing any of this in our marriages, eh ladies. It rather puts a damper on the date night.

Does this mean the husband always gets his way? And he's a big baby and we're the only ones trying in the marriage? That we're the only ones putting any effort into the marriage? Those are valid questions and I would ask you to look at it this way. You are in charge of your children, right? They are supposed to respect your leadership. You get to decide pretty much everything from what they eat to what time they go to bed, especially when they are little. Does this mean you always get your way?

Give me a moment to recover from falling off the couch. I almost hit my head on the coffee table just then.

It is ridiculous for someone to suggest that we mothers always get our way. We know that as mothers we hardly ever get our way. I don't even know what my way is anymore. If I stopped and thought about it long enough, it would probably involve chocolate, lying in bed until 10:00 a.m. and watching movies all day. Wives who don't have children can completely relate to this too because all of us ladies have a huge amount of responsibility. None of us can just sit around getting our way.

A husband has given up his life to head up a family. The Bible says that the husband has to answer to God Almighty for his family, regardless of who's earning money. He would take a bullet in the chest for his family right this second without even thinking about it, if anyone threatened his family. Not my family; your family. Even if I've never met your particular husband I know this is true of him because it's the way he was created. Jesus said whoever would be greatest among you will be your servant. The husband is the leader but he's the greatest servant as well. I don't mean mopping or cooking. I mean he's sacrificing a great deal to be responsible for his family. We wives need to give him the honor his role is due.

Sometimes it has been of medium sized importance. Once, my husband asked me to take our daughter to a certain doctor for an eye problem. I asked him one question, one time, respectful tone of voice: "Do you think doctor Oz would be better than doctor Schnoz?" And he said yes. I disagreed with him. But my job is not to disagree with him.

So I took our daughter to doctor Oz, keeping in mind that there was, after all, a 50 percent chance that I was wrong. (Why do we think only about our husbands' 50 percent chance?) I was thankful that he cares about our daughter, thankful that he makes sure we have health insurance and thankful that he bought us a car so I could drive her to this appointment. It turned out that doctor Oz was wrong, and so a few days later my husband said to go to the other one. On the way there, my daughter said, "Mommy, I thought we should have gone to this doctor all along."

Here's what I said to her: "Sweety? Daddy's right, even when he's wrong."

She didn't go blind, her eyeballs didn't pop out, she was eventually fine. My husband never knew that I wanted doctor Schnoz. I'm not going to do that to him. If he reads this chapter he probably doesn't even have any idea what I'm talking about because it was a non-wife-fussy issue. (Hay babe, looking good in that flight suit.) And anyway, it turns out doctor Schnoz was wrong too and we ended up at doctor Blozz. God is going to honor us wives and keep us and our children protected when we follow our husbands according to His word, even when they are occasionally wrong. And they will be, because they are human.

Now don't bug out on me and start thinking you can't very sweetly ask if he wouldn't mind going a little easier on the air conditioning. It's all in your tone.

Is it: TURN THAT ARCTIC BLAST TO A LEVEL THAT IS DECENT FOR HUMAN SURVIVAL BEFORE A FAMILY OF PENGUINS MOVES INTO THE CLOSET.

You have made him out to be a villain. Or, do you rub his arm and softly say, "Honey, would it be all right to bump up the temperature a little bit for this cold natured little lady of yours? I'm a wee bit chilly." You have turned him into a hero.

We also do not need to take submission to such an extreme that we tell our child he can't compete in Saturday's soccer tournament because Daddy said we're going to go get pizza instead. What a shame that Travis got hit by a truck because I couldn't tell Daddy that I saw a truck coming. No, no, no. Obviously we remind our husbands of the tournament, or we tell them to look out for the truck. We can be sensible and respectfully provide information or facts he forgot or would want to know.

But hold on.

We have to be very selective about those facts and admit that many times we simply have an opinion or belief about something of no great significance, and that is when we must cheerfully yield and nip it. As unto the Lord. Pointing out the "fact" that Interstate 40 is busier this time of day while your husband is driving, goes in the annoying opinion department rather than helpful information. Don't speak it. We lie to ourselves and pretend we are providing information but it's not: it is actually a disguised criticism. What we are really saying to a husband, and what he hears is, "Your dumb decision to go I-40 shows really bad judgment, is wasting our time, and you're very incompetent." Loud sighs or displeased facial expressions communicate the same thing.

No date night is going to fix this.

<hr>

MORE KEEPING YOUR MARRIAGE STRONG

Have you ever wondered why Jesus didn't have a wife? I wonder if it's because His loyalty would have been divided. His enemies could've had an absolute party with trying to divide Jesus between his savior gig and devotion to his wife: "Come down off the cross or your wife gets it."

What Would Jesus Do?

You see the impossibility of it. He would have had to choose between God and his wife, the way Adam did, and failed.

The actor Christian Bale said in an interview with *The Wall Street Journal Magazine* that the only way a taunting, mean spirited reporter was able to get him fired up was by repeatedly harassing his wife. Mr. Bale felt that he had no choice but to defend his wife's honor. He did not want to give that reporter the satisfaction of reacting to him and yet, Mr. Bale said, "he's killing my human-ity and my dignity as a husband if I do not, and he knows that. So you've got a choice."

The interviewer said, "Dastardly, going after your wife to get to you."

Mr. Bale said, "Because that's the most vulnerable thing, isn't it?"

Very well put. These gentlemen speak of a universal truth.

I gave up watching that decorating channel HGTV because it was making me discontent with my house. However, I was in a doctor's office waiting room, and HGTV was on, so I was held captive and forced to hear it. It was thrust upon me. This is what I heard. A bunch of wives with no reverence for the power they have to weaken their husbands and thereby weaken their marriages, that's what I heard.

One husband and wife were about to put an offer on a house. They could afford $168,000 and the husband was very firm on that. I was really proud of him for a while there because, unlike so many other husbands who've had the life sucked out of them, he was standing his ground. The wife fretted that the offer would get rejected, and she wanted to offer $170,000. Back and forth they went, about five times. This wife was bulldozing her husband's opinion, deci-sion and judgment. I was pulling for him the way somebody would pull for his favorite basketball team.

What do you think happened in the end? This is what the husband said and it's the whole point of this chapter. "If they don't accept our offer and we lose the house," he said, "it will always be my fault so that's why we're offering $170,000." He said "always." This husband knew, like every other husband including Adam dealing with a contrary wife, that it was better to deny his own judgment, go into financial strain, and allow his wife to usurp his leadership – blatantly and publicly on national television even – because nothing is worse than living the rest of his life with a wife who would forever resent his decision.

And it made me really sad because this couple was quite young, and yet this husband had learned in a very short time that if he crossed his wife, there would be hell to pay. I'm not using profanity there. I am saying to you that a wife is creating a living hell for her husband when she lords over him the decisions that he has made. They'd be 95 years old with her shuffling along in her bedroom slippers saying, "If we hadn't lost that house then my gall bladder never would've given out and we'd be living in a beach house in California by now."

His whole life. Always.

Adam was faced with this very same quandary with Eve. It's the same quandary that stands to weaken all marriages. The Bible says Adam knew good and well that the fruit was completely wrong and that eating it was disobedience to God. If he had said no to Eve, he would have had to live with a wife who was unhappy with him. It would have been rottenness to his bones.

Guys would prefer respect to sex, if they had to choose one. Men today hardly know this about themselves. They've been bullied by society to think something is wrong with them for wanting leadership when really it's why they were created. They think it's some fault or selfishness on their part to want to make a decision. When in truth, it's their mission from God. We should be the special kind of wives who will never deny them that.

Take Sarah in the Bible. In her younger wife years, she gracefully fell under her husband Abraham's leadership. I keep reading the passages in Genesis and I can't tell if God is pleased or displeased that Abraham asked Sarah to pretend to be his sister when they traveled to a new place. That meant the other fellows in togas thought Sarah was unmarried and available. What matters to us now is that it could not have been what Sarah would've chosen. She must have disagreed about that whole plan. She must have been scared. She must have fretted about all the things that could've happened to her. She could have had quite the discussion with Abraham, pointing out all the disadvantages of his decision. She could have pouted and cried. But she didn't do that. She obeyed and called Abraham "*lord.*" God honored her for that. God kept her completely safe.

If a husband wants to send the children to public school but his wife wants a private Christian school, if a husband wants to send the children to live away at college but his wife is afraid of that, if a husband wants to move to a different city, state or country and she's nervous and worried about that, she can follow her husband with confidence. She can rest in the story of Sarah. No fear, no contention is needed. If we catch hold of the truth that trusting our husbands means trusting God, we'll never need to second guess the guy ever again.

And we don't get to opt out if he's mean, lazy, eccentric or not a Christian. As every military family knows, a soldier respects his boss's position. He doesn't get to decide, "Well you know? That Major Cheeseball is such a hypocritical loser, so I'm not deploying to Iraq." Folds his arms. No, he follows Major Cheeseball's orders as told and he had better like it. Sports teams have a head coach. In marriage, that's the husband.

Our job is to give our husbands the honor they are due as the head of the household. We don't get to think our marriage is somehow different or special. God is *"no respecter of persons,"* meaning: not impressed with our special particular situation. His ways apply to everyone, regardless of hardship, position or status. God's not a meany about it though, He'll help you when it becomes the prayer of your heart. This is where we live: Philippians 4:8 which says whatever things are excellent and good, if there is anything worthy of praise, then think about these things.

It is possible that the water heater he wants is less efficient than the other one and would cost $25 a year more. It is possible that keeping a child up 45 minutes past his bedtime playing video games might give that child cranky fits the next day. It is possible that eating doughnuts is less healthy than eating an apple.

But we have to keep the bigger picture in mind: quibbling over every detail and decision with our men is very destructive. Any dummy can argue with her husband. It takes a pretty cool chick not to argue. It takes character, wisdom, prayer, depth of understanding and self control not to argue. A passage in the book of James tells us that *"the tongue is a fire and your religion is worthless,"* if you use your speech to stir up strife.

As they say in Australia, "what would you rather?" That your child has a doughnut, or your child has a mother who debates with his daddy? The doughnut isn't worse.

SCREEN TIME AND SODA POP

I know all the alarming research about what happens to your children's brains when they look at a video game or TV. It kills most of their brain cells, alters their short term memory and makes them unable to say the ABCs (a slight exaggeration). I know that expensive, organic hormone-free food is better, and that white flour and refined sugar make your teeth rot.[38] I agree with all of that research.

However, I don't care about it.

My husband is the fun guy. If I were in charge of our family, we would all be sitting around eating wheat germ and reciting Latin declensions. Thankfully, I'm not in charge. This household is my husband's kingdom, not mine. Screen time and nutrition for our children have been areas of wifely submission for me. These are two examples for you in which I decided something very important: whatever mild harm the screens or sodas are doing to my children is much less harmful than their having to endure a mother who incessantly frowns at their father. Look at it like this: wifely submission trumps all other convictions you may have.

"Wives, submit yourselves unto your own husbands, as unto the Lord. For the husband is the head of the wife, even as Christ is the head of the church: and he is the savior of the body." Ephesians 5:22-23.

God's moral laws are like His physical laws. We can choose to defy them but with very dangerous consequences. Take oxygen. We can do without it for a little while and see how that goes, to our detriment. The same goes for defying God's moral law of wifely submission. Realizing this has helped me to enjoy seeing my children have treats from their Daddy and play video games. They have a blast. I've even gotten a little competitive with some Mario Kart racing on the wii myself. Why be a fuddy-duddy and miss out on all the fun?

When it comes to nutrition, some husbands seem to believe that doughnuts are one of the basic food groups. The thing that keeps me smiling as my children eat their skittles is the following passage from Jesus. *"Not that which goeth into the mouth defileth a man; but that which cometh out of the mouth, this defileth a man."* Matthew 15:11. This passage puts it all in perspective because it is telling us that whatever is going into our children's mouths is not of great concern compared to what's coming out of their mouths. What are our children's attitudes? What words do our children speak? How is their tone of voice? That is what is truly important.

Guys like toys. Sometimes a husband will have three screens going at once. Aah, that's the ultimate. He's got the game on the widescreen, is tracking the stock market on his iPad and is sending an e-mail on his laptop. Many guys love a good screen. Husbands work hard and this is how some of them relax. If they want to allow the children to enjoy screen time too, then our job as wives is to back up our husbands. (Please see the chapter on good character for more on getting used to social media with children.)

If something like screen time or junk food makes a wife cringe, but her husband wants to integrate that into their family, then God will give her the wisdom and strength to do it. If a husband doesn't want screens at all, is meticulous about nutrition, is passionate about golf, is fond of the outdoors, wants the children to shine in lots of activities, loves to travel, hates to travel, cares deeply about church, or is not big on church, then we wives can keep our marriages strong by diligently applying scripture to support him. He sets the agenda, and we make it happen by being in the world but not of the world.

Laura Schlessinger says in one of her books that if you begin wanting to argue with your husband and resist his decisions for your family, remember the famous saying from men on the battlefield as they fiercely shout this question: "Soldier, is this the hill you wish to die on?"[41] You can tell me the rotting teeth and turning brains to mush research all day long and I would agree with you. But I'm not dying on that hill.

SHORTEST CHAPTER IN THE BOOK, JUST BECAUSE WE CAN

———— ∞∞ ————

In 2 Samuel 19, King David is sitting around weeping and wailing about the death of his extremely rebellious and mischievous son Absalom. That stinker had plotted and schemed to overthrow David. After Absalom's rather gruesome death in battle (he got stuck in a tree okay? ew), King David's trusted helper and right hand man Joab goes to David and very respectfully tells him to get a grip. Sir, Joab tells him, you're acting like you hate your loyal friends when you carry on like this about that loser Absalom. *"Now therefore arise, go forth, and speak comfortably unto thy servants,"* Joab says to David. If you don't, things are going to *"be worse unto thee than all the evil that befell thee from thy youth until now."* The next verse says, *"Then the king arose."*

David listened to his trusted helper's wise counsel. In the same way, a wife can go to her husband and say, "Darlin' I'm on your side. But there is something important that you need to see."

Keep in mind, though, a few chapters earlier in 2 Samuel 3, Joab had gone to David, suspicious about David's decision to trust a colleague. David did not take Joab's advice. And Joab was dead wrong.

CHAPTER 10

MARITAL INTIMACY

───◦◦◦───

There is a time for naughtiness. Namely: having some seriously flirtatious fun in your marriage. We can't be such a little church lady that we neglect this aspect of our lives. Many scriptures tell us to be gracious in our speech, to honor God in our manner, to let no vile talk or jesting be known to come from us, to be sober. As Christians, we cannot talk like sailors and dress all skank, and then expect to share our faith or expect God to hear our prayers. We've got to have some class.

But have you read the Song of Solomon? Whoo, fan the face with the church bulletin. I'm a little lightheaded. That book is rather juicy. My, my.

God wants us to break bad and have a lot of playful naughtiness in our marriages, while still honoring Him completely with everyone else all the time. The Song of Solomon people are married and God put that in the Bible. Marriage is the place where we Christians get to let down our guard and be over the top fun and flirtatious. It's a blessing God gives us. He kind of created the whole reproduction physical transaction thing for marriage, so that it would be a joy to make babies. He thought up that whole interaction, so it's okay with Him to do that in your marriage, regardless of whether your husband's goal is a baby or not.

The world has made a big mess of it all, to the point where people view marriage as the last place you would expect excitement or pleasure. Marriage is considered boring by the world, a drag, or a big joke – certainly not the place where anything smokin' hot is happening. The rest of the world can do their thing and look at it that way all they want, but within our own marriages ladies, you and I can decide we're not going to play along. *"Be not conformed to this world,"* Paul tells us in Romans 12:2.

A woman needs to feel her man's strong arms and adoring gaze. A man needs to have his flirty pretty lady by his side. Husbands frequently need us wives to make ourselves physically, ahem, `available`. If you know what I mean.

Men really need for us wives to be physical with them, often. It's not something optional or extra. It's a strong need he has. People who would like to cash in on this manly need and remove it from the sanctity of marriage have created many products, establishments, publications, and base temptations to lure a man to try to meet this need elsewhere besides from his wife. They don't care about your husband, they just want to make some money. And they're making some money. Billions. They will someday have to answer to God Almighty for the crisis they are causing in marriages for selfish gain and profit.

It's nothing new: harlots were available to men in Bible times. Now this has been expanded to a grander scale through big business in modern times. We have printed or virtual images of women, and degrading establishments owned by men, all of which attempt to grip husbands. Or future husbands. It is all very pitiful and desperate compared to the beauty of marriage. I'm not playing along with it. Neither is my husband, and I love him to pieces for it.

But I am not naïve. I have to stay on top of this issue as a wife and help my husband never feel the need to be tempted. Men are human after all. Let's not be shocked by that. If a husband does give into temptation in some small or even a large way — and ladies it is swirling all around them every time they walk out the front door or turn on the television and it is limitless now through the internet — our job is to forgive them and keep being that source of love, affection and intimacy no matter what.

If a husband is causing you pain in this area, we can't chicken or egg the thing. We don't know which came first. We don't know why he's looking at porn or hanging out at degrading establishments. Maybe he felt rejected by his wife and had to meet the sexy chick thing elsewhere. And then she's hurt and pulls away even more. And on goes the cycle. Or maybe he's just dim and fails to see he's got a flesh and blood hot mama right under his nose. However the destructive pattern got started, we wives have to fight for our marriages.

We fight for our marriages by keeping them exciting and inviting for our husbands. We aren't in control of or responsible for his actions, but we have to fight to do our part. Our husbands' sins are never our fault, ever. We can't carry the blame for his sins. But we can try to set up our guys for success and enjoy this part of marriage ourselves. If we give up on our marital intimacy, then the bad guys who lured our husbands away win. *"Be not overcome of evil, but overcome evil with good."* Romans 12:21.

Remember that God created you to meet your husband's physical need for intimacy. You are God's gift to your husband. God has ordained *you* for this job. You're the foxy lady in his life. I didn't make that up, it's not my big idea: It's very clearly laid out in chapter five of Proverbs. And when he's being physically intimate with you in the bedroom, I promise he's not thinking about your gray roots or cellulite. When you're in a dark, candlelit bedroom, that gorgeous body of yours is looking righteous.[12]

Anyone else who would compete with you to meet this need of your husband's does not have God on her side, and so compared to you, she is a cheap imitation. I don't care how tempting she is or what she looks like. She is a black and white chicken-scratch drawing of a seaweed covered ocean sketched clumsily on a crumpled up piece of paper. You are the actual ocean. No one can touch you in your ability to meet this need in your husband. And there is no expiration date on that, so we don't have to fear getting older and wrinklier.

One day the children and I were making an elaborate breakfast, and we kept adding new things like eggs or biscuits or bacon so we joked that our house was trying to be like Waffle House that morning. We even started shouting like the waitresses do, "Number four. I need a number six plus some hash browns, hun." Then I stopped and said: No, wait, we're not trying to be like Waffle House. It's the other way around. Waffle House is trying to be like us. That's the appeal of the restaurant. It duplicates the cozy deliciousness of a big breakfast made at home.

The same principle applies to any person, product, establishment, image, entertainment, diversion, virtual or in person, which dares to steal the role of your body and physical affection in your husband's life. We all see the magazine covers of the women with perfect bodies, and we can start to feel defeated that we can't ever compete. Especially after childbirth, our bodies can never compete. They're lumpy and motherly.

Just remember, we're not competing with those ladies. They're competing with us. And we've already won, because our wifely bodies are ordained by God to be fulfilling to our husbands.

When I read Homer's *Odyssey*, many emotions stir within me on behalf of Penelope, the wife of Odysseus, who gallivants all over the Mediterranean enjoying steamy interactions with immortal babes. I mean seriously? Tell me Muse, is that an option? The sexual escapades of Odysseus are disdainful, infuriating, self indulging and extremely annoying.

And yet, as I continue to read, I find that the sum of all those emotions toward Odysseus is outweighed by one alone: Compassion. I feel compassion for Odysseus and then for every man, because each is faced with a decision that does not necessarily have anything to do with love. It is a decision that does not even necessarily have anything to do with his particular wife. The decision facing all men, as it was Odysseus, is whether he will choose a wandering life of fantasy with random women, or whether he will choose his wife, who is his home, and that is reality. We cheer for Odysseus in the end because he chooses to go home to a life of reality with his wife, Penelope.

"If this work be of men, it will come to nought: But if it be of God, ye cannot overthrow it," says Acts 5:38-39. That passage from the Bible was written a few hundred years after Homer wrote his poetry. The saintly apostles from the Bible were born into a world of Greek mythology, polytheism and sexual adventure. When applied to the issue of marital intimacy, I believe that passage from Acts is telling us that God wants husbands to have victory in this area of their lives. Everything and everyone that would lure or tempt our husbands away will eventually come to nought. It will never truly satisfy. But our wifely bodies are of God. We were created to satisfy our husbands. No one can overthrow that. They can try. But it won't work.

A wife's motivation to stay hot to trot for her guy in marriage should be to honor God. It can't solely be an act of love for our husbands; otherwise, in the face of any pain or rejection we'll give up and shut down faster than the lady at Waffle House can bring us a gravy biscuit. Ultimately, like everything, our marital intimacy has to be for the Lord. We can't control whether or not our husbands are walking in victory or obedience in this area or not, though we can ask God to give us that. We can't control if or when their blinders will be removed, as Odysseus's were, to see the truth about the only way to be satisfied physically – and therefore emotionally – is with *"the wife of thy youth."* Proverbs 5:18.

What we can control is that when people look at you or me, they might see a wholesome, polite Bible girl who buys peanut butter at the grocery store and reads nice things in a Christian book. But what they do not immediately see is that she is magnificent and lovely Penelope, ready with warmth and open arms.

CHAPTER 11

MONEY

———◦◦◦———

I'd say the best way never to fight about money is never to have a reason to fight about money. Must we become the kind of glam married couple who have so much money that they eat imported crab cakes crumbled atop Angus steaks every night while their children jump in a bouncy pit in their living room that, instead of being filled with those colorful plastic balls, is full of $100 bills?

I think not. Having lots of money isn't the answer. When's the last time we heard of a wealthy famous person's actually being content and joyful? Those high profile people are generally pretty miserable, bless their hearts, unless they know the Lord. The only difference between them and us is: more zeroes at the end of their numbers that they fight about. More money can't stop terminal cancer. More money can't keep a spouse from committing adultery. More money can't fix a rebellious, distant child.

Even knowing this, how can we mere mortals with average incomes and average problems never have a reason to fight about money? It's pretty simple really. We don't place our trust in money. We place our trust in God. Not trusting God? Just go ahead and put on a t-shirt that says: Marital Financial Crisis Waiting to Happen. Instead of wearing that t-shirt, we Bible people often gravitate toward the Proverbs for wisdom regarding our handling of finances and this is good and right.[39] We'll get to a couple of those in a moment. But for now let's consider what the Psalms tell us about our attitude toward this money we are managing so Biblically. Hate to break it to you but Psalm 52 says the righteous will laugh at *"the man that made God not his strength; but trusted in his riches, and strengthened himself in his wickedness."*

113

Another Psalm warns, *"if riches increase, set not your heart upon them,"* Psalm 62:10, and then the next verse says that power belongs to God. The entire chapter of Psalm 49 blasts people who *"trust in their wealth, and boast themselves in the multitude of their riches."* Let's just say it's not a pretty picture God paints of them in those 20 verses. The most convicting part of it might be verse 11 which says, *"their inward thought is that their houses shall continue forever."*

So where do we find our security, where do we place our trust, rather than in a paid-for house, college savings plans, healthy investment portfolios or other wealth? We place our trust in God. What does that even mean? Well, if it is blessings we are seeking, the math formula for that is clearly laid out for us many times in the Bible and here is one example. Psalm 40:4 says, *"Blessed is that man that maketh The Lord his trust."*

We need to make a lifelong commitment to refuse to get caught up in the love of money, which the Bible says is the root of all evil. Love of money is what made Delilah betray Samson, the most buff man who ever lived. Love of money is what made Judas betray Christ, the only perfect man who ever lived. Wives? Don't love money to the extent that you contradict, fight against and thereby betray your husband, who is your true love and the only man in this world who matters.

When we speak of loving money, we are talking about being gratified by it, pleased by it, placing worth in it, being delighted with it, believing that it can make us happy or unhappy. We are strongly attached to it, we're even afraid of it, in the sense that we have begun to worship it. It has power over us.[47] And so all of those attributes of loving money need to be re-directed back to loving and fearing God instead.

Here is a basic, healthy attitude toward money:

- God is the provider, not the husband, who is simply the hard working guy. (Philippians 4:19)
- It is God's money and we get to keep some of it too. We don't think of it as ours. (Colossians 1:17)

- A woman tells herself and her children "no" a lot. (David should have told his son Adonijah no, 1 Kings 1:6)
- She doesn't buy or do things she can't afford. (Luke 14:28)[13]
- She doesn't daydream much about what she wishes she had, or what she wishes she could buy. (Hebrews 13:5)
- She knows that this world is not her home, and she keeps her eyes fixed on heaven which is her eternity. (Hebrews 13:14)
- She tries to be a financial asset to her husband in spending money carefully, or by earning money if he would like for her to. (Proverbs 31)
- When you haven't dug yourself a big financial hole, there's nothing to dig yourself out of. (Proverbs 22:7)
- Being a contentious wife is rottenness to a husband's bones and defies the word of God. (Proverbs 25:24)
- She submits to her husband in all things. (Ephesians 5:24)

All of that is to say, we must try to apply Biblical principles to our attitude toward money. We need to be familiar with the Bible and respect God's ways, rather than wanting to get our own way. This is Proverbs 3:5 *"lean not on your own understanding,"* applied to real life.

That last bullet point about a wife's calling to *"submit to her husband in all things,"* is crucial in not fighting about money in marriage. A husband is only human, so he might make financial missteps. It's a somber time when this happens. It weighs on a wife's heart. And yet a wife can remain his admiring cheerleader. How is this possible? It's because ultimately she is yielding to and adoring her God.

That's real trust. And it also displays a heart of contentment. We don't gotta panic, y'all. Any sensible husband who knows he has his wife's respect will talk to her about money, consult with her and ask her input all the time. As my friend Pam says though, if there's any disagreement, the husband is simply the tie-breaker.

This is when we begin to enter the supernatural. Do we truly believe that God is not confined to numbers and He will bless or not bless whomever He chooses, based on that person's pure or impure heart? Do we realize that blocking our husbands from leading could be striving with God's holy purposes?

If a wife starts to fear or distrust about not having enough money, she can ask herself: How much does a 2 year old fret about the electric bill's getting paid? Never crosses his mind. If a husband is too crazy spendy with money as if there's no tomorrow and he's just throwing iPhones and lobsters out the car window at people while you don't know how to pay the water bill, we as wives yield to him and trust God. The Bible says for us to have that kind of childlike faith. We see in the Bible that God miraculously cares for and even prospers those who fear Him. God provides manna from the sky. God sends food through ravens. God makes oil not run out when poured into jars. God squeezes water from a rock.

Or, opposite problem, if a wife wants to get argumentative with her husband over wishing they'd spend more money, she can imagine a couple of toddlers grabbing a stuffed animal back and forth and screaming at each other, "Mine! No it's mine. I want it! I had it first." If a husband is a tightwad down to the store brand paper towels and the $3 rebate from the drug store when you know full well there's a big fat pile of paper sitting in the bank, crying out to be spent and enjoyed, we yield to him and trust God.

Ladies it's idolatry if we think buying stuff and spending money are going to bring us true joy. We know we're right onto something else after a couple of days. If we are ever tempted to shop excessively, one thing that helps is to look at that item and ask: If this was two years old, dusty and in a little pile buried under old gloves and shoes in the garage, would I still want it? Spending money for pleasure might give us a little happy boost, that day, but it can never truly satisfy. *"Delight thyself in the Lord,"* the Bible tells us (Psalm 37:4). A relationship with Him is the only place to find lasting joy and fulfillment. We can fight this truth, but that's like trying to go somewhere on an exercise bike.

Proverbs says that a prudent wife is from the Lord. And so God would have us make wise decisions and not be flighty or careless with money, whether it's shopping, vacations, standard of living, generous contributions to charity or something else we really can't afford. If we are careless with money then we are seriously sucking the life out of our husbands. We are a huge drain to him instead of an asset. We are making him have to figure out how to overcome his high maintenance wife, rather than being blessed by her. It's reverse snobbery – or maybe it's just snobbery, someone do the math – for a wife to believe that only the worrying husband is worshiping money. But then she excuses her excessive spending by saying the Bible says not to worry about money. They're both the love of money. Let's not be another reason our husbands are worrying about money.

I've been seriously strapped at times in my life, and God carried me through. As a young single lady, I ate a baked potato every night for dinner and it wasn't because I liked baked potatoes. Once, I needed a new bed. I bought the mattress one month and the covers the next. It was all I could afford. When my husband and I got married, I was down to my very last dollar. But I didn't bring any debt to our marriage either because my parents had taught me to live within my means.

I get money's being tight. I understand free falling and not knowing how to pay the next month's bills. I know that twisted knot in your stomach when you're walking through the grocery store. Shame and pride are taking punches at you from different directions at the same time. But I also know my God. He is mightier and stronger than numbers. He knows you need food. He knows you need a place to live. He knows you want to enjoy life. Fall to your knees and ask Him.

CHAPTER 12

DIVORCE

⸺⸺⸺

After visiting for a while with a kindly elderly couple in a doctor's waiting room, I asked them, "What is the secret to a long, happy marriage?" Without even looking up from his magazine, the husband said, "You put up with each other." The wife smiled in agreement and said, "Commitment."

I want to offer hope in the midst of a storm. I went through my Bible, every page, and wrote down the scriptures that would address pain and heartache in the context of marriage in the face of divorce. Please read those by clicking on the Divorce Scriptures button on the welcome page of TriumphantChicks.com, if you are considering divorce. Please read them, before you make any decisions. Please read them, and decide to fight for your marriage with God as your strong Father.

Stop right here and let me say to anyone who has been through a divorce: Our loving God adores us and gives us a fresh start every time we ask Him. This chapter is not to debate about what's been done. If you want to see somebody get real feisty, real fast, judge my dear Granny who went through a divorce in the 1950s. This chapter is for married women or ladies who have not gotten married yet. Here we go.

Jesus says divorce is not an option, unless the wife committed adultery (Matthew 19). And even then, in the Old Testament, God says *"I hate divorce."* The King James says, *"I hate putting away."* First Corinthians tells us that wives should never separate from their husbands.

- We need to be obedient to God's word, including divorce. This is not about your relationship with your husband at all but rather is about your relationship with God.
- The scriptures are our road map; we don't have to wonder what His will is for us.
- When we accepted Christ, we were saying, "The Lord is on the throne of my life now, I'm no longer on the throne."
- It's a scary place to be in to try to take that throne back; we can even call that rebellion to God.
- Many scriptures warn us to avoid rebellion, to fear God instead and not follow our own hearts but to obey and observe God's ways.
- Sometimes we obey out of sheer will, sheer submission to God, not based on our feelings or what we think is best.

If a wife chooses to put herself out there in the midst of pain and blindly obey His word, God will honor that. He won't forsake you. God wants you to be joyful and live a fulfilling life. This may not happen overnight. It might take a lifetime. In the book of John, Jesus said: *"But the counselor, the Holy Spirit, whom the Father will send in my name, will teach you all things and remind you of everything I said to you."*

The world is going to tell you, "you go girl" and "you deserve better." But God Himself is the Wonderful Counselor (Isaiah), through prayer and His word. Sometimes our circumstances are too hard for us. But do you take God at His word that it's not too hard for Him? (Jeremiah). Do you believe Him when He says He can "teach you all things?"

God's commandments, not just the Ten Commandments, but His ways, are unconditional. And the Bible tells us that His commandments are not burdensome, that they are not too hard for us. They are for everyone, regardless of the circumstances under which you got married. Regardless of whether your husband is a Christian. Regardless of any sin or pain after you got married, it is a holy contract to be honored. The marriage relationship is so sacred that it is the relationship that God compares to His relationship with us.

Ever since Adam and Eve, God has let us decide to obey or not, and obeying Him is really the only way to get to happiness. An artsy gardener in our town has a plaque by the plants in his nursery with the following words scribbled in chalk: "If you escape, you have to end up somewhere." Leaving a marriage in order to seek happiness is the reason people consider divorce after all, right? They think it's how they'll finally be happy. After divorce, we would still be seeking happiness. No more husband problems, but different problems that are just as unbearable apart from God.

The best marriage advice I have ever gotten came from a pastor's wife who says you must forgive in marriage as a matter of the will. Then ask God to catch up your feelings. Here is a rhetorical question from God to Jonah: *"Doest thou well to be angry?"* Jonah 4:4. People who tell you not to forgive, that you have a right to be angry and then recommend divorce are not going to pick up your children from school, throw the ball with your son, help your daughter with math homework or hold you at night when you have cancer. The people who say divorce is awesome will vanish.

No, we do not stay married for the sake of the children. However, if we stay married for the sake of obedience to God, then that is passing on a Godly legacy to our children and down through the generations in ways we cannot even begin to imagine. Our testimony to our children will be: Look what God did for me. I obeyed and trusted Him when my marriage was difficult and He gave me a joyful life.

Have hope. People do change. The Bible says, *"I the Lord do not change,"* but people, his creation, do change. Satan himself began as an angel, and now he is the very definition of unangelic. King Saul started out wisely in seeking God but changed into a desperate coward. Solomon started off so wisely that he wrote most of the Proverbs but in the end became a worshiper of idols. King Josiah was an excellent king at an early age under wise instruction but ended up worthless under bad influence. Peter was an awkward bumbler who could hardly put two words together and then after Jesus' resurrection became smashingly articulate. Paul's conversion in the New Testament is a powerful example of a guy who started off self-righteous and "religious" as he stoned and imprisoned believers, but he ended up writing much of the New Testament and gave his life to preaching the Gospel.

Ask God to help you put up with each other.

Not Really My Wife

Women can get a little competitive. I can't even enjoy board games because I am so competitive. We have got to rein that in for the sake of our marriages. We cannot look around at what another woman has and try to force our husbands to emulate her family. If a wife does this, she is following another woman. If a wife lets her own mother run the show, she is following another woman. Two women are in charge of the family.

A recent magazine article told a story about a woman who got married and her husband did not want children. He was very clear about that. The wife went against him, stopped using birth control without his knowledge, and had a baby. He left. He divorced her. The purpose of the magazine article, which sympathized only with the wife, was to elevate her and commend her for picking up the pieces of a shattered life. I am in anguish for her myself and am proud of her for carrying on.

But a husband is a person too. Guys need to feel ownership of their families. When a man divorces a wife who isn't following his lead, he feels that she left first. She wasn't following him. She was following someone else, some other person or philosophy, some opinion or desire. So in his mind, she was not "his" wife at all.

He is divorcing nothing.

When a husband says, "You are my wife," that "my" matters. He needs to feel ownership of his family or else his heart begins to detach. When we clean our own house or weed our own garden, it's work but we are happy to do it because it's ours. Cleaning someone else's house is a huge act of sacrifice and kindness. We might like to get paid for doing it because we don't feel ownership. When a woman says that is "my" husband, it is not ownership but more of an admiration of his strength. But for men, the need to feel ownership of their families is crucial.

The devastating pain caused to a man by a wife who doesn't follow him is the same devastating pain that a wife would experience if her husband was sexually unfaithful to her. Let me say it plainly: A woman is committing emotional infidelity in her marriage every day that she follows someone else's leadership other than her husband's. He is crushed. He is in despair. He would rather go somewhere he is needed.

DIVORCE PREVENTION: DON'T CULT OUT ON ME NOW

If someone gave your husband $5 million today, would he say, "Nice knowing you babe"? And then leave you and spend all his time at work? Of course not. He would drop the job in a heartbeat and keep you. Even if a husband and wife both work, everything our guys do is for us. They want to be the hero.

All guys. Even pastors and the very nice guys at homeschool organizations. I'm going to use homeschooling as an example to make a point, simply because it is familiar to me. The men at homeschooling support organizations pour their very lives into their cause. My family is extremely grateful to have such valiant, honorable men speaking on behalf of homeschooling. They are engaging in spiritual warfare in our nation to keep liberty alive for families, not just now but for future generations. They are the good guys. So please don't anyone come cart me off in a black Suburban for what I'm about to say.

Wives, we need to understand that the men at homeschooling organizations — or at any organization, church, or cause — are doing their job ultimately for their own wives. Not for me. As dearly as the homeschooling advocates love the cause, and as much heart as they pour into it, they love their own wives more. It's a labor of love, yes, an honorable ministry even. But these guys are getting paid. Not just from our memberships, but also from advertisers. The higher their membership numbers, the more appealing they are to advertisers. Non-profit organizations do have paid employees; don't let the name mislead you. And every human being is driven by a certain level of pride in knowing he has followers and admirers. So as much as these men care, it's a job. It's a business. It can be a little bit of an ego trip. They're not paying your electricity bill. They're paying their wife's electricity bill.

So naturally they're kind of invested in having us all keep participating in their movement. They are not going to lay out all the disadvantages for us. The homeschool advocates are not trying to force or pressure anyone to homeschool, but in being supportive of those who already are homeschooling, they sure do make it sound wonderful. They make it seem very Biblically sound. And it is, for those who are called by God to do it.

Wives are listening to them speak at conferences. Wives are reading their magazines. Wives are following them on social media. The wives get pumped. And if the husbands are on board too, then great. But homeschooling is a bunch of hogwash to a lot of manly men who work with their strong hands and aren't big readers or activist types. Then the wives are following the homeschooling advocate's lead, perhaps over their own husbands' lead. It's almost like she's married to the homeschool advocate guy or pastor, in her husband's mind. The husband is having to compete with some total stranger for his own wife's respect and admiration. This is a very humiliating war for a man to be asked to wage.

I'm grieved to see that a foundation has been established to help single homeschool mothers. Sometimes their husbands are deceased, but sometimes these women are single because their husbands have left. They have divorced their wives and left their families. And then these husbands are frowned upon by the Christian community. Perhaps there is a connection. Did these men even want to homeschool in the first place? Did anyone ask them? Maybe the wife was super sweet and the husband was a big awful scoundrel and he left out of nowhere and we hate him. I don't know. But I have to wonder.

Some husbands cannot articulate their objections to homeschooling as well as lawyers can articulate the benefits of homeschooling. Some husbands are more math or mechanically oriented in their gifts and are not as verbal as lawyers or pastors or other public speakers. Don't make your husband compete with these guys who are debaters as a profession, sometimes even in front of the Supreme Court. It's hard to outslick them. If your husband says he doesn't want to homeschool, then that is argument enough.

Maybe God told you to homeschool. God showed me this one passage in Deuteronomy that I didn't even know was famous among homeschoolers at the time. He spoke to my heart. And that was real. But if your husband says not to homeschool, then that is what God is saying to you now. I love homeschooling. But I don't place my hope it in it. After all, I went to public school myself and I'm adorable.

Colossians 2:8 tells us to *"Beware lest any man spoil you through philosophy and vain deceit, after the tradition of men, after the rudiments of the world, and not after Christ."* We ladies constantly have to be evaluating if we are in fact following our husbands, or if we are following someone else's husband. We can get a little too gung-ho thinking that family size, donations, activities, church, homeschooling and causes become a sort of cult mentality and we lose sight that it is God guiding our family, under our husband's leadership, not the homeschooling community or any religion or philosophy.

A man should never abandon his family for selfish reasons. We can all agree to that. Dolphins can stay under water for a while. But they're not fish, they're mammals, and eventually they have to come up for air. They can't stay underwater or they start to die. A man who is not a homeschooling father and is forced by his wife to be one, can take it only for so long. He's created to lead and no one in the family is following.

Buck up and be a man, you say? Make them follow? Perhaps. But have you dealt with stubborn, disobedient children or pets before? Have you ever tried to get chickens into the coop during a thunderstorm? Neither have I, but they've got to put up a terrible fuss. Did you see what a joy Moses did not have with all the resistance from the Israelites? Hello Adam giving into Eve in the Garden of Eden? It's not that easy. A man should not have to overcome a stranger's leadership in his own family, any more than a wife would want to overcome a strange woman in her bed.

DIVORCE PREVENTION: GRATITUDE

I have been guilty of jealousy at times, when it comes to my marriage. This jealousy has nothing to do with my husband. It's 100 percent silly, unrealistic pride and competitiveness with other wives. I don't like thinking some other chick has it better than I do.

An envious attitude is destructive to a marriage. It's hard for a husband to stand it. Proverbs 27:4 tells us: *"Wrath is cruel, and anger is outrageous, but who is able to stand before envy?"* When I first got married – and occasionally since then, until I realize this is what is happening – I wanted my husband to have all the admirable qualities of every man I'd ever seen or heard about since I was 4 years old, and none of the bad qualities. This is absurd. That guy doesn't exist, not for any wife.

A husband can't drop canned goods from his fighter plane during a missions trip while presenting you with a diamond necklace he bought during your anniversary trip to Paris, before initiating family devotions for your 12 children, implementing scripture he memorized in Hebrew along with a poem he composed for you the day he planted a row of leyland cypress trees which you really wish he had arranged in a more staggered fashion but whatever, it's too late now because this afternoon he's working on his dissertation about better internet laws for minors, and you will be glad when he's finished with that and begins his benefit 10K run so that he will come home and load the dirty dishes into the dishwasher, which he recently repaired MacGyver style using popsicle sticks and liquid iodine.

Perhaps he would simply like to watch the football game?

We laugh and tell ourselves that no wife could be quite that diva. No wife would have ideas and thoughts that are quite that high maintenance. True, maybe not all in the same paragraph. Maybe not all in the same day. But what about over a span of three years? What about a span of 10 or 35 years? A wife could hope that her husband would do every one of those things.

She had better not invite those thoughts in to have tea. Otherwise, her personality begins to take on a critical attitude of wishing her husband would do things that she thinks other husbands are doing. She is wishing her husband is different. A husband translates that into meaning his wife wishes she had married someone else. Ouch. He's just been handed a discouraging existence. The Bible says to *"take every thought captive to the obedience of Christ."* 2 Corinthians 10:5. If we wives think about our marriages in a competitive, jealous and comparing way, it equals a lifetime of frustration for a husband, who feels he will never measure up.

Not fun.

Husbands are designed by God to slay the dragon and win the girl. A husband slays the dragon as he tries his best every day to provide for his family. He needs to know he's won his wife's heart and that, no matter what, it will stay that way.

Little eyes are watching their mothers all the time. Children, whether 18 months old or 23 years old, are experts in detecting disappointment and jealousy in their mother's attitude toward marriage. Nary a word need be spoken. The children see it in her frosty facial expression toward their daddy. They hear it in her tone of voice toward their daddy. Their world is in confusion and their hearts are breaking.

Most of all, we wives don't want to let down our Heavenly Father. Ephesians says for wives to give reverence to their husbands. Nowhere in the Bible can we find anything that suggests a wife must first make sure he's a buff Mister Rogers astronaut ninja. We obey the scripture unconditionally, out of love for our Lord and Savior Jesus Christ. After all, Jesus Christ is the only perfect man who ever lived. Jesus Christ is the object of our worship. He is the source of our strength. He is where we get our identity. We love our husbands, we honor them, and we respect them. But a wife has to accept that her husband, ultimately, is just a guy. He's a guy, who used to be a little boy and is trying to have a family now. He needs his wife's ongoing approval and admiration.

In that perfect Garden of Eden, things weren't quite good enough for Eve. She had to go there with the fruit. We don't know for certain what made Adam cave and go along with her. It might have been because nothing is worse for a man than a wife who is always wishing things were different. The opposite of jealousy could be gratitude. This can be a wife's opinion of her marriage and it's plenty: "I have a good man who loves me."

This page is for you to cut out or photocopy for your marriage or any other couples who might benefit from it. You have to promise me one thing though. You will try to keep in mind that, ultimately, the way for a wife to find true joy is not in his but in hers.

....

His

"Husbands, love your wives, even as Christ also loved the church, and gave himself for it ... so ought men to love their wives as their own bodies. He that loveth his wife loveth himself. For no man ever yet hated his own flesh; but nourisheth it and cherisheth it."
Ephesians 5:25-29

Hers

"Wives, submit yourselves unto your own husbands, as unto the Lord. For the husband is the head of the wife, even as Christ is the head of the church ... Therefore as the church is subject unto Christ, so let the wives be to their own husbands in every thing ... let the wife see that she reverence her husband."
Ephesians 5:22-24, 33

....

Triumphant Womanhood: God's Never "Whatever"
by Jennifer Houlihan

PART IV. CHILDREN

"Above all we appeal to the mighty army of our German youth...
The work and care of education must begin with the young mother."

Adolf Hitler, *Mein Kampf*, Volume 2, Chapter 2

CHAPTER 13

YOU JUST HAVE TO
LAUGH (AND CRY)

My 5 year old said, "Mommy? I like my school work. It takes away my stupid."

Every mother has been entrusted with the weighty honor of molding eager young hearts and minds. You are the expert on your child. Many excellent parenting books have already been written, so this is not another one of those. My favorite parenting book is the book of Proverbs. In this section, I want to laugh and cry with you about the joys and sorrows of motherhood, and then help point our children to God.

Of course I realize that fathers do exist and are very important. In fact, statistics show that it is fathers who make the crucial difference in whether a child turns to a life of crime.[56] That's one reason it is so urgent that we keep the dads happy in all that marriage talk we just had together. In discussing children, then, if I ever make it sound like it's all about the mothers and the responsibility lies only with us, please understand that I'm operating based on the Bible's guideline that the aged women are to teach other women. Now that I'm in my 40s I consider myself aged enough to do this. Someone else can boss the men around but it won't be me. I very much dislike the idea of women reading a bunch of hoopla about fathers and then being disappointed with their husbands. All we can really ever do is apply what we read to ourselves.

The best parenting advice I have ever heard came from author and speaker Marilyn Boyer at a mother-daughter conference. Mrs. Boyer has written some amazing materials on instilling good character in children, and she has used these materials with her own family. She told us at the conference that she asked her grown children how it is that she and her husband have such strong, happy relationships with all of their children, while some other families do not. She wondered specifically which methods or lessons had made the difference. "What did your father and I do?" she asked her grown children. One of her sons said, "You delighted in us."

Similarly, my friend Vickie, who later died of breast cancer, was years ago answering my unending questions about how to be a good mother: What do I do, how do I do it, what list do I follow, what books do I read, how do I get it right? After patiently answering my questions for quite some time, Vickie finally looked at me and said, "Jennifer? I was 16 years old when I had my first baby. I don't know if I did everything just right. But I loved him."

HELPERS IN THE KITCHEN

The good news is, my daughters have practically taken over my kitchen. The bad news is, my daughters have practically taken over my kitchen.

I made a decision a long time ago to endure chaos and mess in order to raise young women who will know their way around a kitchen when they get married. I don't necessarily like that they are currently running my kitchen. Sometimes it makes me cranky. On Thanksgiving morning, my Dad ran out to the store on an emergency bacon bits mission, just to end the tense discussion my daughter and I were having regarding whose recipe was more deserving of the last of them. I still vote for my broccoli casserole.

I was to blame for not being more kind hearted about my daughter's cooking. I have told my girls that I am aware of the problem and that I'm calling on Jesus to help me be more gracious. I want to love that they cook, I want to embrace the cooking chaos and gladly share my kitchen with them. They do respect that I have final kitchen authority and they yield to me graciously (usually).

But mercy. If I go in there, I bump into at least two people and can't open a cabinet or use a knife because someone else was about to use them. My measuring spoons are never clean when I want them to be, and if they were clean they wouldn't be in neat nesting stacks by size, the way I used to keep them when I had a kitchen. I haven't found my vegetable peeler in three weeks. The appliances are always plugged in and firing up. Then sticky afterward. Flour is everywhere. Bizarre pulp and shavings of unknown origin are constantly sitting in my sink. Dried goo is stuck to my stove top. I really could do without the frozen heart-shaped orange juice molds sticking to everything inside the freezer.

My daughters had a lively discussion this very week, verbally and in writing, regarding the freshness of a jar of apple sauce and whether it was worthy to be salvaged. When I open the freezer, ziploc bags full of sliced bananas jump out at me and fall on my feet. One of my daughters uses them to make banana smoothies called "monkey shakes."

I don't even have dominion over my grocery list anymore. My husband came home from the grocery store with a large assortment of expensive meat one day, not having realized it was one of our daughters who circled all this on the grocery list rather than his wife. I resorted to banning them from cooking Mondays through Thursdays. They can have at it on the weekends.

Right on the heels of these two daughters is another wave of daughters, who as toddlers are now embarking on the joys of cutting up strawberries and stirring batter, then dropping most of it on the floor and dripping it all over to the table from the counter in a large falling glop. A new generation of little chefs is budding before my very eyes. With all these women in the house, it's going to be a couple of decades until I get my kitchen back.

On the other hand, my house smells like homemade bread right now. While I was at an appointment this afternoon, my daughter rolled out yeast bread dough into four loaves and let it rise. She baked them while I was relaxing. I'm about to go slather some butter on a piece in a minute here, once they've cooled. We're taking a loaf to a friend at church this weekend as a gift.

My girls are probably at the point where, if something happened to me and I was sick or debilitated for a while, they could keep our whole family well fed without me, three meals a day no problem.

A passage in scripture says, *"Where no oxen are, the crib is clean: but with much increase is by the strength of the ox."* Proverbs 14:4. If my kitchen had no children in it, then it sure would be clean and tidy. But then the passage goes on to say that much strength comes from the oxen. I don't think God is saying don't have a cow. He's saying your helpers are well worth the mess and trouble. The notes in my Geneva Bible interpret the passage to mean that "without labor there is no profit." We ladies are working hard to raise our children and with that comes great profit. Your children help you gain or increase so much more, they strengthen your family so much more than if the house was empty and quiet, and you were the only worker.

The kitchen in our house is sometimes a female hormonal war zone. It's never quiet in there. Heaven knows it's never empty. I'm sharing it with other females for a season of my life, and that's going to create liveliness. But these girls know how to cook. They're only 13 and 15. Think what they can do when they are 23 and 25.

WIGGLY LEETLE BOYZ

The only way I could cut my son's hair when he was a toddler was to give him a big bowl of ice. The ice cubes shocked and surprised him just long enough for me to dash around like a Japanese chef with butcher knives, slashing away as fast as I could at that hair before my 45 seconds were up.

Little boys are very busy. Mine is almost a young man now. He's delightful. I'm crazy about that boy. But Lord have mercy, he sure did slam dunk me into motherhood. Complete wildman. Sweet as could be, but that child was wide open. He was not a gentle introduction to motherhood. Little boys never stop. If they are awake, they are moving. When he turned about 6 or 7 years old, he started to chill out. It was a huge change, a huge relief. I no longer felt as if I was living with the Tasmanian devil. Entire minutes would pass without any jumping, darting, throwing or crashing. Then, hours started going by where nary a thrash could be found. Now he goes all day behaving like a respectable Earthling.

When he was still little, I would see those kid-sized recliner chairs in stores and wondered why anyone would buy one of those. The child never sat down. My 2-year-old daughter is always into everything, but it's as if she is moving in slow motion compared to what her brother was like at that age. He didn't walk, he ran. He bounded.

I don't think I heard a sermon for four years. Too busy chasing that child around in the back of the church or outside. He did math drills while running around the circle of our floor plan downstairs. "One-fourth, one-half, three-fourths, one," through the kitchen and around to the living room and back out again.

Crayons were for throwing, dolls were for target practice. The couch was for vaulting over, the stairs were for leaping down five at a time. Jeans lasted a few wears before holes got in the knees. Strollers were for sissies, and getting strapped in the car seat was torment and anguish. The more daring the better: headfirst down the hill on a skateboard, climbing 30-foot-tall trees, swimming all the way across the pool without taking a breath just to see if he could do it.

Boys are exponentially active. I bow down in solemn reverence to any woman who has a plural number of them. When my son was younger and bouncier, his friends would come over and I could do about 30 minutes of having them all inside the house. They feed off each other. We know a large family with many children and one of the daughters said something about her two brothers one time. I said to her, "There are only two of them? Seems like there are more than that." She knew what I meant.

Those boys never seem to stop karate chopping each other. They're a tangled, blurry flash of color tumbling and shouting by, with arms and legs sticking out now and then. Our friends across the street have four boys, and we see one of those boys out running laps around the cul-de-sac sometimes, having been sent outside to blow off a little energy.

My son slowed down quite a bit once he left the toddler stage and learned to read. If boys have books that actually interest them, they'll read. He always loved Davy Crockett books, Boxcar Children books, biographies, mysteries. He still loves a good *Ranger's Apprentice* novel or a *Warriors* series book. The slowing down has been gradual, but the spunk hasn't gone away completely.

Our pediatrician is a confident, tall, booming Russian whom we are very fond of and who loves to give my son a hard time when we bring him in for injuries. Which seems to be often. A couple of years ago, my son fell off a trampoline and saw tweety birds and stars. Our doctor said, "You're four-theeeen. Four-theeeen is supposed to be creating eeeen-ter-net web sites and these things. These trampoline, these is for leeetle keeed."

Once, I told on him for not wearing an arm brace. The doctor threatened to put him in a cast, just to make a point. "A smarth person, would wear brace," he said to my son. "A smarth person, would not use arm. A smarth person, would take care of eeen-jury."

The last time I took my son in for an injury was when he was wearing Vans instead of basketball shoes while shooting hoops, and he damaged the growth plate in his ankle. On the ride to the pediatrician's office, we both wondered what the doctor would say this time. In his best Russian doctor voice, my son said to me, "We're not paying heeem for these comedy. We're paying heeem for methical athvice." We sat in the waiting room with Thomas the Tank Engine movie playing and a bubbling fish tank, hoping we wouldn't have to go get a cast.

The doctor walked into the room. He didn't say a word. He put his hands on his hips, looked my son square in the eye and shouted, "You know. Zee best game? Is chess."

INTERRUPTING YOUNGSTER

Knock knock.

Who's there?

Interrupting cow.

Interrupting c—

Moo-oo.

Young children tend to interrupt. And it's about as funny as that bad knock-knock joke when it happens. Seems like there are two categories of interrupting. Number one, something or someone explodes and you are truly needed. And then, number two, rude interrupting.

My friend Susie has a brilliant way of handling the latter – the rude interrupting. The things that can wait. The stories about their cat toy pretending to jump and scare their horse toy, while you are standing there talking to another mom about her dad's leukemia treatment. That is in the rude interrupting category and Susie handles it like this. You train your children to put their hand on you. They stand there and wait with their hand resting on your arm, or whatever they are tall enough to reach, so that you know they are waiting to talk to you. Even an extremely meek and polite, "May I please tell you something, Mommy?" is interrupting.

With your child's hand resting on you and waiting, you can keep eye contact with the big person you are talking to, while hugging the child into you so he knows you do truly care about his toy cat, but that it will have to wait until the serious big person conversation is over. After all, children have our attention so much of the time, and they need to learn that they have to wait. So with that kind of interrupting, we are talking about good manners.

With the other kind of interrupting, you do have to stop what you're doing; otherwise, the whole kitchen goes up in flames. Or conflicts escalate, is more likely. We must intervene when we hear voices becoming unhappy so that our children do not have to come to blows with one another. We stop what we are doing to help them resolve conflicts before it gets ugly.

It helps to have the expectation around the clock that you will not in fact complete anything from start to finish. Then you're not as surprised or frustrated. Your mindset is: I'll be so thrilled and happy if I can fold these shirts so they won't wrinkle, and the random socks can wait when I get interrupted. It's a mindset of "when I get interrupted" rather than "if I get interrupted." God is pleased with this kind of readiness to deny oneself, as He loves to see that we mothers are truly giving up our lives. Every moment of every day, you are ready for that not to be your moment but rather given to someone else.

When I sat down to work on this chapter, my then 1 year old was trolling around nearby. I said to myself: I'll be amazed if I can write a little bit, and when she interrupts me I'll go sit in her floor with her and read a book while she plays and crawls in and out of my lap. So I had a backup plan.

All of this talk about interruptions begs the question: interruption from what? Blink.

What are we supposed to be busy doing with our time? Serving God. Glorifying Him. Honoring Him. Being about our Father's business. With no thought for our own pride, pleasure or recognition. Delaying or denying our own plans or needs to help our own child, day after day, in the privacy of our home where no one else but God will ever see that you did it, is exactly that: genuine, ongoing service to Him. We could even say it's the very definition of serving Him. No newspaper's going to report it, no worldly reward will come, there is no applause or paycheck. It's truly and sincerely for God. Graciously responding to interruptions from our own children is one of the highest tributes to God from a woman. The eternal, heavenly rewards are beyond anything we might ever think or imagine.

The English word "interrupt" comes from the Latin word "inter" which means "between." It's the kind of Latin preposition that has to do with motion or movement,[27] not as in two frogs sitting on lily pads staring at each other, with one taking a nap in between those two. It suggests instead an active sort of between, where something is happening, something is moving in between something else. The Bible has told us we are to care for and nurture our children as ministry to God. So when we say our child interrupts us, we cannot really say that at all. That would be saying that our ministry to God is coming between us and our ministry to God. Most of the time, what we could admit is that our child is simply coming in between us and our selfishness. Perhaps our children are not an interruption after all but rather they are the destination.

You will be pleased for me to report that my wee one toddled in just now to see me for the first time, and I got to write without interruption for a while, like a big girl. I am pleasantly surprised and grateful for that. Someday soon, we as mothers will long for their voices or their busy hands. But for now, life's one big ol' interruption and God can help us react graciously by seeing that interruptions are actually our raw and beautiful service to Him.

Screaming

You know that passage in the Bible where Jesus says, *"Ye have the poor always with you"*? Matthew 26:11. God tells us that, unfortunately, in this world until He returns, we'll always have the poor. My husband alludes to that passage when he says, "You'll always have the screaming."

When you have little children, there's screaming. It's a way of life. The trick is #1 to ask God to help you be gracious about it and #2 to decipher between screaming that needs correction and screaming that needs affection. Either way, your reaction needs to be loving. James 1:5 says that God will give wisdom to everyone who asks Him. He can give you wisdom to know the difference. One way is to ask Him, when they start getting revved up: "Lord, is this fussing and crying because of some sin on that child's part that needs correcting? Or is it just his being a child and annoying me."

Sometimes it's the latter. They can't help it, the wee ones. They fall apart and can't help it. They need compassion. They need us to scoop them up in our arms and love on them. They can't even say all their words right, they can't read yet or draw a straight line, their feelings get all bottled up, and they don't have the maturity to react well yet. When the tiny people are falling apart and can't help it, I give them a healthy snack or I sit down on the floor and smile at them and hold my arms out to them. They pile in my lap and hug on me and cry their hearts out a little bit longer to tell me all about it and poof they're done. We talk or I'll read them a book or let them show me their toys. All better.

On the other hand, sometimes they can help it and are being little toots. They need some corrective discipline. Disciplining our children takes some serious discipline. Like it or not, we are always disciplining our children.[14] If we tell a child to stop jumping on the couch, he keeps jumping, and nothing happens, then we are disciplining that child that it is marvelous for him to do exactly as he pleases.

If we do correct that behavior, then we are disciplining the child that disobedience to authority has consequences. This morphs into helping him later: if you try a drug with a friend, that has a consequence. If you go 80 in a 55 zone, that has a consequence. If you get physical with someone before marriage, that has a consequence.

The consequence for these behaviors is never: someone will talk to you and talk to you and talk to you. You will hear all about someone's feelings and thoughts. If you speed and the policeman talks and talks and talks, what would you learn? You wouldn't be able to tell me because your head would have long ago crashed onto the steering wheel as you fell sound asleep.

What would you learn if the policeman slammed your car door and got right up in your face and screamed at you, then screeched away in a rage doing donuts out into the next three lanes of traffic? You would learn that this guy has some serious issues and you could tell the family at dinner that night all about the wacko who made a fool out of himself on the side of the road.

Children need a very real, concrete and calm result from a rational human. This is why, with children, if a mother doesn't really mean it, then she shouldn't say it. If she is not willing to follow through to the death at that very moment, then don't say it. Does it really matter if they put on their shoes right that second? If not, carefully word a suggestion instead: "Y'all might want to wear some shoes if you don't want to get bitten by the fire ants." There is really nothing to obey or disobey at this point. She's just giving them a heads up or a preference. If she does give a clear command, she had better mean it and be ready to see it through: "Please put your shoes on now."

Boom, she said it. If the child does not obey, then a specific consequence needs to happen such as taking away an older child's cell phone. Get 'em where it hurts, girls. Once my teenager strongly refused to turn over his phone. I went around the house and found all the chargers. The phone died a slow death and the child eventually surrendered. Diligent mothers are making sure that something happens every time a child disobeys or treats his authority with disrespect.

When we speak of discipline we are talking about educating, instructing, cultivating certain attributes, correcting, preparing, governing, training in subordination to authority, chastising.[47] All that good stuff. The stuff that creates productive, God-fearing adults. One of King David's big failures was never telling his own son Adonijah "no." King Rehoboam foolishly ignored the wise men who told him to rule with kindness and not harshness.

Ask God to help you not get drawn in to the children's screaming and end up pitching the biggest fit of all. We have to rise above their irrational ways rather than join them. I've mellowed out a lot over the years. But when I was a younger mother and was not yet broken in on the screaming reality, the children's naughty outbursts made me see red. A cool mom named Claudia told me that she would drop down and do push-ups whenever she felt herself getting angry at her children. You get this adrenaline rush of anger when your children are provoking you, and doing push-ups gets rid of that. Also, when the children look over and

You Just Have to Laugh (and Cry)

see: Whoa, mommy's doing push-ups, they think, "maybe we should chill." Right there in the living room, I would do push-ups rather than interact with them.

I'd get on my knees and pray right there in the living room too: "Lord please help me with these children." And He did. We aren't on TV, the queen is not dropping by, we're not sitting in church, this is our home and we have to do whatever it takes to get it together if we're angry at our children. It doesn't always look neat and tidy. It's very humbling to do push-ups and bow to our knees, but this is spiritual warfare and it's probably good for your children to see you doing these things to manage your anger, rather than pretending you have it together all the time.

I've heard it said that anger has to do with disappointment. And disappointment has to do with expectations. We need to have the expectation that, if there are babies and young children in the house, there will be crying and yes sometimes there will even be screaming. There's nothing wrong with your young children if they are loud or sad or crying. Your family is just like mine. In fact, if anyone were to challenge my small children to a screaming duel, we'd win by a landslide. We're 98th percentile on loudness at our house.

The Out of Control Five Year Old

When my 5 year old has reached a state of complete desperation and emotional confusion, and it's not because she is sleepy or hungry, I tell her it is time to go and read the Bible together. She will kick and fight her way to her room with me, as I take her to go and read the Bible. She is absolutely out of control. I'm calm and I bring her near to me with my arm around her as she screams. I open up her Bible with pictures and stories that are familiar to her.

She keeps crying and saying things that don't make any sense. I don't get drawn in to that irrational bumbling. I turn to the first page and she sees Adam and Eve. She is protesting and wailing but remembers as I read and she says through her tears, "I don't want to be like Adam and Eve." I keep reading, she keeps crying. I turn the page and by the time we get to Noah she is more quiet and says, "I want to be like Noah." Tears are still streaming down her face but she is breathing more normally now. I keep reading. By the time we get to Abraham and Sarah she is very calm and she remembers that she wants to follow God like they did.

By this point she has forgotten all about whatever it was that pierced her heart minutes before and is asking to skip ahead to "the Baal dudes." We are laughing now at how silly those guys were to worship someone besides the real God. We don't want to be foolish like that.

She talks rationally about what was bothering her now. She starts crying a little but we talk about what happened. We talk about how she can't insist on her own way. We need to forgive, wait our turn, be patient, obey, can't throw fits, use a gracious voice. She asks to read Esther, so we read Esther. I have to get back to cooking or laundry but by then my child is right with the world. There might be a follow-up punishment, corrective discipline, an apology from her, hugs to a sister, some closure on the problem. Her heart is ready for all of that now.

And her entire life, she will know that whenever the world is crashing in on her, God's word is where we go.

OUR PROPHETIC PILLOW

I was slumped over in a chair, with my face buried in my hands as I wept to God. Years ago my husband and I were having some monumental struggles with one of our children. Nothing scandalous, just some special needs that grieve a mother's heart such as violent emotional outbursts over schoolwork and chores, and a puzzling chemical imbalance that I couldn't whip.

No one else seemed to be having problems like this. Some well-meaning relatives had just had meltdowns of their own, unhappy with the way I was handling these challenges. The doorbell rang, and even though my face was red and tear-stained, I went to the door. It was my beautiful friend Robyn, holding a gift bag. What I didn't know was while we were having these difficult struggles with one of our children, and had been enduring much weeping and gnashing of teeth and crying out to God on this child's behalf, He had done a miraculously kind and loving thing for me.

He told Robyn to sew a pillow for Jennifer. There it is, pictured. Robyn did not know about the problems we were having with our child. She had never heard God be so specific about sewing before, but she knew it was a serious thing. He even woke her up in the night to tell her about this pillow to sew for me. She went to look at her fabric and God directed her to the fabric, which she didn't even know she had. She had never remembered seeing this fabric before. But there it was, and so she got to work on this pillow for Jennifer.

As she sewed, she felt the gravity of the situation and was talking to God about the details of it, asking Him about the trim and the size and the shape. She opened up her Bible and came to a passage that said, *"And it shall be a square."* This was probably some Old Testament instruction about building the tabernacle, but it gave Robyn quite a shiver to read that. She made the pillow into a square. And she brought it to me that day that I was feeling so defeated and hopeless. When I first saw that pillow, I started crying again, but this time they were tears of joy.

Only our first three children had been born at this point, and so you see pictured in the pillow three children. In studying it, I believe the blooming large roses underneath represent my other children, who had not yet been born. Two of the three roses are our fourth and fifth children, and the sixth is a baby we lost in a miscarriage.

Robyn and I had learned to bake homemade bread together. It sounds impressive to grind your own wheat but honestly it's not like I'm out in the backyard stomping out grapes to make wine. If you can grind coffee beans, you can mill grain. Robyn and I had ground wheat together and rolled out dough together, shared loaves of fresh bread with each other, visiting as sisters in Christ and trying to make something healthy for our families.

The children on the pillow are gathering grain. When you read the Bible, you know that God talks a lot about harvest, and He knew I needed to see that my children would someday be happily and abundantly gathering a great harvest. He was telling me my sorrow would be short-lived – it was; this child is doing great now – and that soon I would see rich fruit from all my children's lives. I'm talking about the fruits of the spirit found in Galatians 5:22 and 23. The good stuff, the character stuff that comes from knowing Him: *"love, joy, peace, longsuffering, gentleness, goodness, faith, meekness, temperance: against such there is no law."*

A church is in the background. My husband and I weave Godliness and Biblical truth into every day we spend with our children. In putting the church there, God was telling me He sees that, and He is always going to honor that, by being there for us, faithful and strong and guiding us. I am so thankful that Robyn did not argue with God, like Jonah, but rather obeyed Him. It would have been so easy for her to dismiss what God was telling her to do as just a kooky silly thought and not want to embarrass herself in front of her friend. But she obeyed Him and sewed me a pillow.

If you are faithfully raising your children according to His word, the picture on that pillow shows the beautiful harvest to come. I used to think this pillow was a miraculous show of love, just for me. Now I see that it is for all of us.

CHAPTER 14

BIBLICAL WORLDVIEW

—∞∞∞—

I have in my hands a bumpy-textured, burgundy-colored book roughly the size of a thank-you note. I love to flip through this little book and run my fingers over it. It's called *The New England Primer* and as I understand it, that's pronounced "primmer" as in "slimmer." This little volume is how all the great men in our nation learned to read in the late 1600s and through the early 1800s. Children were taught the alphabet using this book, like so:

A   Adam's fall. We sinned all.
B   Heaven to find, the Bible Mind.
C   Christ crucified, for sinners died.
D   The deluge drowned the Earth round.
E   Elijah hid by ravens fed.

And on it goes. These are the ABCs of Christianity that once were easy and familiar to every American child. This alphabet speaks of Job blessing God in the face of pain, Lot fleeing Sodom, Moses leading God's people through the Red Sea, the global flood of Noah, great young kings Obadiah, David and Josiah, Peter's bitterness after denying Jesus, Queen Esther saving the Jews, Ruth leaving all for truth, young Samuel fearing the Lord and being dear to Him, Timothy, Vashti, Jonah, Xerxes and Zaccheus.

Most children today are not being taught who any of those people are. It is all quite foreign to them. In America, the basics of the Bible were once taught alongside the basics of the English language. After the alphabet is learned, sentences are taught in this book quoting passages from the Bible and they begin in this way:

A wise son maketh a glad father…
Better is little with the fear of the Lord…
Come unto Christ all ye that labor…
Do not the abominable thing…
Except a man be born again…

This is how the sentences all begin, all through the alphabet. Each of these sentences is taken from scripture. These are the first sentences the founding fathers of our nation learned to read. After this primer came the McGuffey readers, which were used by Laura Ingalls Wilder in school,[53] and these are still in print today. They contain Biblical truth, they contain prayers, they distinguish between right and wrong character, they're not afraid to say the word "God."

Up to as recently as the 1950s, as any grandmother can tell you, scripture was recited and memorized in school. The Ten Commandments were posted on the classroom wall. Teachers would read aloud from the Bible, or students stood in front of the class and read a chapter of the Bible. Classes regularly studied great portions of the Bible. Of course one must know and be familiar with the Bible. It was all very basic. It was considered very "duh."

This is gone now. Children today are not being taught anything about the truth of the Bible in public school. Our country's final generation who were taught in school the things of the Lord is fading away and almost gone. It's an emergency because Jesus said many times to his clueless accusers, *"Haven't you read?"* Don't you know the scriptures? And then He would quote passages from the word of God. Our own generation and the next generation are Biblically in the dark and *"haven't read."*

We need to realize this is happening. We need to understand the times. And we have to take seriously that our job is to fill in the holes left because our children are no longer being taught by the collective society. American education used to impress this on children's eager and pure minds:

1. $2 + 2 = 4$
2. Rebellion to God will lead to misery.
3. ABCDEFGHIJKLMNOP…
4. Scripture says that the humble will be exalted.
5. Christopher Columbus sailed in 1492.
6. Moses was the meekest man on the face of the Earth.

And so on. Modern education has removed every Biblical reference so that it looks like this instead:

1. $2 + 2 = 4$
2.
3. ABCDEFGHIJKLMNOP…
4.
5. Christopher Columbus sailed in 1492.
6.

In Ezekiel 22:30, God sought for someone who would stand in the gap for Him and there was no one. We can raise our hands and say, Me, Me, Lord, call on me, I'm there for you. I will stand in the gap. It's the same thing Daniel's, Moses's and Samuel's mothers did so beautifully. Those mothers taught their sons the things of the Lord in a time when God's ways were under attack. And so can we.

We can't sit around and bemoan why this is our country's condition or cry about it. In fact, Ecclesiastes 7:10 gives us something important to obey and that is, *"Say not thou, what is the cause that the former days were better than these? since it is not wise of you to ask this."* All throughout history man has rejected or embraced the things of God, and we American ladies living in the 21st century happen to have found ourselves plunked right down in the midst of a rejecting time. Full on attack actually.

Our government's agenda is not merely to remove Biblical teaching but rather to combat it, to fight it, to contradict it. They replace Christianity with religions of their own and then call it neutral. Religious neutrality does not exist. Religion is simply a belief system based on faith. No one can re-move religion from education. What can be done is to remove one certain religion – Christianity – and replace it with other religions such as socialism and environmentalism.

No biggee. Unelected government officials can do that all they want. They lose. We simply teach the truth to our own children ourselves. Regardless of where our children receive their formal education, we mothers are to teach our own children the truth of the Bible. Modern education has bizarre, mischievous goals. But it doesn't matter. Our goal is very clear regarding the ways of God and that is to *"teach them diligently to thy children,"* Deuteronomy 6. The anteced-ent of "them" is referring to God's statutes, God's character and a life of honor-ing Him. And the passage says for us to teach this to our own children.

No one can stop people from believing God's truth. As Jesus says in Luke 19:40, *"if these shall hold their peace, the stones would immediately cry out."* Our schools have textbooks that deny the Lord Jesus Christ with all their might but that's okay. The very rocks will cry out about Him instead.

Sunday School is marvelous but it does not necessarily produce a Biblically literate child. Often the materials are based on the happy parts of the Bible, the New Testament, or watered down versions of the Old Testament. The materi-als can be written by people who have not read the whole Bible themselves. Youth devotions are sometimes written by people who disgrace God in their own lives. Church can supplement us, but we can't rely on church alone. Some churches do not even consider the Bible.

I've heard it said that the Christian church is about two decades behind the culture in rejecting God's ways. As this book was being finalized for pub-lication, the Presbyterian Church (U.S.A.) announced its official acceptance of same-sex marriage. This decision strongly contradicts Biblical teaching. Ironically, the Church's announcement was made on St. Patrick's Day 2015, a day to honor the saint whose love of Christ led him to spread the gospel and Biblical truth throughout Ireland. St. Patrick, who quotes the wazoo out of the Bible, speaks in his *Confessions* of the importance of leading a holy life and distin-guishing between good and evil. "So be amazed, all you people great and small who fear God," St. Patrick wrote. "You well-educated people in authority, listen and examine this carefully ... The flesh can be an enemy, dragging towards ... doing those enticing things." Today, many church leaders are extremely confused because they are Biblically illiterate. It really is up to each mother to teach the Bible to her own children.

When I first discovered everything I am telling you, I felt like the blind leading the blind for a while there. I myself was educated with the Bible completely absent from and contradicted in the classroom, and not very thoroughly taught in church – or maybe I wasn't paying attention. I was vaguely familiar with the Bible but as an adult I found myself having to catch up. I had to re-educate myself. I tried the public library but figured out pretty quickly the unfortunate reality that the library, funded by our government, is not going to be carrying children's books with a Biblical view of the world.

Now, the library does have some cute little board books about baby Jesus in the manger or whatever. They are in the holiday section along with the Easter Bunny and Groundhog Day. If a believer busts out into the mainstream such as Dave Ramsey and his financial books, then the library will carry those. And of course our man C.S. Lewis was skillful enough to bury Biblical brilliance into his Narnia books in a way that was palatable to the secular world. They never even knew what hit them.

There is buried treasure in the library. Look hard and you will find remnants of Christianity. Find any book written before 1970 and what you have there is an author educated in or before the 1950s. That book most likely will, at least to some extent, reflect the nature of God. The older the better. Even though the classics are no longer discussed from a Biblical viewpoint in modern education, the classics all contain Biblical truth and lessons in morality, and so our family tries to gravitate toward those.

If the library shelf is slim pickin's then that's okay because there is only one Book we ultimately need. Read the Bible, the whole Bible, with your children over and over and over, all throughout the 18 years you have with them. It's very simple but that's the answer.

I humbled myself down to a tiny speck of nothing when I first began reading the Bible with my children. They would ask me questions such as, "Why did Queen Vashti not get to be queen anymore?" I know the answer now but at first

I did not. (The king needed to set Vashti's disrespectful 'tude as an example to all the other wives in the kingdom in order to prevent some trickle down rebellionomics. Our girl Esther took over.) Somehow my children still respected me greatly as I would respond, quite a few times actually, "I don't know. That's a good question. Let's read more and find out." We've learned the Bible together.

So we must read good children's versions of the entire Bible like there's no tomorrow. And then when it comes to specific academics, just spin it baby. You can take those hollow modern textbooks that have no mention of our God in them and give them a Biblical outlook as you discuss them with your children. Let's talk about the three subjects of science, history and math. And please always make sure your husband is good with anything I ever say or I'm banishing you from Triumphant Womanhood.

SCIENCE

We are in the midst of this amazing, breathtaking world that we can't even begin to understand or try to measure or imitate, and then mainstream science experts are so smart that they've become not. They insist that the world made itself. Did it now? The pyramids in Egypt did not build themselves. As scientist Ken Ham points out, the pyramids are the handiwork left behind by someone we can't see anymore. The Earth was created by Someone we can't see. The idea that the world appeared by accident is important to some because they need for there to be no Creator. Otherwise, they are faced with their authority, which means they are faced with their own inadequacy. And that's not fun. Unless they understand grace someday.

Apparently we are fortunate to have a planet exactly the size of Jupiter sitting exactly at its distance from Earth because a whole bunch of asteroids are pulled into Jupiter all the time rather than landing on us in parking lots. Now God could have decided a solution to that would be: no asteroids. But there are asteroids. And they are hitting Jupiter instead of Earth. The only explanation is that God would like us to notice how much He loves us. If the sun were even a tiny bit farther from us or closer to us, life would be impossible. The precision of God's creation and therefore love and concern for us are astonishing.

All right ladies. If someone tries to tell our children we evolved from monkeys, here are two things we can say to our children later: "One, he has quite a strong faith about that interestingly bizarre story eh? I thought he didn't want anyone to mix faith and science. And, two, if monkeys turned into people, then why are there still monkeys around today?"

Scio is the Latin word for "I know." You conjugate that to the third person plural future "scient" which means "they will know." God is omniscient, "omni" meaning all. So we have "all" + "they will know." God is all they will ever know. He knows everything, so He might have some idea about maybe what those bright things are up there in the sky floating around, and His book the Bible might have a few things to say about that too.

When people say you can't mix science and religion, that statement is meaningless. That's like saying you can't mix Leonardo da Vinci with the Mona Lisa. All that statement does is display that whoever said that would like to leave the Creator out of the creation.[18] You can subscribe to *Creation Magazine*, which my husband heard about from another pilot. And we found out about Answers in Genesis at a homeschool conference. Looking at these organizations' websites with your children is very educational, and it's free. We can offset all the evolution indoctrination that our children are bombarded with everywhere else they look.

⟨∞⟩

HISTORY

If science is the study of the stuff God made, history is the study of the people He made and their actions. History is seeing God's hand in blessing people or smiting people, depending on their respect for Him or their rebellion to Him.

It is a crying shame the way the public schools have rewritten history. It reminds me of George Orwell's book *1984* where a whole staff of employees was paid to change historical facts in order to keep the people ignorant. A friend told me her daughter's public school history book contains six pages on some little known multi-interesting person's contribution to our nation, while George Washington was mentioned maybe twice in passing. No disrespect to that fascinating person, but our children need to know the whole truth.

They need to know that George Washington referred to God as "the Divine Author of our blessed Religion, and without an humble imitation of whose example in these things, we can never hope to have a happy Nation."[47] Our children need to know that Christopher Columbus knelt down and prayed when he hit North American soil. They need to know that he sang Christian hymns every night.[40] They need to know that the founders of this country, while not perfect as no man is perfect, all knew the Bible left and right. Knowing the Bible used to be one of the basic marks of an educated person. Our children need to know that the Native Americans were often paid for their land by white settlers, who many times shared the gospel with them. My own great great great grandfather Gideon Pond translated the Bible for Native Americans.[10]

My children understand very well from Bible stories that when it comes to history, God doesn't play. He makes nations rise and fall. He establishes and brings down leaders. It makes one feel rather small and in awe to view history that way, but also full of hope because He always takes care of those who are faithful to Him. Daniel and the lion's den? That's what I'm talking about if China comes and enslaves all of us. Our nation owes China something like infinity-trillion dollars and eventually they might ask us to pay. I'm teaching my children not to be afraid of captivity the way Daniel and his buddies weren't.

When you read the whole Bible with your children, this is God helping you pass on to them the truth about history. They learn not to fear tyrants or bureaucrats. They learn to fear and trust God.

MATH

The math books all speak for themselves when it comes to the Bible. I'll tell you what I mean by that. Suppose someone who likes to pick on Christians as a hobby were to say, "There's no right and wrong. How can you prove there's right or wrong? It's all up to the individual." Then you can wonder if that person's math teacher agrees with him.

Math reveals the existence of right and wrong. There's no almost right answer. Ten plus six can't be 45 one day, and the next day be zero, depending on how it is feeling. It always has to be 16. Math by definition is a very beautiful display of God's physical laws. And of course, math is the language of science.

Math must be unchanging and constant, which is to say true. If someone claims, "There's no absolute truth. Each person gets to decide the truth for himself." You can wonder, "You believe that to be true?" Maybe he will someday see that he needs for truth to exist in order to claim that anything that he wants to say is true.[8]

When my children and I marvel at some amazing phenomenon in math, we'll stop and say, "Isn't God so cool?" A simple example is that any number whose digits add up to a number that is divisible by three, will itself be divisible by three. I think God did that for fun, just to delight us.

In Isaiah 10:15, we are asked to consider this: *"Shall the ax boast itself against him that heweth therewith? Or shall the saw magnify itself against him that shaketh it? As if the rod should shake itself against them that lift it up, or as if the staff should lift up itself, as if it were no wood."*

Numbers did not decide to be the way that they are. Does the Pythagorean theorem work every time in measuring right triangles and then boast itself against God? Does pi work every time on measuring the circumference of any circle, and then lift itself up as if it were its own idea?

No one in the general public would ridicule a mathematician or scientist who had done all he could without acknowledging God and then reached the point where he stopped, sat back in his chair and said, "Perhaps all this time my main assumption has not been correct." Colleagues would snicker, but don't they always? Such a person would gain great respect by most everyone for refusing to dismiss the notion that the orchestra is being conducted by God.

Regardless of the math curriculum, and my family's is secular, numbers are a beautiful example of God's brilliant order, God's vast knowledge, God's law that there must be right and wrong, and the fact that there must be truth.[32] One of the very last passages in the Old Testament before we get to Jesus says in Malachi 3:6, *"I am the Lord, I change not."* And, I would add, He plays not.

CHAPTER 15

GOOD CHARACTER

—∞∞—

Years ago, whenever my clothes dryer buzzed, I would groan in a way that sounded like Chewbacca had gotten stung by a hornet. I was super annoyed that the dryer was calling me to come fold clothes when I was busy. I was totally unaware that I was making this sound. Until ... one day my daughter was annoyed about something, and she made exactly the same sound. Children sure are little mirrors. Ever since then, I smile and scurry to fold the laundry cheerfully like a cute little Ewok.

We can't bark at our children sarcastically, roll our eyes at our husbands, frost a telemarketer on the phone, and then think that compartmentalizing a seven-minute lecture on Godly character is going to get very far with our children. So the pressure is on as a mother, isn't it? If the wee ones are awake, we're on the clock. We're setting the example of Godliness in our home. And it's not something you can fake. I've tried that and failed. We also want to equip our children to rely on Him as much as we do. My relationship with Him can't be their relationship with Him. They have to have their own God thing going.

George Washington believed that God would bless or curse his army depending on how they all honored Him, feared Him and cried out to Him. Washington wasn't Jesus sewww ... his life wasn't perfect but this man feared God Almighty. We can read letters he wrote to his generals saying: Yo, we have to do this or that, or else God's favor won't be upon us and we'll lose the war with England.[35] I just know in my heart it's because his mother had him believing this at a very early age.

Perhaps we could say Washington feared and loved God in such a way as to care about being naughty or nice. Speaking of Santa Claus and toys, I've been on the dark side in public relations and I can tell you that you're not crazy. It's not your imagination. People really do sit around conference room tables talking about how to get children in a frenzy over products. They do not ever consider your child's character. It's a non-issue. They're just trying to make money by saturating the market with brand loyalty, especially with licensed toys and trinkets. This behavior threw me off for a while because a marketing employee is your average, everyday very nice person who is married with children of his or her own. There was a disconnect between what they professed to believe for their own families and how they applied that to their professional lives.

The question among the marketing people is always, "How?" never "Should we?" Books that are spun off of TV shows – or even shows themselves – can be one big marketing promo rather than real literature or valid, wholesome entertainment. I can smell those when I pull into the library parking lot. Boo-yah, we go on the counter-offensive and try not to let our children be exposed to their market saturation. The products are mindless drivel with no serious content.

Big screen films and many TV shows, on the other hand, do take their content almost as seriously as making their cool million. Their agenda for your child's character might not be the same as your agenda. Their agenda might actually be destroying yours.[16] Regardless of the cultural stance you and your husband take, we mothers are more savvy than the marketing and film people. We understand that our children are very impressionable and so we use this for good instead. We promote the Lord Jesus Christ. We launch an ad campaign in our homes for the Lord Jesus Christ.

We want our children at a very young age to see that God is their heavenly Father who blesses and curses. He is not just some big aloof guy in the sky with a red coat and jolly face and maybe sort of created the world, and then has been taking a nap ever since. Let's look at two modern examples, social media and video games.

SOCIAL MEDIA

The Bible doesn't contain the expression "social media." But the Bible addresses socializing. All we have to do is apply scripture to social media the way we apply it to every other area of our lives. Things were much simpler in our day, when all we had was maybe an Atari with that Pac Man or Asteroids game on it. Allow me to walk you through my daughter's experience with the now obsolete Starland social media application (app) so that if your children begin to use social media, you won't feel like you've been hit in the head with an actual asteroid.

Starland was basically a combination of Instagram and Twitter for teenyboppers. It was like Facebook but more brief verbally, and available only on handheld devices. Imagine scrolling down and seeing all of your e-mails on a single screen, with pictures and text. This is what social media looks like. It is interactive because everyone in a group sees everyone else's posts in their "feed." Subscribers to Starland had a personal profile and could post pictures along with text up to 600 characters. (I found that to be a cruel and unusual limit.) They had followers who saw their posts in their feed, and they followed people whose stuff they saw. They could "like" other people's posts and people could "like" theirs. They could make their account private or public. Joining most apps is free because the creators of apps make their money from advertising. Here is how my husband and I applied Biblical principles to our daughter's participation in social media.

1. Our daughter was 12 years old and asked our permission to have Starland, just as she would have asked our permission to go to a birthday party. Our answer was yes. She also asked to have Instagram. Our answer was not yet. We allowed our son to have Instagram at age 15. (*"Children, obey your parents in the Lord, for this is right."* Ephesians 6:1.)

2. After we said yes to Starland for our daughter, I set up a Starland account for myself. I joined it too. This way, I could stalk my daughter while also having fun with her and try to understand her heart. I "liked" all her posts and learned more about her. I've learned that she

is wonderfully creative. Actually, my daughter set up my account for me because I had no idea what I was doing. Your children are the gizmo experts, and they love it when we ask them to help us. *("Know well the condition of your flock."* Proverbs 27:23.)

3. My daughter wanted her account to be public because she truly had some adorably cute ideas to share with the world of young ladies. We allowed that, but we didn't allow her to post any pictures of herself. She posted only pictures of her stuffed animals and their escapades. If she has a private Facebook or Instagram account some-day, then she can post pictures of herself. If it's public then her dad or I will want to approve her pictures before she posts them. She didn't see what the big deal was at first, but I explained to her that the world contains people who are creepy. *("Keep yourself unspotted from the world."* James 1:27 and *"Do not throw your pearls to the swine."* Matthew 7:6.)

4. I asked her to exercise caution with deciding whom she followed. Once she clicks "follow," then that person's posts will forever appear in her feed. We're not trying to hurt anybody's feelings or insult anyone around here, and it is a serious downer when you follow someone and then have to unfollow them. Just don't follow them in the first place if you aren't sure they are going to be honoring God and keeping it clean. *("Above all else guard your heart, for it is the wellspring of life."* Proverbs 4:23 and *"He that walketh with wise men shall be wise: but a companion of fools shall be destroyed."* Proverbs 13:20.)

5. My daughter was using the expression OMG in her posts. Yes, there are much worse expressions in the world. Still, I challenged her to get extreme and do something more ridiculous than Shaun White's first snowboard run at the Winter X-Games. I asked her to try not to say OMG very often. *("Do not take the Lord's name in vain,"* Exodus 20:7.)

6. My daughter posted a few "Oh wow can you even believe I have this many followerrrrrrs??" posts. She took a picture of her screen showing all her many "likes" and "followers." I asked her to remove those messages. I told her that God wants us to be humble, modest and not showy-offey. *("Let the one who boasts, boast in the Lord."* 2 Corinthians 10:17.)

7. She once spoke about her dad in a joking way that could have been seen as disrespectful. I asked her to delete that. *("Honor your father and mother."* Exodus 20:12.)

8. All of my teenagers and I had some lively discussions regarding the moral soundness of my daughter's plan to award prizes to other subscribers for participation in her contests. I'm still not sure, but I think I lost. *("Take every thought captive to the obedience of Christ."* 2 Corinthians 10:5.)

My daughter cheerfully went along with my micromanagement of her first experience with social media. She did respectfully tell me a few times that she was only doing what everyone else was doing. Well now let's see. Parents have been hearing that lame plea since the beginning of time. We must trust our instincts and stand up against anything that doesn't sit right with us.

Starland turned out to be a really fun and creative outlet for my daughter. She was kind of amazing actually, and I was sad when the app was cancelled. She posted a picture of her "marshmallow army" once while she was making fudge. She held sewing and drawing demonstrations. She held fun games for girls: "Guess which stuffed animal this is, now that her face is covered up with a purple moon." The girls all told each other "Super cute, great job." It was a friendly, uplifting place.

VIDEO GAMES

When I was a young lassie growing up in North Carolina, my beloved Granny had come to visit from Tennessee. One morning, my brothers and I said good-bye to her as we left for school, because she was leaving to drive back to her house. When I came home from school that afternoon, my Granny's white car was still parked in front of our house. Happy but surprised, I walked inside and called out, "Granny? Are you still here?" She didn't answer, but from our downstairs den this is what I heard. Frogger music played. My Granny's voice said, "Offpt. Well shoot." More Frogger music played. My Granny said, "Ack. Oh no." More Frogger music. "Dag nabbit," said Granny.

I walked downstairs and there was Granny, sitting in front of our Atari, determined to win at the video game Frogger. There is no telling how many hours she had been glued to that game, trying to conquer it. My Granny was a highly educated elementary school principal, world traveler and community volunteer. She was a strong Christian lady. But that Frogger game had her mesmerized.

Video games sure can pull us right in. Even the best of us can get hooked, although my Granny did eventually turn the thing off and drove home. God doesn't say anything about wii or Nintendo in the Bible. Here is what He does say: *"A child left to himself bringeth his mother to shame."* Proverbs 28:15. If a husband and wife decide to allow electronics in their family, then they mustn't give their child the gizmo and walk away. We set limits and stay involved.

We take seriously the sicko violence thing too and stay away from stuff that is way sinister. The Bible addresses that in Proverbs 13:2: *"The soul of the unfaithful feeds on violence."* My friend has a special blow-up world for her son on Minecraft, so that he will stop blowing up random stuff his siblings have built in other worlds. I have told our children they cannot play Minecraft if they are going to steal from, trap, or otherwise torment the villagers. (If you have no idea what I'm talking about, be very glad.) No, the villagers are not real and they don't have feelings. But we treat people well not merely for humanitarian reasons, but to honor God.

Years ago, one of our video games became a serious addiction for our son. My husband and I saw that the Playstation (PS3) was completely different from other video games, in the way it was affecting our son. Unlike our other video games, the internet-linked ones provide children – especially boys – with a false sense of accomplishment.

These games are very powerful. The game that grabbed hold of our son was called Zombies. Which is funny, or not, because it turned my child into a zombie. After a few months of seeing our son not be himself, and seeing him isolate himself on a destructive downward spiral, we felt God telling us to take his game console away. "Get rid of it," I heard. I went into my son's room and unplugged the PS3 one day. Just unplugged it. I packed it up in a box, never got it back out again, and later my husband sold it on eBay.

I sat down with my son to ask if he would share with other families what he learned from that experience.

Jennifer: *What would you say to other families about Playstation or Xbox games?*

Son: It's kind of like a drug almost. Especially with multi-player games. You can get sucked in and waste your whole day without even realizing it. When you're 24 and applying for a job, it's not going to help you later in life. There are people who have spent 2,400 hours or more playing these games. It's so dumb because you could be doing other stuff with that time.

J: *You didn't realize this while you had your PS3?*

S: I didn't realize that until my PS3 was taken away and sold. The video game companies are taking so much money from kids. You buy the game and then two months later they release a map pack, and if the company was honorable it would be available for free. But they're getting $120 for this map pack or a new weapon from a lot of people. Then something new comes out a few months after that.

J: *How are the real time, internet games different from other video games?*

S: Playing video games with friends in the room is different. It's fun, it's a social thing rather than you by yourself with a headset on.

J: *I think a lot of families will appreciate your explaining this to them.*

S: Parents should know that they have power over their kids, and they can take it away. The kid might be saying, "Oh poor me, I got my game taken away," but they really didn't take anything away from them at all because it's all virtual.

J: *Do you miss your PS3?*

S: I'm a whole lot happier and well off now. I don't miss it at all.

Teenagers: Test Flight

As I tried to care one morning about the fretful studies in the newspaper that droned on and on about troubled youth, crime and warped humanity, my mind wandered to the only relevant thing I know. My mind wandered to you. Devoted parents are instilling character in the next generation. We are quietly preventing the problems of our society, one child at a time in our own homes.

Sometimes my husband practices in a flight simulator for his job, as ongoing training to stay qualified as a pilot. If he begins flying a new aircraft, he has to study many hours and spend time in flight simulators. That's how a mother can think about instilling Godly character in her children. Her home is 18 years of flight simulator. Her child's life after that is the actual airplane. The whole time she has had this child in her care, her job has been to simulate where Godly obedience or Godly rebellion leads. We schwack our children with consequences when they stray from God's ways, and we bless them with joy when they're right with Him. They are being given 18 years of practice, with their parents doing later what a relationship with or without God will do. They learn that when we are tight with God and abide by His ways, we have joy.

This is why we are surrounded by tragic, disturbing news. Many children have grown up without any time in a spiritual flight simulator, and now they are adults flying a plane.

It seems so intimidating to consider parenting teenagers when it is far off. Years ago, I truly disliked all the times people would fill me with dread about The Teenage Years. It's a lot like women who've not yet given birth having to sit through childbirth horror stories at a baby shower. Once you've gone through childbirth, you realize most of the stories were exaggerated and although birth was kind of unpleasant, you know that you can handle it. A young child is like a puppy dog who follows you around adoringly. A teenager is like a cat. He is marginally aware that he needs you, but he is aloof.

Having teenagers has been different, I've had a lot to learn, and we've had a bit of heartache. But there's been no more to learn, no more heartache or difficulty than when our children were much smaller. The most challenging time I've had as a mother was with a newborn baby. And you've already done that. You will do very well with your teenagers. Besides, you have the advantage of having been a teenager.

Women sometimes freak younger women out by telling them, "Just wait. Teenagers are harder than toddlers." I have both right now, and I have at least four things to say about that statement. One, it is not true. Two, it is a cruel thing to say to a young mother. Three, the claim that teenagers are more challenging than toddlers is about as accurate as saying that sitting in a malfunctioning massage chair is more of a hardship than running five miles. In the snow. Without shoes. Four, be gentle with anyone who says this to you because, most likely, she authentically has forgotten what a 2 year old is like.

I want to encourage mothers with young children by telling you that teenagers are the gratifying outcome of all that hard work you did when they were little and impossible. My 15-year-old daughter helps me run our household, is very hard working, offers to help, delights in her younger siblings, and loves reading her Bible. She exercises and eats well. I've never had to tell her to practice her violin and she's been playing for five years. She practices every day. She and her 13-year-old sister both love to cook (I'm not grimacing). The three of us knock out cleaning our entire house every Saturday. It used to take me all day to clean the house by myself. My 13 year old volunteers to show up an hour early to her dance studio each week to help with a toddler class. I look at my daughters and I see future Godly women.

Our 17-year-old son is responsible, thoughtful, excelling in academics and in his part time sales job. He changed a blown out tire the other evening in the dark, by himself, with no phone service. He is always very respectful to his father and me. He gravitates toward people who want to have good clean fun and not get into trouble. A friend said something about getting high once, and my son never hung out with that guy ever again. Last Christmas my son kept telling me he wanted to buy me a pair of tall brown leather boots. I said, "Please don't do that." I didn't want him to spend his hard-earned money on me. My husband said, "Let him buy you the boots. It will make him happy." So I did. He gave them to me for Christmas. I cried.

Our teens have gone against our rules a few times, yes. They have very nearly broken my heart a few times. God has had to help me get up out of bed in the morning a few times, over the grief they have placed on my heart. But in being diligent, and in seeking God over and over again, my husband and I have kept them in line and they have never shouted at us, never gotten out of control, and they are drawn to the things of God. The Holy Spirit seems to be present and active in my children's lives.

When our son did make some bad decisions once, my husband and I had good talks with him and gave him some tough consequences. We asked him what went wrong. Our son said, "I hadn't read my Bible in three months." That was a good answer. He didn't say, "I should have tried harder to be good."

One of my daughter's English assignments was to take notes, in outline form, on the sermon at church one Sunday. Our pastor gives some meaty sermons with lots of scripture references and specific examples. So I knew she would be able to come up with a really good outline.

At home after church, I asked to see her outline. I glanced down at it while I was busy in the kitchen, and my heart sank because all she had written was one sentence. I was disappointed because this was unacceptable, and I knew she would need to try again the next Sunday. Before I spoke to her about it, I finally got around to reading the one sentence she had written. I got teary-eyed and decided what she had written was perfectly fine. We can learn about outlines later. What she had written was profound and wonderful and displayed a spiritual understanding that many people live a lifetime without achieving. This was her sentence:

"If you believe that God is in charge, then you will be happy."

CHAPTER 16

A MOTHER'S BEAUTIFUL HEART

———∞∞∞———

My 2 year old Rebecca is such a serious handful that lately we have begun refer-ring to her as the anti-Rebecca. Wee ones are so yummy when they're born, but you've given up your life. The Bible says that when you lose your life, that's when you gain it. Motherhood forces us to do this. Motherhood leaves us no choice. There's this desperation to meet your own basic needs just enough to function. Then gradually as they grow, they start to get into everything and have quite the attitude. It's exhausting and intense. Having a young toddler is like having a raccoon in the house, only cuter.

Rebecca decided three days ago that she hates taking a bath. She used to love her bath. Now, bathing this child is like fighting with a baby seal who's be-ing attacked by a panther. Squirming slippery fury, is what she is.

When you have tiny children, you can grow tired of the battle. They're naughty and busy. They fall apart emotionally at the most inconvenient times. The massive power of their sin nature threatens to engulf you. And then you are faced with your own sin nature, in reaction to theirs. Psalm 51:17 says that what pleases God is a broken spirit: *"...a broken and contrite heart, O God, thou wilt not despise."* God's not all that impressed with all the sacrifices or striving or trying from us. He's impressed when we come to Him crying out with a broken spirit.

When my first three children were ages 4, 2 and newborn, I would get them all asleep at night and fall on my knees to God in utter exhaustion and bro-kenness, saying, "Thank you so much Lord for getting me through another day."

Once, when they were all under age 7 my husband was about to deploy to Kuwait. I didn't have a "staff" back then like I do now – my older children are enormously helpful with my wee ones. I said to God that I couldn't do it. I couldn't get through the deployment. Forget the deployment: just getting through the day with children that age can be very difficult for any mother. I was overwhelmed with anxiety and told God I didn't know how I'd get through each day.

I felt the Lord say to me, "Stay in constant communion with Me."

That answer really twerked me. I started to cry. I shouted to God in my heart: "Is constant communion with you going to school the children, make the meals, give the little ones their baths and be my husband's arms hugging me?"

And God said, "Yes."

I don't become speechless very often, but I was mighty quiet right then. And it turned out to be true. Constant communication with God did get me through that time and many other times too. I don't know how to get us around the difficult times of having a baby or toddler or a troubled youth. I don't think there is a way to make it easy. We have to charge right through and embrace it. It's not pretty. It's not easy. But as we do this, motherhood breaks us of our pride and we become even more of a Godly woman, if we will let it.

Braces hurt, but teeth are straight afterward. As every gardener knows, sitting on the couch all day is easy, but you don't have fresh tomatoes afterward. Not going through the exhaustion and difficulty of having children sure would be easier. But I don't know of another way to end up with a heart that beautiful. Every battle you overcome each day with your children is God's way of shaping and molding your heart. He's refining it and making it more and more beautiful.

Your own heart is forever changed and molded in ways it never could've been any other way, except through motherhood. You can't get this kind of beautiful heart from reading about it in a book. You can't get it from talking to anyone else or watching a movie about it. The way to get it is by going through motherhood. And it never goes away. God lets you keep the beautiful heart even after the children are grown.

Ecclesiastes 8:12 says that, "... *yet surely I know that it shall be well with them that fear God.*" I can tell you that it will be well with you if you stay in constant communion with the Lord. Your heart is going to be gor-juss after going through the tough times and hard work of motherhood.

Sprinkled throughout an old journal of mine are the following prayers. If I had not been an exhausted mother, I never would have had these thoughts. My thoughts would have been more along the lines of, "I wonder if I should thinly slice the onions or coarsely chop them?" In the midst of these prayers, I also wrote in my journal that my young child said to me one day back then, "Mommy? You have a beautiful heart."

Here were those prayers to God:

- Please reign over this household today.
- Please bring a peace over this household.
- Please make my words gracious.
- Teach me your ways through the Holy Spirit.
- Give me a huge, overflowing supply of love and patience for my children.
- Please soften my heart.
- Please calm my heart.
- Grip our hearts with Your word.
- Give us a thirst for Your word.
- Give me wisdom to raise these children as unto You.
- Give me a sense of humor.
- Please give me courage and strength.
- Keep me connected to You.
- Help me to be selfless.
- Help me to be lighthearted.
- Help me to pour myself out for these children.
- Help me to treasure the children and enjoy this day with them.
- Please invigorate me as if today's the last day I have to do it.
- Help us to glorify You.
- Give me the heart of a servant.
- Mold me into the woman You'd have me to be.
- Change whatever needs changing in our hearts.
- Give me dignity.
- Redeem my yuckiness.

- I'm crying out for strength, peace and harmony in my household.
- Remind me to turn to You when it gets stressful.
- Surround us with Your love and might.
- I trust You.
- I believe You.

THE SHUSHING GUYS

When my husband and I toured the Sistine Chapel in Italy recently, I didn't expect for tears to roll down my cheeks the entire time. I found it very moving. Painted on the ceiling are Michelangelo's famous paintings of creation and the Bible. I don't entirely agree with his interpretation but I forgot all about that when I saw the paintings with my own eyes. I didn't want to leave. I wanted to make a little bed in there and stay and look at those paintings forever. Michelangelo agreed to do the paintings only if he could paint excerpts from the whole Bible, not merely the Catholic saint guys who were highly respected at the time. I looked up and saw Adam, Daniel, Ezekiel, Zechariah. All my peeps.

The Sistine Chapel is such a sacred place with Michelangelo's priceless artwork, that my husband had warned me that professional shushers are there all day, shushing all the visitors and asking them to be quiet out of reverence. They also have a dress code, which is strictly enforced. That's what I'm talking about. Nothing above the knee or off the shoulder is allowed, and silence is constantly requested. And don't even think about taking a picture. One man nearby us had the nerve to take a picture and the leetle Italian shusher man rushed over and sternly made him delete the peek-ture and put his camera away. If he pulled that again they were fixing to drop kick him out of there.

The men who work in the Sistine Chapel are fully aware that every single day, thousands of people are going to walk through the chapel and break their rules. They probably have little staff meetings: the public is going to come in and talk loudly, they're going to take pictures, they're going to need to be given something to cover up their legs and shoulders. And every single day, the professional shushing guys diligently, forcefully, confidently and unapologetically fight to maintain their rules.

The whole time I sat and wept over Michelangelo's paintings, the shushing guys were saying, "Shh. Quiet please, sacred place. Shh, quiet, silent. No pictures, sacred place. Quiet." They handed out fabric to cover up any lady who did not meet their dress code. They watched the crowd closely to make sure no one was taking a picture. These guys don't back down. They keep a high standard. They fight to protect the priceless Christ-honoring artwork by requiring reverence. The Vatican pays these men to take this job seriously. And so ultimately it's the Catholic Church that is fighting to keep this high standard.

The next day, when my husband and I walked through the city of Naples, we saw in that town's square a little Vatican wanna-be church. It was at one time quite magnificent and vibrant in that city. Over time, it has been completely neglected and is not even used as a church anymore. Rallies and protests are held there, and tourists like my husband and me go to visit. Graffiti is spray-painted nearby. Contrast that with the Vatican and the Sistine Chapel, the place where I could hardly control my emotions as I beheld the holiness and the beauty. Naples gave up. The Vatican is not giving up.

Neither can mothers. We are the shushing guys. Our children are the Sistine Chapel. The Bible says that a believer's body is the temple of God. Our children are a sacred, holy dwelling place. Like the professional guardians of the Sistine Chapel, we know that our children are going to break our rules, make mistakes, not meet our standards, try to get away with going beyond our boundaries. Every day, we must remind them swiftly and confidently of those standards.

"Precious child," we say day after day, over and over, "share with your brother and sister, no hitting, speak respectfully to your parents, honor God with your life, obey, read your Bible, say thank you, put others before yourself, that skirt is too short, respect your authority, speak graciously," and on and on. As we do this, we are pointing our children toward becoming future men and women who can reflect the sanctity of our Lord and Savior Jesus Christ because that is what will have been ingrained in them, over and over, each day.

PART V. PAIN

———⊷———

The actor Robin Williams, first loved by America as Mork,
admitted to having done "mountains of cocaine"
while filming the *Mork & Mindy Show* in the 1970s.

In the time leading up to his death in 2014, widely accepted as a suicide,
Williams was quoted in *Rolling Stone Magazine*
as saying he could not find peace or joy.

CHAPTER 17

PAINFUL RELATIONSHIPS

———◦◦◦———

People who have never even cracked open a Bible know that Jesus said to *"turn the other cheek."* He did say that. But if this is the entire scope of our Biblical counsel when dealing with painful relationships, that's about as clued in as the airport security people who have had to frisk little old ladies as possible terrorists.

Yes, Jesus did say not to lash back at someone who's blatantly mistreating you out of nowhere. But what did He not say? Jesus did not say to pursue this relationship, spend all your time and energy in trying to win this person over to a kindly friendship. You don't lash back. You forgive. Whether or not they asked you to forgive, you still forgive. You bless that person. You pray for him or her. Then if you've done nothing wrong that needs to be apologized for yourself, you pretty much get away. Jesus Himself escaped from those who hated Him many times. He told his disciples to shake the dust off their feet and go to a different city when met with contempt.

Jesus gives us a three strikes you're out guideline in Matthew 18 if our brother wrongs us. We confront our brother a couple of times and then if he doesn't come around we consider him a heathen. This is the Biblical version of "forget you then." The Latin literally says "brother."[6] So we can't apply this passage to everyone and their brother. Random friendships or even other family relationships don't necessarily deserve this sort of sincere time and effort.

Many times we ladies altogether bypass this first part that says to go to him and him alone and we blab instead to everyone and their brother. (I'll stop, last time, do you see what my children have to endure?) This passage in Matthew has to do with a brother cheating someone, as far as I can tell regarding money because the connotation is "debt." So we are talking about a serious offense, not just: Oh child you rolled your eyes at me three times so now it's on. We'd just be searching for a reason to blow someone off because we didn't like them in the first place. That's not the heart of God.

No one drives from one city to a new one without a road map. The Bible is our relationship GPS. Let's fire it up. We will consider five people from the Bible and how they reacted to wrongdoing: Jacob, Moses, Nehemiah, David and Ruth. None of this has anything to do with marriage, which is our one flesh relationship that we fight for until the day we die. Pain in marriage is so much more complex and we are not talking of that here. Also, none of this has to do with warring with another nation, which many times God ordains. This has to do with personal relationships that are not marriage.

Jacob was seriously cheated by his brother-in-law Laban who repeatedly did him wrong. Jacob put up with it for a long time and was pretty subtle himself. One day Jacob suddenly decided he knew he must get away from Laban, and he moved his entire family away from him in the middle of the night. This is why: Jacob saw that Laban's *"countenance is not toward me as before."* Genesis 31:5. Jacob understood from the hostile vibe Laban had begun sending him that it was a done deal. We're enemies now. He had to get away.

In much the same way, we know from the famous story of Moses begging Pharaoh to ... what? Please be nicer? Please be my friend? Please love me for the grunge *Duck Dynasty* bearded dude that I am? No, Moses begged him to let the entire Jewish population get away from him. They probably would have up and pulled a Jacob and run away without permission but they knew Pharaoh would chase them down and kill them all. Thus the conversations between Moses and Pharaoh. God told Moses what to say, told him what to do, gave him Aaron to help, performed many miracles, parted the Red Sea and boom they were out of there. God miraculously got them away from their enemy.

You hear about these wealthy brain surgeons who give up years of their life to live in some shabby hut in a third world country as a missionary doctor. That's our man Nehemiah. We love him. He gave up his cush job as cup bearer to the king to go to work for God, rebuilding Jerusalem's wall. He barely even responded when an enemy accused him of all this nonsense just to bring him down, distract him and stop the wall from being built. Nehemiah knows this guy is up to mischief and when asked to come and talk it over with him, this is what Nehemiah does.

He writes him a letter. *"There are no such things done as thou sayest, but thou feignest them out of thine own heart."* Nehemiah 6:8. And then he got back to work and refused to go visit him or talk about it anymore. Look, he was saying, you've made this all up, homie. I've got work to do for the Lord and you don't get my attention. I'm too busy serving God to deal with your drama because your motives are clearly to tear me down. And that was the end of that.

Sometimes this is hard. David says in Psalm 55, I thought you were my friend. In this passage David realizes he has been betrayed by a friend who has really been his enemy all along. As painful as it is, David accepts that relationship for what it is and understands that it's over. He's torn up over it. He's in anguish. It was you, my faithful friend, he says. We used to hold sweet conversations together. David has come to realize that, *"The words of his mouth were smoother than butter but war was in his heart: his words were softer than oil, yet were they drawn swords."* Psalm 55:21. So how did David deal with this pain? He poured his heart out to God. He wrote about it. And the passage reveals that he was not planning to seek out this person ever again.

Ruth got it right too. We don't know that her blood relatives were necessarily mean to her. Maybe they just ignored her, and that is its own stinging kind of pain. We don't know because she never wallows in it. But when her mother-in-law Naomi moved away, Ruth *"clave"* to her and went with her. The Bible says it's because she knew Naomi was of the Lord: *"thy people shall be my people, and thy God my God,"* Ruth 1:16. Ruth wisely moved away from her own family (meaning her parents and siblings; her husband had died) to be with more distant family whose hearts were about the things of God. God prospered her greatly, and she became David's great grandmother.

There is a fine line between loving and stupid. Did you know that right after Jesus said to love your enemies and turn the other cheek, in the very next chapter of Matthew, He says not to cast your pearls before the swine, and then says to beware of someone in sheep's clothing who is inwardly a ravening wolf?

Titus 3:10 says, *"A man that is an heretick after the first and second admonition reject ..."* We can be very loving but not actively pursue a relationship with an "heretick," which can be defined as a person who is determined to hold strong opinions that are contrary to scripture.[47] How can we identify such a person? Jesus said, *"By their fruits ye shall know them,"* Matthew 7:20. Bottom line is, I'm not frolicking with toxic people.

The difference between a kind hearted person and the rest of the world, in breaking away from someone, would be at least three things:

1. We are grieved and kind hearted rather than feisty.
2. We do not gossip about that person.
3. We are ready to welcome her with open arms if she comes around to embracing God's ways.

The stories in the Old Testament and the wise words in the New Testament are the key to how God would help us react to people who are hostile toward us or not building up our lives. These people in the Bible all seemed to have forgiven their enemies, even though as far as we know their enemies never apologized (except for Laban, sort of). They didn't harbor bitterness or keep themselves in a tizzy trying to fix it.

How? They knew God Almighty. They knew that God always gets the last word. *"'Vengeance is mine: I will repay' saith the Lord,"* Romans 12:19. Yes that's New Testament and these guys were Old Testament but Paul is quoting Deuteronomy and God doesn't change, so we can apply all of scripture to anything. Cutting themselves off from these people wasn't a revenge thing. They probably kept their hearts open for reconciliation if the other person came around. But it was wise for them not to keep pursuing or figuring out these harmful relationships. They got away and closed the door, and left any fixing up to God.

Whenever we are tempted to set the record straight or get even with someone, the thing that can keep us from doing that is this. The Bible says to show kindness to your enemies and insodoing you are *"heaping coals of fire upon their head and the Lord shall reward thee,"* Proverbs 25:22. The Bible also says that whoever touches me, *"toucheth the apple of the Father's eye,"* Zechariah

2:8. We can fear and trust Him enough to understand that if we set it straight, He probably won't. We don't want to beat Him to it, because however God would take care of someone who has hurt me, is going to be far more effective than anything we would ever think to do or say. Sit back and watch God make it right. Maybe not in this lifetime, but eventually that person has to answer to God Almighty.

An important question here is: what is happening to the relationships in our lives that could be joyful and bring glory to God if, meanwhile, all our time and energy are spent ignoring Biblical counsel such as this? It would be tragic to allow ourselves to stay embroiled in trying to figure out futile relationships with enemies, when sweet family and friends are available and waiting. Find your Naomi.

COULD I BE LABAN?

Jacob wisely got away from Laban when he understood Laban's countenance was decidedly against him. We can relate to that all day long. We can see ourselves in Jacob's position no problem. But I have a harder question for us to consider. How unkind is my countenance toward certain people? Am I the one causing someone pain? Is anyone scurrying to get away from me?

Many scriptures command us to be gracious, kind and merciful. These are not suggestions. This is an order from our God, whether it's fun or not, whether we like certain people or not. We are warned not to harbor bitterness and anger toward people, and we cannot act maliciously (Ephesians 4). No one likes to think she is behaving maliciously. We all sometimes have shamefully malicious thoughts. We can't act on those. God does not want us to nurture a spirit of revenge, harbor ill will, daydream about or actually inflict pain on someone, paint others in a negative light or feel gratified when they are emotionally injured. All of that is malicious.[47]

The Bible says that it is easy to extend kindness to those who are kind to you. Even the dirtiest, most corrupt mafia guys in trench coats can be nice to the people they like. And compared to being kind to people that you really don't like, giving time or money to charities is easy. Anyone can do that. It's generous, but it's not necessarily kind.

Except for Jesus who was perfect in every way, the Bible is full of examples for us of people behaving both wisely and foolishly. The same people do both. God sets these stories before us to show us what happened with them and then see how we ought to live.

Yes, Jacob was done wrong pretty badly by his family member Laban. But in the very next passage in Genesis, we see that Jacob was in the wrong about something else. Jacob had tricked his own brother Esau out of his birthright and lied to their father about it years ago. Esau was angrily coming toward him with hundreds of men. Jacob had wrestled with God all night before this. He wisely sent gifts ahead to meet Esau and his men before they got to him. Jacob set a tone of reconciliation and apology. Sent some flowers or a fruit basket or something. Then Jacob fell on his face and said I'm so sorry for what I've done. Is there any way you could forgive me?

This is huge.

After all, Jacob's mother had told him to lie. "It's the way I was raised," he could have said. God had said for him to be the heir, not Esau. "I was only doing God's will," he might have said. Jacob could've used that as a big fat excuse his whole life and justified his actions. That dumb old burly Esau probably grated on his last nerve anyway. Family can be like that. Jacob could have denied his own wrongdoing and sympathized with himself the rest of his life. But he didn't. He took responsibility for what he'd done.

Jacob admitted his sin and genuinely apologized. Esau received that. Gave Jacob a big ol' hug, it's all good bro. Esau forgave him and welcomed him with open arms. And, just between you and me, I have to wonder if God allowed that whole Laban misery in Jacob's life as a consequence for his own dishonesty and ruthlessness with Esau. That situation with Laban must have humbled Jacob just a little bitty bit, by the time he saw Esau again.

Previously we also talked about King David, and how heartbroken he was at being betrayed. He was acutely aware of his own pain when someone hurt him. But one day, he lazed at home neglecting his kingly duty of war, seduced and impregnated Uriah's babe of a wife Bathsheba, tried to pass it off as Uriah's baby, and when Uriah was too honorable for that to work, David had the poor guy killed in battle. You can't make this stuff up and put it on daytime television. And yet we love David.

We are going there to point out that somehow David wasn't crying in his pillow over all that. David wasn't pouring his heart out writing Psalms about that – yet. He was thinking only of himself and was trying not to get caught. He was stone cold busted and finally admitted his wickedness when God got through to him by sending a prophet to call him out on his sin.

David was finally remorseful but it was too late. He had ruined Uriah's and Bathsheba's family. God punished David in this way: the first baby born from Bathsheba died. God is merciful and forgiving though and He saw David's remorse, so a later son from Bathsheba did live and that was Solomon, who wrote all those kickin' Proverbs. David messed up really badly and faced it. He came around and admitted his sin, accepted his punishment and God calls David *"a man after my own heart."*

Let's consider Pharaoh, the guy in charge when Moses pled with him to let the Israelites leave Egypt and stop being Pharaoh's slaves. Pharaoh abused and bullied an enslaved Israel and refused to listen to God through Moses, to the point that all of Egypt was completely and utterly destroyed. Pharaoh refused to see his own sin. He would not back down or face his mistreatment of those people. His sentiment was: Hey, they're my employees, I own them, how dare they complain? He was stubborn, cruel and hard hearted. This led to his ultimate destruction, unlike Jacob and David whose hearts God softened. They were not only forgiven but were ancestors of Christ, along with our girl Ruth. The Bible says that God hardened Pharaoh's heart. God's purpose as I understand it was to destroy Egypt and to show His might on behalf of His faithful people.

Did Pharaoh even ask God to soften his heart?

We'd all like to think that we are never in the wrong. We'd like to think we are always good and they are always bad. We sympathize so much with ourselves. We see our point of view so clearly. It's easy to think that we are always the victim but it's not so.[9] We see in the Bible that the very people who God anoints and mightily uses are also capable of great sin. God deals with that sin. And He will deal with ours. If we truly fear Him and love Him, we'll try to get a jump on that and pour our hearts out to Him on behalf of anyone we have hurt.

Some relationships might not come easily to us, but it would not be okay with God to roll with those feelings. As women and queen of our families, this is very important for us ladies to take seriously. We have some power in our families. The guys are focused on guy stuff and work. Meanwhile we ladies can grant or deny access to the children.

An elderly clerk bagged my groceries for me at the store one day and we began visiting. As she walked me out to the car and smiled fondly at my small children, she explained to me that she never sees her grandchildren, who live three miles from her. Years ago her son's wife wrote the family a letter saying she was not having anything to do with in-laws. This wife never even gave her husband's family a chance. She was all about her own self preservation and assumed the relationship would be too painful to put up with. Too much trouble to have these random people all up in her space.

How would this wife like it if her husband decided to implement that same policy and not have anything to do with his in-laws? That's her parents. "Sorry babe," he might say, "I know you've got the table set for your folks coming over for dinner tonight. But I woke up this morning and decided: I don't do in-laws." Perhaps her own sons' wives will have the same policy 20 years from now, and what will she think of it then? Such an arrangement would be familiar to her sons after all.

This is *"do unto others"* at its scariest.

We stood in the grocery store parking lot, crying together. This elderly lady told me she wished she'd had a daughter. She is growing old, her life is coming to an end, and she is cut off from her family, because someone doesn't have room for her in her heart. I told her to keep hope in God.

I don't want to make a habit out of tormenting people in grocery store parking lots so I didn't say this to her but I will say it now: I wonder when she was younger if this lady treated her own in-laws with adoration and acceptance when it was her turn. Maybe she did. I don't know. Maybe she perpetuated a painful excluding in-laws legacy from which she is now suffering. Older women say awfully rude and cruel things about their own mothers-in-law, and then, almost in the same breath, lament for themselves pitifully how their daughters-in-law disrespect them and exclude them. We can't have it both ways.

All of that is up to God to keep straight. Whether we are talking about in-laws, siblings, neighbors, children, or any other relationship that doesn't come naturally: you and I should not end up going off the deep end with our own selfish desires and pride as David did when he ruined Uriah's family. We should not get to the point where we are tricking people and twisting the truth and ruining families the way Jacob did. At least those guys felt bad about it and tried to make it right. We certainly don't want not even to care, like Pharaoh who was consumed with bitterness and stubbornness. We should not pounce to stir up strife like Nehemiah's pugnacious, jealous enemy.

No one should be crying out in anguish to God because of us, writing in her prayer journal or lying awake at night because of us. Sitting with her head in her hands weeping because of us. Move to a different city because of us. We might have to ask God to soften our hearts toward certain people. We can ask Him to create in us a fondness for them. We can ask Him to help us see things from their point of view. That's the definition of compassion.

CHAPTER 18

DRUGS

—⁂—

The thing about drugs is, they're nothing but a product like anything else. We just have to be a little more sly than the people trying to get us to use their product. They tell us only half the story. Yes if someone tries a little hit of this or that then she's going on a magic carpet ride. We can't argue with that. But here's what they don't tell her.

Yeah it's great that night and she liked it, but she kind of crashes a little the day after that so she wants to do it again. She does it again, only this time it takes a little more to give her that surge. Then the next day she crashes a little lower. Every time she uses the drug, she is building up an appetite and a tolerance so that before you know it she needs this thing. She needs it to feel normal. She doesn't even get fruity off it anymore.

It's taking some money and it distracts her now that it has become her only goal to get it, and she becomes a little desperate to get more money. She does some stuff she shouldn't do but she has to have this thing. She loses her job and destroys relationships with people she's stolen money from, all in an effort to get the drug. She doesn't even like it anymore. It doesn't even get her high anymore. She just needs it to feel normal again.

Well shoot. She was normal to begin with. She's trying to get right back to where she started. We can feel normal right now without going through all that. Can't we. So sugar, don't touch the stuff.

Here are a few reasons someone will ask us to try a drug:

1. Money. Buh-bye, they just want your money, they don't care about you, this is obvious.
2. Have you ever had a friend invite you to a movie but you get the feeling she doesn't really like you very much; she just doesn't want to go to the movie by herself? Some people are looking for someone else to get lit with because it's not as fun doing that alone.
3. People truly care about you and think the drug will give you an escape from your troubles.

If a friend tries to get us to "try something that'll make you feel really good," our answer is, "Nah sorry, I'm not really into that. Not my scene." Keep repeating that as many times as necessary. Physically run away if you must. Sometimes this is very hard because we know we can no longer be friends with that person. Hanging with people who are into drugs is never going to have a happy ending. Read the Proverbs. It's all there.

Well-meaning doctors offer pain killers for chronic pain. Hellew, those are addicting and it's "no thanks" if our condition is not a short term issue. The same goes if someone suggests drugs to fix emotional pain. Someone who cares about us might truly want to get us away from that pain. They care about you and they want to rescue you.

By now you have an advanced degree in triumphant womanhood and you could have written this chapter yourself because you know what I'm going to say. The Lord Jesus Christ and His living word are where we go for lasting, permanent, unchanging comfort and to be rescued from our emotional pain. It really works, it's not a joke and what have you got to lose trying it? It won't give you a hangover or an addiction and it's free.

RADIANT

One particularly unpleasant day when my husband was deployed, I happened to walk past a mirror. I'd dumped my hair up into a boofy clump on the top of my head in a big clip, and my gray roots were growing in. Between that and the extremely exhausted and defeated look on my face, I scared myself. I looked like a female villain from a Disney movie. That got me thinking how I could have gotten to such a low point in my countenance.

I realized I had been depending on my flesh instead of on God. During my husband's deployment, or any crisis that sends us way beyond our human ability, I still could have had joy and peace that day. I should not have scared myself when I looked in the mirror.

Psalm 34 says, *"Look to Him and be radiant."* Normally I love the King James Version best, but that particular translation is huge to me. If we are looking to God and spending time with Him, then we will be radiant, regardless of the chaos, heartache, or difficulty that is swirling around us and threatening to engulf us. The King James puts it this way, that the people *"looked unto Him and were lightened."* I got on my knees and told my heavenly Father all about it. I poured my lil heart right out to God. Prayer is our communication with Him.

The Bible is His communication to us. Hook yourself up to some intravenous Bible. God's word can pull you out of times of despair, illness, heartache, betrayal, mistreatment, financial crisis, loneliness and anything else life throws your way. Carry that Book around the house with you like you're dragging around an IV. Read it and read it and read it as if your life depended on it. The God of the Bible is your lifeline. When you are in despair, shoot up with some Bible. Bust open a six pack of Bible. Take a hit of Bible. Find passages that relate to your pain and drink those up until the anguish gradually begins to fade.

As for the day that I scared myself in the mirror, I was still broken and exhausted. The deployment did not let up or get any easier. My circumstances stayed the same. But I was tight with God and my countenance was radiant.

"When thou art in tribulation, and all these things are come upon thee, even in the latter days, if thou turn to the Lord thy God, and shalt be obedient unto his voice, (for the Lord is a merciful God;) he will not forsake thee." Deuteronomy 4:30-31.

ADDICTION

My church's music director, Paul, once shared the story that he and his buddy, as young boys, made a homemade boat together when they were growing up in Florida. The two boys were out on their boat one day, having fun in a lagoon that led to the ocean. After a while, they wanted to throw in the anchor so they could stop and eat their lunch. Paul was busy on one side of the boat and his friend, without telling Paul, tossed the anchor into the water. What his friend didn't know is that the anchor's rope was caught around Paul's leg. The anchor quickly splashed into the water, and so did Paul, before he had time to take a breath.

As little Paul hit the bottom of the lagoon, trapped there by the anchor attached to his leg, he looked up and could see the surface of the water and the sunlight shining down at him about three feet away. The anchor held tight to his leg, keeping him on the bottom of the lagoon, and twice Paul strove with all his might reaching up, up to try to get back up to the surface and out into the sunlight. He was running out of time and realized after his second try that the only way he would ever get back to the surface of the water again would be to go in the opposite direction of the light, down to the anchor. He swam down to the bottom of the lagoon with what little energy he had left, untangled the anchor's rope from his leg, and was free. He swam to the top of the water. He climbed onto the boat and promptly beat up his friend. (Not really. I'm sure he felt like it.)

Paul told our church this story to illustrate that if we are drawn to God and are reaching, trying, striving with all our strength to get to Him and His light but we can't get there, it is because we must first untangle and detach the anchor in our lives.

That anchor is named addiction.

As long as you keep going back to that drug, as long as you are keeping it close to you and keeping it in your world, it is smothering the life out of you and keeping you separated from God. You have to cut yourself off from it completely, and only then will you be able to reach a life of light with God. Cut the thing off.

How can someone do this? She doesn't. God does.

My cousin Butch was hooked on cocaine many years ago. He wanted to stop, but he knew that the addiction was more powerful than he was. Butch was in the hospital one day recovering from a bad cocaine overdose. As he lay in the hospital bed, going in and out of consciousness, he looked over on the nightstand and saw a Bible. His mama's sister had brought it to the hospital for him. Butch had been taught the Bible and knew that it was powerful, but he was not able to read it right then because he did not have the strength. He was very nearly dead. Butch was able to reach over and pick up the Bible. He laid it on his chest and held it close to his heart. He felt the life draining out of him and heard the medical staff saying "we're losing him." He started reciting Psalm 23 in his mind. Then Butch said, "Lord, I don't want to change your will, but if you would give me a second chance, I'd appreciate that," and at that moment he started feeling the life come back into him.

What happened at that moment was the same thing that happened to Saint Augustine in about 400 A.D. when he was desperate to leave his destructive, sinful life and heard children singing in Latin outside his window, "tolle et lege, tolle et lege," which means "take up and read, take up and read."[27] Augustine, like all learned men of his time, had read the Bible before. He had always found it to be less clever than Cicero, who seeks wisdom without making any mention of Christ. But this time, Augustine got over himself and listened.[3] He opened up the Bible and read. His life was changed.

The "tolle" part was enough for Butch, who held the Bible dearly to his chest and asked God to remove the craving for cocaine permanently. God did it. Butch has not touched drugs since the day he placed that Bible on his heart in the hospital and prayed. If you ask Butch how he stopped using cocaine, he would tell you he didn't do it. God did.

Oh, and he married his nurse.

In his book *A Better Way*, John Barrow describes his life of crime, pain, drugs, violence and prison. One day, at age 25, he got thrown into a month of solitary confinement, again, for selling marijuana to a prison mate. They give you one meal a day, barely, and Mr. Barrow describes the hole as the bottom of the bottom, a prison inside of prison. He doesn't remember how, but this time he ended up with a Bible in his tiny dark cell. For 28 days straight he did nothing but read that Bible from cover to cover. "For the first time in my life," he writes, "I truly surrendered my will ... My heart was truly pierced by the Scripture and the word finally became alive to me in the midst of all the pain."[5]

Mr. Barrow had some faithful prayer warriors in his life, including a wise and determined grandmother. So did Saint Augustine and my cousin Butch. Ladies, do not stop praying for the people in your life who are troubled. When Mr. Barrow came out of those 28 days in solitary confinement, he was a new man, because he had fallen in love with God's word and therefore with God.

He then did something very important. He gravitated toward other people who were drawn to the things of God, and distanced himself from his friends. It's not that he thought he was too good for them. He just had to give himself some time to get his spiritual legs underneath him before he could help anybody else. "Stay away from old friends who don't walk, talk, and think like you do, even if you like them," he wrote. "The Bible says: Bad company corrupts good character. And believe me it does," he said. Once Mr. Barrow had stopped doing drugs and given up his old life, he knew that the spiritual enemy would try to bring him back down again. Why? "Because, like a tree," he said, "if you can kill it off before it takes root then you will not have to worry about it once it is full grown."[5]

Mr. Barrow now has a thriving ministry that helps men who are struggling with addiction by leading them to Christ. But right at first, he could not help anyone else until he was stronger and well grounded. So he turned God into his best friend at first. God is always there, always listening, always faithful and always ready. If you've been at the bottom like my cousin Butch, Saint Augustine or John Barrow, that doesn't have to be your identity now, even though it used to be.

One of the things I love about God is how merciful He is. In fact, "... *His compassions fail not. They are new every morning."* Lamentations 3:22-23. I like knowing that He fails not. Even though we might. This means if you've done recreational drugs, depended too much on pain killers or anything at all you're ashamed of, and I mean anything, you can decide today that you're never going there again. Ask Him to give you the strength. Ask God to do it for you.

We think there's no way to get past our awful sin, we feel that we're trapped with no way out and we see how unworthy we are to seek God or pursue a relationship with Him. That it would be dishonest to go to church or claim to be a Christian, knowing everything we've done. We know what we are. But God doesn't see that. It's just the opposite. *"I came not to call the righteous, but sinners to repentance,"* Jesus says in Luke 5:32. I used to think when He said that, that there were two groups of people: one group of good people and one group of bad people.

I understand now that we are all born into the bad group. The only difference is whether or not we realize it and ask Jesus Christ to make us righteous through His death and resurrection. He can't, or I suppose won't, help people who think they are all right without Him. God is going to help us when we realize we need Him. And so if you are ashamed of anything in your life, this is actually very wise.

One way not to stay enslaved by past sin is to realize that when we become a born again Christian, it is a new birth. The Bible says you're a new creature. You're a new person. Claim this in the fullest sense. Anything I did before? That wasn't really me.

CHAPTER 19

STRIFE AND DEBATE AMONG WOMEN

There is something irresistible about being right. Am I right? Heaven knows we need intelligent public debating going on in this nation. Please give us more of that from articulate, kind hearted Christians. On a personal level though, when it comes to expressing our viewpoint within our relationships with other girls and women, the Bible is rocking my world in convincing me that debate with one another is almost always hostile to His ways. When we ladies debate with someone else about her life, we have basically declared war with her. Them's fightin' words. In war, somebody's fixing to get injured.

Sometimes it pays to be nosy. I discovered the following clever list while flipping through my child's logic textbook, titled *The Thinking Toolbox*. This book does a marvelous job of sorting out for us the different kinds of conversations that are flying around in our relationships. It goes something like this:

1. Discussion: we're just talking.
2. Disagreement: our opinions are different.
3. Argument: we defend those positions.
4. Fight: we want to take the other person and her opinions out. We go on the attack. This is almost always done with unkindness and strong emotion. It is hardly ever appropriate and is very destructive.[54]

I'm thinking let's stay away from number 4. Number 3 might be out too. Actually maybe we should not even be up for number 2 very often. We might as well go ahead and agree with someone, be supportive of her viewpoint and brighten her day. Jesus Himself said, *"Agree with thine adversary quickly,"* Matthew 5:25. Only the Holy Spirit can change someone's mind.

When I stare at my Bible – the inside, the part with words – what starts freaking me out is debate and strife keep showing up together. Genesis 13:7 tells us that the whole reason Lot and Abraham (then called Abram) parted ways was because their little worker people were fussing and fighting. The Bible puts it this way: *"Also there was debate between the herdsmen of Abram's cattle, and the herdsmen of Lot's cattle ... Then said Abram unto Lot, Let there be no strife, I pray thee, between thee and me."* So there you go. They just could not co-exist and had to part ways.

A good definition of destructive debate would go something like this: pressing my annoying opinion onto the ladies in my life. This includes sisters, mother, daughters once they're grown, cousins, aunts, and friends. *"If anyone stirs up strife, it is not from me."* Isaiah 54:15 (ESV).

A very tragic situation involves a loving, caring mother who has completely destroyed her relationship with her daughter. Her daughter's husband does not want children. Her daughter didn't take the situation lightly. She knew when she married him that she was signing up for a childless life. She decided she loved this man, wanted a life with him and would follow his lead on what their life would look like. Sounding pretty Triumphant Womanhood to me. But her mother, for many years now, has fought for victory on the issue of their having children. Every time she is around her daughter and son-in-law, she contentiously opposes their decision about children. Outwardly or on the sly. You know how we women operate.

This woman is engaging in emotional combat with her daughter. But she really doesn't have a chance to do this very much anymore because her daughter has fled the relationship. Can't say I blame her. She has had to make the extremely painful choice between loyalty to her husband and loyalty to her mother. The husband wins. Now the mother gets to sulk in self pity that no one ever visits me, no one cares about me, no one wants to be around me. In debating with her daughter, she has created a life of being right, all by herself.

When we sow discord with other ladies, we want to prove that our opinion is right. And maybe it is. But we and our "right" can die all alone at age 83 with our cats, while people flee from the painful controversy we are causing. Isaiah admonishes *"the men of thy strife, for they shall be as nothing."* Isaiah 41:12. Now that's cold. But God loves us enough to sock it to us. We need to know these things so that we don't become as nothing to someone we love.

In Isaiah 58:4 our prophet buddy tells us, *"Behold, ye fast to strife and debate, and to smite with the fist of wickedness."* Isaiah is blasting anyone who devotes herself to strife and debate to the point of fasting for it. Fasting is this big serious thing and he's saying: Cut that out when it comes to strife and debate among your- selves. Otherwise, you are smiting someone else's life with your fist of wicked- ness. Are you hearing that in a creepy whisper? Your fissst of wickednesssssss.

Second Timothy 2:23 is shaming me for real when it says, *"And put away foolish and unlearned questions, knowing that they engender strife."* Our relationships cannot afford for us to come to other girls and women questioning their life. It's foolish and not only that, we don't know what we're talking about, which as that last passage puts it, we are "unlearned." We should get King Jamesy and say it like this: Un-Learn-Ed. Either way, it's time to let it go.

Paul gives this big scary list of all the awful and horrifying things anyone could do and guess what's in this list? That's right, debate. Check it out:

"Being full of all unrighteousness, fornication, wickedness, covetousness, maliciousness, full of envy, or murder, of debate (told ya!), *taking all things in the evil part, whisperers, backbiters, haters of God, doers of wrong, proud, boasters, inventors of evil things, disobe- dient to parents, without understanding, covenant breaker, without natural affection, such as never can be appeased, merciless."* Romans 1:29-30.

I'm gathering from this list that Paul would have us chill on the debating in the sense that we are selfishly promoting our own views and beliefs against some- one else's. When we do this to someone, we want to exert superiority over her. We might as well pick something else terrible from that list up there in Romans.

By the way, if we ladies ignore all this Biblical counsel and continue engag- ing in conflict and strife with one another, what are the guys debating? "Dude can you even believe Tim Tebow got traded to that other football team?" The guys figure, hey the debating is taken. It's covered. The men aren't that engaged in debate where we need them as leaders of our community and nation because, as they see it, the women have more than checked off that block.

⚬⚬

YOU SAY POTATO, I SAY TATER

It took me four babies to come to the following realization at 2:00 a.m. one night: "You know? I'm the one up at night with this baby. I'm going to do it my way."

You are doing the work for God. Do it your way. God's word says some will teach, some will preach, some will write winsomely poignant works of non-fiction. My Dad grew up in the rural South and likes to joke, "You say potato, I say tater. You say tomato, I say mater." We need to respect one another's ways of serving God and encourage one another. I didn't say anything goes. I said encourage one another's ways of serving God. I didn't say: you say tomato, I say crystal meth. It's like any family. A father who requires obedience and respect from his children will, while staying true to his character, allow them to have a personality.

We know that God really doesn't want us to debate about other ladies to each other. That would be gossip. In Proverbs 25:8-9 God tells us, *"Go not hastily to strife, lest thou know not what to do in the end thereof, when thy neighbor hath put thee to shame. Debate thy matter with thy neighbor, and discover not the secret to another."*

He's saying, Look if you have legitimate quarrels with folks, specific conflicts that need to be resolved, work it out amongst yourselves and don't go slandering the girl to everyone else. Christ is helping us resolve our problems and that is great but listen. Debate here isn't recreational fun. It's not for sport. It's not an ongoing lifetime thing. You're looking forward to its end.

It can be extremely painful when people judge each other by saying, for example, someone else shouldn't work because the Bible says to be a keeper at home. Perhaps going to work is keeping her home. She is earning money to buy toothpaste and shoes for her children and would much rather go on their school field trip given the choice. Or the flip side: A woman says another woman has no idea about even starting to serve God because she stays home in that perfect little shell of hers and doesn't have to work. Maybe she is quite lonely and is treated as if she had no brain or worth because she is "just" a stay at home mom.

It reminds me of Eris, the goddess of discord in Greek mythology, when she came up with that mischievous idea to present the golden apple as the prize for the most beautiful goddess of all. She got comfy and sat right back and watched the show. All the heartache that followed among the goddesses was a big delightful party to Eris as she let them fight amongst themselves. The goddesses forgot that none of them had started it.

There is an enemy, a force of evil, and if we are busy debating about the details of other people's lives then our greatest enemy – that old serpent Satan – has thrown us all a golden apple and he is sitting back like Eris, relaxing in his hammock, eating popcorn and sipping lemonade, and getting a real kick out of watching the show.

⚬⚬⚬

THE ATOMIC BOMB OF DEBATE

Just when we think we understand everything there is to know about debate, Jesus drops the debating bomb. Here's our one example of when we need to jump back and see that Someone can debate all He wants to about Himself while we stand there looking at one another in a hushed silence. *"Think ye that I am come to give peace on earth? I tell you, nay, but rather debate."*

Nay. I'm not always Mister Fun, there will be debate, He says. The connotation of that word "debate" is something like "division." This is Jesus speaking in Luke 12:51 and we know whenever He speaks it is time to listen up. Our concept of Jesus is erroneous sometimes because we like the sweet stories about Him that make us feel warm and fuzzy inside. That is only part of who He is. Yes, He loves us more than we can ever imagine. He knew temptation Himself and truly sympathizes with our struggles. But He is also declaring war regarding what's going on with our hearts. His purpose in coming to earth was to save us. And so He is saying in Luke 12 that debate and division are what will

197

naturally follow because mankind declares war on Him as His goodness exposes our sinfulness.

If we dare speak up in a controversial way about someone else's life, or about our own, it should ultimately be regarding our relationship with the Lord Jesus Christ. That's the worthy topic. Because if you think about it, anything we are concerned about falls under that category. First Peter 3:15 says, *"Always be ready to give an answer to every man that asketh you a reason of the hope that is in you, with meekness and fear."* It is all right, then, to defend our faith. We do not need to apologize for our faith.

If we see something that is sinful, objectionable or very worrisome to us then it really comes down to whether that person is tight with God or not. We don't need to debate with her about her behavior or what we are seeing on the outside because those are just the cobwebs. We have to go for the spider. We point her toward a relationship with God. Point her to His word. Then the Holy Spirit does its spirit thing (or not). God decides to fix problems from there. He's just getting us to help Him. It's never our doing, always His. Sometimes God would not have us say anything at all but just pray for that person. If we do think He has placed it on our hearts to speak, then notice that the passage in 1 Peter says that we have to handle this sort of sacred debate verrrrrrry delicately, very lovingly, with humility, with meekness, relying on the guidance of the Holy Spirit, and not taking ourselves too seriously. Which is why I agonized and wept so, over the words I've written in this book.

CHAPTER 20

NONE OF THIS IS WORKING

———— ◦◦◦◦◦ ————

Pop quiz. What have you not found in the *Triumphant Womanhood* book?

a) Charming hilarity and cheeky metaphor.
b) A paragraph containing the words "Aristotle" and "muffin top."
c) The observation that when the author doesn't fix her hair she resembles Moses, or
d) The promise that if you do everything in this book, then life will be great.

I'm sorry friends but the answer is d).

"It isn't working," you might say. "I've done everything this book has said. I'm sweet to my husband, I read the Bible all the way through, I eat cashews, I was nice to my mother-in-law, I teach the Bible to my children every day, I give God my utmost. Your book isn't working."

If you've turned this book upside down and shaken it but you are still waiting for your circumstances to change, I can tell you the truth. It's not necessarily going to happen. I could lie to you and say pretty things that are profound and sound like they would work. But I'm not doing that to my girlfriends. The only if/then statement anyone can offer you is this one: If you fully devote yourself to the Lord Jesus Christ, then you will have true joy.

Authors, speakers and TV personalities who assure us if we will only do what their big ideas are then we'll have victory in certain areas of our lives, seriously need to admit that their solutions ultimately amount to chasing after the wind. We all appreciate a medical doctor who reaches the point where he will look at his patient and say, "I'm sorry. I don't know."

There are important female topics I didn't cover such as racism or the frustration of losing control from Alzheimer's. I stopped writing because you don't need someone like me. We ladies need to let go of the habit of relying so much on man's wisdom when we have challenges. Once I had read the Bible all the way through for the first time, I was so empowered that I rarely use Bible devotions any more. Um, such as this one. Why keep going to some random political adviser year after year when the President of the United States is standing right there behind him, smiling and waiting for you to talk with him? Good Bible studies have their place, especially when they bring us together to hang with other Godly ladies. Christian books can be interesting and uplifting. But God and His very own word are right there.

The Knowledge of God[32]
(if it could ever be contained in a circle)

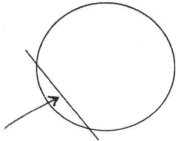

All man will ever know
(I'd say that's a generous estimate)

I hope that something I have written points you to seeing that God and His word are our answer. When paving the way for Jesus to come, John the Baptist said, *"I am not the Christ,"* John 1:20. Neither am I. Not even close. My book is one microscopic speck on that big circle diagram. And barely even that.

---

[32] Nickel, James. *Mathematics: Is God Silent?* 2001

Chart used with permission from the author.

I will consider myself a smashing success if the following happens: someone stops going to books like this one so much and spends the rest of her life reading and delighting in the Holy Bible. Every page. Preferably the King James Version. God can become your source of joy, knowledge and wisdom. Fall in love with God and His word. That is your Answer. There's not necessarily a reliable way to change your circumstances if they are exceedingly bleak. Perhaps "how can I improve my circumstances?" is the wrong question to be asking.

⊸⧟⊷

THE SO-THAT'S

One last thing stands to finish off a faithful, God-fearing person. It's the one thing that can push us off the cliff and create unbearable torment in our hearts. It might drive us to suicide. It's the thing that threatens to make us give up hope. It's the so-that's.

> I am a submissive wife <u>so that</u> I will have a glorious marriage. [He cheats on me.]
> I have integrity with money <u>so that</u> I will have financial peace. [I lose my job.]
> I diligently teach my children <u>so that</u> they will honor God. [They are out of control.]
> I dress modestly <u>so that</u> I will marry a valiant man. [No one is noticing me.]
> I do what God says <u>so that</u> my relationships will be healthy. [My family is cruel.]

Every one of those statements is an honorable, Biblically based statement. Unfortunately, God sometimes confounds us and has other plans we do not understand. This is when it gets tough. You realize it's not about trying harder or doing anything that you can muster in your flesh. So you obey God's ways, do everything in His strength and believe the promises that are right there in scripture plain as day. Yet nothing changes. Circumstances become even worse.

It took Noah a mighty long time to build that ark. In all those years, he must have thought once or twice, "This rocks." It's what I'd be thinking every day. "All these insane, wicked people who mock me today are totally going to come to their senses and join my God-honoring party in this ark. I wonder how many people my ark is going to have in it, to save them from this flood? One hundred? One thousand? One hundred thousand? Can't wait to see what God's going to do here." It turned out to be zero. Not a single person came onto the ark, besides Noah's own family. It wasn't God's purpose. Noah never did get any glory or fame from those people. God had a much greater purpose than that. He began all over again with humanity.

The prophet Elijah gave God his absolute all. Barely anyone listened. The king and queen hated him and gave him death threats. He could not immediately see the fruit of his labor. "It isn't working," he must have thought. Elijah was so discouraged that he sat down with his head in his hands and asked God to let him die. Ultimately, God did do huge things through Elijah. His great works are in the Bible for crying out loud. It doesn't get any more successful than that.

Where did it get Mordecai to raise his niece Esther in the fear of God and then wisely send her to be queen? Where did it get him to save the king's life by revealing a plot to kill him? Where did it get Mordecai to refuse to bow down to anyone but God? Where did it get him? The king did not reward or promote Mordecai. He promoted Haman, who hated Mordecai and all the Jews. The king listened to Haman and sent out a decree to kill all the Jews including Mordecai. But that wasn't the end of the story at all. God turned it completely upside down eventually, and Haman was hanged on the gallows he had built for Mordecai.

What about Job? God singled him out specifically when Satan was in the mood to pick on somebody. You just could not have found a more upright guy than Job. And yet he lost everything he had, all his possessions, his family, his property, his own health, his reputation, everything. All in the same day. The Bible says that before one messenger was finished speaking, another would run up and tell him more bad news. Can you imagine that? "Lady your toilet exploded and your house burned down—" then someone else runs up and says, "Your children are all dead and your car caught on fire—" then someone else runs up and says, "Your coffee maker had a seizure and you lost your job."

That's the kind of day Job had. His friends are all sitting around taking turns telling Job it's his sin and his fault that this happened to him which is not true at all. His wife tells him to curse God and die. He had some funky skin condition going on too. But Job remains faithful and this is what he says, *"Should we receive good but not evil from God?" "For I know that my redeemer liveth."* Job 19:25.

In Job 19:23 he says in his despair, *"O that my words were written in a book somewhere."* Which is amazing now because they are written in *the* book and you just want to shout at your Bible and tell Job to hang on, don't worry, sit tight Job, God is going to make it right and what happened to you will be read about throughout all of history. Job was in such desperation that he said several times that he wanted to die. He might have thought about killing himself but he said no. No matter what happens, *"blessed be the name of the Lord."*

The question for Noah, Elijah, Mordecai, Job and all of us who are truly living the Christian life but seeing 100 percent futile and dismal results becomes as follows: "I live an upright and blameless life that honors and obeys God, and where did that get me?"

Yes, where did that get you? I'll tell you where it got you. It got you right in the middle of God's purposes. God restored everything Job had and then some, so Job's suffering and tragic circumstances were a painful detour but not the end. It was God triumphing over Satan through Job. It was light triumphing over darkness. The way to survive emotionally when a Biblically sound "so that" is going in a very confusing, painful or destructive direction is, I believe, to come to the point where something must happen.

I honor God <u>so that</u> nothing.

Only then can we can add to our circle from the beginning to make sense out what is happening to us in the following way:

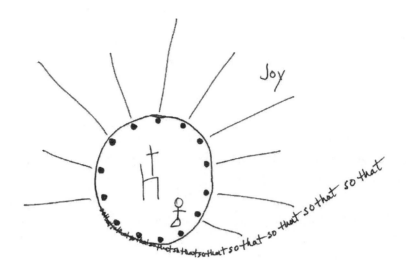

This circle explains the intriguing Proverb that says, *"Commit your works to the Lord, and your thoughts will be established."* When we commit to Him the work we are doing, when we truly release our efforts to Him, and we have no personal expectations other than that His purposes are where we'll end up, then He will give us thoughts that do not torment us and do not ask us the hopeless question, "Where did that get me?" He will instead give us thoughts that are established, confident, firmly fixed, settled, at peace, and strong. God then allows glimmers of light, of true joy to peek through to us and shine out of us. We would never have been able to experience that, if we had continued to cling tightly to the binding, enslaving chains of our own plans. Our lives will shine brightly as the sun, bringing joy to us and glory to Him.

Adversity, then Eternity
"Nay but, O man, who art thou that repliest against God?"
Paul asks us in Romans 9:20.

The times of adversity in life are what give us any sort of depth of character. Vacations, luxury and wealth give temporary pleasure but they are not going to satisfy. A fun, relaxing day at the beach has done nothing for me spiritually. If it weren't for the times of crisis in my life, this book would be about decorating and recipes. I would have nothing else to offer.

My Dad used to tell me life is like a tapestry. If you stand right up close to it, with your face almost touching it, all you can see are ugly, disorganized colors and messy threads going every which way. When you take a few steps back, you realize all those colors and threads were working together to create a beautiful work of art. I believed Dad during hard times and I see it now.

So does Paul in Philippians 1:12 when he says, *"But I would ye should understand, brethren, that the things which happened unto me have fallen out rather unto the furtherance of the gospel."*

Through the pain and heartache in life, God has, as my friend Rose said, "shaken off the dust so we can shine a little brighter." She said that after her husband barely survived a motorcycle accident that split him in two. And so who am I to question? Who am I to reply against God on what heartache or adversity He is allowing in my life? We have to accept that He has a greater purpose, beyond anything we might have even imagined.

God sees you and loves you the way he did the beggar Lazarus when Jesus Himself said of a happy rich man, *"Remember that thou in thy lifetime receivedst thy good things, and likewise Lazarus evil things: but now he is comforted, and thou art tormented."* Luke 16:25.

This is what life will look like at the end, when we finally meet our Creator and Heavenly Father face to face in heaven. There will be no more circles. There will be no more dots. There will be only Him, and you. Triumphant. For all of eternity.

Part VI. The Bible is Ninja

───❧───

"You don't have to go to university and do a Ph.D. to understand this stuff. You just go to the person of Christ."

Bono, lead singer of the rock band U2
In an interview with Focus on the Family, summer 2013

CHAPTER 21

LOVE ME SOME BIBLE

—— ⨒ ——

I fell in love with my Bible when my husband was furloughed from his airline job. Furloughed is a pleasant sounding word that means no money. You are laid off without pay until the airline can afford to bring you back. During that time, I clung to my Bible for dear life. I read the entire Bible from start to finish twice in one year, and I am not telling you that to be impressive but rather to demonstrate my state of brokenness. I've been reading it through ever since. It was good for me that I was broken, because it got me to learn the Bible. Psalm 119:71 feels me: *"It is good for me that I have been afflicted; that I might learn thy statutes."*

I started out with a more modern translation at first. I decided to get jiggy with it and tackled the King James Version a couple years after that. When I first read the King James, I was like hold up. `Hold right on up`. It was very different and, I believe, gets to the heart of God's character. Once you get used to the stuffy pronouns, the King James rocks.

The New King James is also very good. Any Bible is better than no Bible, but some of the more modern translations such as The Message and even the New International Version scare me in that they are so watered down, you're barely even reading the Bible anymore. I'm sure those editors mean well and want to make the scriptures accessible in modern language, but they have destroyed the original meaning in many cases and are actually changing the theology. Not to mention removing the beauty of the language. Understand that if you are reading one of those versions of the Bible then you are getting more of a commentary or interpretation of the Bible, rather than a straight-up translation of the Bible. When I read the Bible, I don't want to know what someone thinks about what God said. I want to know what God said.

EPHESIANS 5:22 FROM THE MESSAGE (YAWN.)
"Wives, understand and support your husbands in ways that show your support for Christ."
What does that even mean?

EPHESIANS 5:22 FROM THE KING JAMES VERSION (OH SNAP.)
"Wives, submit yourselves unto your own husbands, as unto the Lord."
That inspires.

I also caution you not to rely exclusively on any form of a digital Bible. One, if you are looking at your screen thingie, you're in danger most of the time of getting distracted. Something's always squawking at us on those gizmos. Two, you can't feel the pages and make marks or underline parts that speak to you. And three, you're missing a chance to inspire other people who can't tell you're reading a Bible. All they see is someone staring at her phone or tablet.

If you are pressed for time or have a long commute, you can find Bible MP3 versions or CDs that are recordings of someone reading the exact words of the Bible. I highly recommend the free pod casts from Bibletrack.org. A while back, someone broke into my husband's truck. My husband is convinced that this person left without taking or destroying anything because he saw Bible CDs lying on the seat. That's right, shoo, shame on him.

For your children, my friend Mary Jane gave our family a wonderful book called *The Picture Bible* by Iva Hoth. This book makes Bible stories very interesting in a comic book-type format. It's a step up from a babyish Bible, but not the real deal quite yet. We loved it so much that we wore out to shreds the *Picture Bible* that Mary Jane gave us and have replaced it at least twice. Our children are very familiar with all the Bible stories because of this book. It gives you and your children a good solid familiarity with all the events in the Bible and a deep respect for God's sovereignty.

When you've read the Bible all the way through, you see the world differently. You can hear things like "God helps those who help themselves," and you can say, "That's not in the Bible." Benjamin Franklin said it. You will know that the word Trinity is not in the Bible. A good church leader guy made it up later. It is a Biblically sound idea, and you will know that too. When you have read the entire Bible, you see the big picture. You know more about the word of God than many pastors. They do not have to read the whole Bible in seminary school to become a pastor, or to publish a Christian book. Scary right?

I've heard it said that if you read three chapters a day, plus five on Sunday, you'll finish the whole Bible in one year. And we don't get bonus points for starting in January. I'm not telling your 5th grade teacher that you started in July. Don't worry if you aren't understanding everything at first. We never will. It will take a lifetime to understand a microscopic smidge of what the Lord knows. Do we really need an entire chapter in Leviticus about skin scabs? I don't understand why that is in the Bible. We can ask when we get to heaven. Until then, in reading the entire word of God the first time, and the time after that and the time after that, you will start to know Him.

Bust it open and read it girlfriend. I go Genesis through Revelation with my bad self and it has never given me a seizure or a sprained ankle to read it that way, even though it is not strictly chronological. I'm over it, just give me some Bible. Some people love a good reading schedule because it holds them accountable, but I don't use one because if I miss a day, I feel defeated. I go at my own pace instead. It's just me hanging with the Lord.

BIBLE PEOPLE

When we start talking Bible, we've got some categories of people. Which is good because I needed one last list before we go Bible in a second here.

1. Those who consider God and His word to be completely irrelevant. It's as if, forgive the illustration, they have never heard the word "piano" and would not know a piano if one fell off a balcony and landed on their heads.
2. Those who are sincerely drawn to God but aren't at all familiar with his word. This is like enjoying and appreciating the sound of piano music but never having learned to read music or play.
3. Those who genuinely love God and His word but rely on books like this one and sound bites from the New Testament. This is like a piano player who knows only the treble clef.
4. Those who passionately love God and know the Bible in its entirety inside and out. These are the accomplished concert pianists whose music leaves one "astonied," as the Geneva translation says.

When we discover how wonderful the Bible is, the first thing we want to do is to get the people we love to love it. Don't make me drag you back through all that stuff about respecting your husband and not thinking you're above him. Or girls, don't be thinking you're smarter than your parents. You will disrupt your marriage or relationship with your parents if you try to get them to switch categories. I'm writing all this to you, and I do not try to get my own husband or parents to read more of the Bible. Don't do it, or you'll be shooting yourself in your triumphant foot with a stupid gun.

Here is one thing you can do though. Girls, smile at your parents and obey everything they say. Or wives, smile at your husband and agree with everything he says. When asked what your deal is, you can reply sweetly, "I'm just following the Bible."

Forever imprinted on their minds will be these two words: "Bible, good."

CHAPTER 22

OLD TESTAMENT TALK

The Bible contains 66 books. We don't need to go seven-volume *Harry Potter* today, so here are some selected highlights that speak to us as women, with my commentary for special ladies just like yourself. So here we go. The rest of this book is dedicated to delighting in His Book. And delight we shall.

GENESIS

GENESIS 1
"In the beginning God created the heaven and the earth." Genesis 1:1
Of course that was just the beginning for us. God has no beginning or end. Our little brains can't really wrap around that one because we are linear in time unlike God.

Genesis 1:16 simply says, *"He made the stars also."* Just made 'em. No biggee. Astonishing and baffling for us. Pinky finger for God.

After creation, He rested on the seventh day. God chillaxed on the Sabbath and if it's good enough for Him then it's good enough for us. Yesterday was Sunday, and I knew I should take a break from writing, so I stuck a post-it note on my computer screen. It said DAY OF REST. Whenever I started to think about my writing, I would tell my brain DAY OF REST.

GENESIS 2

"*And the rib, which the Lord God had taken from man, made he a woman, and brought her unto the man. And Adam said, 'This is now bone of my bones, and flesh of my flesh: she shall be called Woman, because she was taken out of Man.' Therefore shall a man leave his father and mother, and shall cleave unto his wife: and they shall be one flesh.*" Genesis 2:22-24

This is God's plan for families, right there on the first couple of pages of the Bible.

GENESIS 3

After the fall of man, once Satan got Eve all confused and questioning God, here is the consequence God gave to Eve and all of womanhood with her:

"*Unto the woman he said, I will greatly multiply thy sorrow and thy conception: in sorrow thou shalt bring forth children: and thy desire shall be to thy husband, and he shall rule over thee.*" Genesis 3:16

Eve sweety. Seriously with the fruit thing though. And by the way, is there a serpent in your life? Someone who is questioning God? Tell him "shoo."

GENESIS 4

"*Sin lieth at the door. And unto thee shall be his desire, and thou shalt rule over him.*" Genesis 4:7

Those "him" pronouns are referring to sin so God's saying we have to master sin rather than sin's mastering us. Holler back?

GENESIS 8

Noah gets busy on the ark, got a hammer and a slide rule or something, massive building project here without so much as a calculator so don't tell me the ancient guys weren't smart. People think he's whack, had to float around on that ark for days and days with stinky animals, and he and his family came out and started life again but here is what God says after that:

"*I will not again curse the ground any more for man's sake; for the imagination of man's heart is evil from his youth: neither will I again smite any more every thing living, as I have done.*" Genesis 8:21

Okay that strikes me as puzzling. God said before the flood that the reason He was about to do it was because people's imagination in their hearts was evil. Then right after the flood when everyone except Noah, Mrs. Noah and the Noah sons and their wives was killed by the flood, God says the exact same thing. That He's not going to wipe out the Earth ever again because the imagination of man's heart is evil. He did the flood because man's heart is evil, and now He won't ever do a flood again because man's heart is still evil.

It's not as if God can learn anything. Perhaps God is saying to us: Look, there's nothing you God-fearing scripture reading faithful people can ever do to wipe out evil completely. I've already tried in a global flood way that you could never do and even that didn't work.

I mean the very next passage after the flood was when Noah's son Ham was weird and lewd about Noah's nakedness. By the way, Ham's descendants are Sodom and Gomorrah. And those guys highly angered God. After the flood chapters, there's a genealogy chapter, and then the tower of Babel situation. God dealt with those high-minded guys with selfish intent by confusing their language.

So God's not saying: whatever, give in to evil because we know it's what's in the imagination of everyone's heart. He's saying we absolutely resist it, He's got it under control. But ultimately until Jesus returns in the second coming, no one can wipe out evil completely, and God is choosing not to wipe it out completely. Sorry but this means that whole world peace thing ain't going to happen.

GENESIS 15
Abraham was chosen by God to be the father of a great nation, Israel, and ultimately of the Christian faith. *"Fear not Abram, I am thy shield, and thy exceeding great reward."* Genesis 15:1

GENESIS 18
"Is any thing too hard for the Lord?" Genesis 18:14
Well newwww?

GENESIS 24

I love when Isaac's servant goes to find a wife for him, and he's feeling the pressure and wants to do well with this task. He explains his prayer communication with Rebekah and her brother Laban and when he's finished, he asks Laban, can Rebekah come with me and be Isaac's wife: so what do you think Laban? Here is what Laban says: *"The thing proceedeth from the Lord; we cannot speak unto thee bad or good."* Genesis 24:50. Laban is all: doesn't really matter what I think. The thing comes from God. I can't really say anything about it one way or the other. Pretty cool insight coming from a guy who cheats his nephew later on. If it weren't for all that later, I'd say Laban starts out being a good man. He obviously has taken good care of his family member Rebekah who is a respectable young lady who has never known a man, as in a virgin.

GENESIS 33

Isaac's son Jacob is traveling away from Laban who has gone slightly bonkers. While they are traveling, Jacob says, *"My lord knoweth that the children are tender ... I will lead on softly, according as the cattle that goeth before me and the children be able to endure."* Genesis 33:13-14. This teaches me to be patient and go at a pace the children can handle because they do not have as much endurance.

GENESIS 45

Jacob has 12 sons, and Joseph was his favorite. Do siblings like it when there's a favorite? No. Joseph's brothers sold him into slavery in Egypt. He ends up saving his family and all of Egypt when God tells Joseph in a dream that seven years of famine are coming. Joseph stores grain for this famine, and Pharaoh makes Joseph second in command. Guess who comes a-crawling to Egypt during the famine? His brothers. They bow down to Joseph and don't recognize him until later when he weeps bitterly and says, *"I am Joseph."* When the brothers apologize – and guys y'all better start apologizing, am I right? – Joseph forgives them and this is what he says to them:

"So now it was not you that sent me hither, but God." Genesis 45:8

GENESIS 50

Joseph also says to his brothers: *"But as for you, ye thought evil against me, but God meant it unto good."* Genesis 50:20

——— ⚬⚬⚬ ———

EXODUS

EXODUS 1

Along came a new Pharaoh who apparently did not pay attention in history class because he doesn't know about Joseph or his family. He enslaves them. God sends Moses and his brother Aaron to get the Israelites out of there.

Here's a passage that reminds us that as believers (as the Hebrews) we are set apart from the rest of the world (Egyptians.) The bad guy king was trying to get all the midwives to kill all the male Hebrew babies at birth but they feared God and refused to do it.

"And the king of Egypt called for the midwives, and said unto them, Why have ye done this thing, and have saved the men children alive? And the midwives said unto Pharaoh, Because the Hebrew women are not as the Egyptian women, for they are lively, and are delivered ere the midwives come in unto them." Exodus 1:18-19. I like that. The Hebrew women are lively. Some translations say "vigorous."

EXODUS 8

Pharaoh was extremely stubborn, would not listen to Moses and so God sent all these unbearable plagues such as turning the Nile River's water into blood. It's amazing how God drew this line so that swarms of flies stayed in Egypt and didn't bother His chosen people. Exodus 8:22-23

EXODUS 10

Memo from God to Pharaoh when he wouldn't let the people go: *"Thus saith the Lord God of the Hebrews, How long wilt thou refuse to humble thyself before me?"* Ex 10:3

Also known as: Hey Pharaoh, lighten up and listen to God, would ya? He never did. Moms, it wasn't because Moses did a bad job. It was because Pharaoh's heart was hardened and God had a very great purpose, a bigger picture.

Exodus 14
The Hebrews were about to cross the Red Sea, which God parted for them so they could cross on dry land, and it's just astonishingly miraculous, I totally disagree with the smartie pants scholars who try to explain this away as tidal patterns or a tsunami. It's not a natural phenomenon, okay? The Bible is very clear about that, see Leviticus 19 coming up. We might as well believe it:
"Fear ye not, stand still, and see the salvation of the Lord, which he will shew to you today. The Lord shall fight for you, and ye shall hold your peace." Exodus 14:13, 14

Exodus 15
"The Lord is a man of war." Exodus 15:3 also translated, *"the Lord is a warrior."* Military families can take comfort in that. God's fighting our battles alongside us. But that passage is for everyone, for every battle when we turn to Him. Emotionally or otherwise.

Exodus 18
Ladies we have to ask for help when we need it. Moses's father-in-law Jethro encouraged Moses to delegate the work by appointing some helper people. Now with a good ol' boy name like that, we have to listen to this guy. Jethro said to Moses, *"Thou wilt surely wear away...for this thing is too heavy for thee."* Exodus 18:18

Exodus 32
God had been verrrrrrry clear about not worshipping idols or building and then bowing down to any sort of special statue. Lame excuse award goes to Moses's brother Aaron: Dude I threw in some gold or something and like, *"out came this calf."* Exodus 32:24

EXODUS 33

This next passage kind of blows me away, when I see that the Bible says this of your average, normal guy Moses:

"And the Lord spake unto Moses face to face, as a man speaketh unto his friend." Exodus 33:11

Moses to God: *"Shew me now thy way, that I may know thee, that I may find grace in thy sight. And he said 'My presence shall go with thee, and I will give thee rest.'"* Ex 33:13-14
So when we are troubled, we know that God's presence will be the place we can go to get rest from the heaviness of heart.

LEVITICUS

LEVITICUS 10

"And that ye may put difference between holy and unholy." Leviticus 10:10
Anything goes? Newwww. We must discern between what is of God and not. Sometimes I think the book of Leviticus is in my Bible by mistake. And then I read passages like these and I'm like oh okay.

LEVITICUS 19

"I am the Lord your God, which brought you out of the land of Egypt. Therefore shall ye observe all my statutes, and all my judgments, and do them: I am the Lord." Lev 19:36-37

LEVITICUS 26

"If ye walk in my statues, and keep my commandments, and do them; Then I will give you rain in due season, and the land shall yield her increase, and the trees of the field shall yield their fruit. And your threshing shall reach unto the vintage, and the vintage shall reach unto the sowing time: and ye shall eat your bread to the full, and dwell in your land safely. And I will give peace in the land, and ye shall lie down, and none shall make you afraid." Lev. 26:4-6

We have here an "if, then" statement from God. We can take comfort knowing that if we are respecting God's ways, He'll respect us. As my girl Donna says, "You deny Him, He'll deny you." To me this is not works-based theology which would be about salvation. That is a separate issue which can only be had by giving oneself over to Christ, but rather these passages are telling us how to have peace in *this* life. He is saying I will take care of you, I will defend you, when you fear and love Me. Which we do. It's so simple that it's baffling.

Numbers

Numbers 6
Well here we are in Numbers, and it's good to know those benedictions, which I used to hear as we adjourned at my childhood church affectionately referred to by my brothers and me as First Prez, were taken from scripture.

"The Lord bless thee, and keep thee, The Lord make his face shine upon thee, and be gracious unto thee: The Lord lift up his countenance upon thee, and give thee peace. And they shall put my name upon the children of Israel, and I will bless them." Numbers 6:24-26

Numbers 12
Moses's sister Miriam got a little uppity and tired of having Moses in charge. Miriam, sweety? It is not about you, so just step back and listen to Moses, your brother from the same mother. Numbers 12:1

"Now the man Moses was very meek, above all the men which were upon the face of the earth." Numbers 12:3
God chose the meekest guy to lead so I'm seeing here that God digs humility. God didn't go find some type-A Goliath kind of guy to do the job. So when we are meek/humble/weak then God is at work in us and has some mighty cool plans brewing for us.

NUMBERS 13

"And Caleb stilled the people before Moses, and said, Let us go up at once, and possess it; for we are well able to overcome it." Numbers 13:30

Caleb's like, Hey we got this. He had faith and confidence when everyone else was saying no way can we beat the bad guys. This is Caleb having confidence in God that they could defeat the enemy and take their land but nobody else saw it that way and were all scared so they didn't go for it like God had commanded them. God was chafed. Let's pronounce that "Chafe Ed." Just for fun.

NUMBERS 14

Check out what God says about Caleb a couple of verses later:

"But my servant Caleb, because he had another spirit with him, and hath followed me fully, him will I bring into the land whereinto he went: and his seed shall possess it." Numbers 14:24

So God rewards us when we seek Him and trust Him.

Then God is blasting everyone else:

"And the Lord spake unto Moses and unto Aaron, saying, How long shall I bear with this evil congregation, which murmur against me? I have heard the murmurings of the children of Israel, which they murmur against me." Numbers 14:24 and 27

Then He says some serious, wroth stuff to the people regarding their complaining and murmurings and punishing them in a way that has to do with their carcasses. When God starts to talk about their "carcasses" He generally means business. So I'm just seeing here that God rewards those who seek Him and trust Him, and who have a "different spirit," as in a heart that is fully turned toward the Lord.

NUMBERS 15

"Remember all the commandments of the Lord, and do them; and that ye seek not after your own heart and your own eyes, after which ye use to go a whoring." Numbers 15:39

Ouch, does it really say that?

NUMBERS 16

Enough with the murmurings. Now it's not like Moses to get snippy but apparently he was "very wroth" when some people rose up against him. No worries, God opened up the Earth and swallowed up the complaining people. Numbers 16:15

NUMBERS 21

"And the Lord said unto Moses, Make thee a fiery serpent, and set it upon a pole: and it shall come to pass, that everyone that is bitten, when he looketh upon it, shall live." Numbers 21:8

This is possibly sort of a foreshadowing kinda thing of looking up to the cross of Jesus later. Sometimes I wonder if the people in the Old Testament got their salvation the same way we do: trusting in Jesus' resurrection. Only for them, it was trusting what hadn't happened yet (the hope of Christ in the future), and for us it's trusting that it already did happen (the hope of what Christ did in the past + He will come again). Either way none of us was actually there so we are believing in something we didn't see with our own eyes but rather trust in our heart. I mean David had to go to heaven right? Daniel, Ezekiel, Moses, Noah all those good God fearing guys. Not through their own righteousness but through their belief in the coming Savior. So they were all about proclaiming what would happen whereas the apostles taught about what previously happened. Either way on the time scale slash number line, salvation comes from the resurrection.

And one final thought: it's kind of deep, so you might want to take a moment and get in the zone. Shekels, offerings and peeps. I'm thinking they call it the book of Numbers because there was a lot of numbering going on.

Deuteronomy

Deuteronomy 4

When God says *"take heed,"* I'm finna take heed. *"Only take heed* (also translated 'be careful') *to thyself, and keep thy soul diligently, lest thou forget the things which thine eyes have seen, and lest they depart from thy heart all the days of thy life; but teach them thy sons, and thy sons' sons."* Deuteronomy 4:9

This passage says to teach the ways of God to your grandchildren, as in your son's sons. For those of us who have grandchildren to teach and influence, I'm taking that to mean we do not get to spoil those youngins.

"But if from thence thou shalt seek the Lord thy God, thou shalt find him, if thou seek him with all thy heart and with all thy soul. When thou art in tribulation, and all these things are come upon thee, even in the latter days, if thou turn to the Lord thy God, and shalt be obedient unto his voice: (For the Lord thy God is a merciful God) he will not forsake thee." Deut. 4:29-31

Deuteronomy 6

Years ago, I didn't know this is called the The Shema. I just knew God was telling me to homeschool:

"Hear O Israel, the Lord our God is one Lord: and thou shalt love the Lord thy God with all thine heart, and with all thy soul and with all thy might. And these words, which I command thee this day, shall be in thine heart: And thou shalt teach them diligently unto thy children, and shalt talk of them when thou sittest in thine house, and when thou walkest by the way, and when thou liest down, and when thou risest up. And thou shalt bind them for a sign upon thine hand, and they shall be as frontlets between thine eyes. And thou shalt write them upon the posts of thy house, and on thy gates." Deuteronomy 6:4-9

So there's The Shema, then Jesus quoted this verse later to Satan:
"Ye shall not tempt the Lord your God." Deut 6:16

DEUTERONOMY 8

"Beware that thou forget not the Lord thy God, in not keeping his commandments, and his judgments, and his statutes, which I command thee this day…Then thine heart be lifted up, and thou forget the Lord thy God…But thou shalt remember the Lord thy God; for it is He that giveth thee power to get wealth." Deuteronomy 8:11, 14, 18

This is why we read and study the Bible all the time, friends. Ditto on the next passage:

DEUTERONOMY 12 AND 17

"Ye shall not do after all the things that we do here this day, every man whatsoever is right in his own eyes." Deut. 12:8. *"And it shall be, when he sitteth upon the throne of his kingdom, that he shall write him a copy of this law in a book out of that which is before the priests the Levites: and it shall be with him, and he shall read therein all the days of his life: that he may learn to fear the Lord his God, to keep all the words of this law and these statutes, and do them; that his heart be not lifted up above his brethren, and that he turn not aside from the commandment, to the right hand, or to the left; to the end that he may prolong his days in his kingdom, he, and his children, in the midst of Israel.* Deut. 17:18-20

DEUTERONOMY 20

Military families, take comfort:

"Hear O Israel, ye approach this day unto battle against your enemies; let not your hearts faint, fear not, and do not tremble, neither be ye terrified because of them; for the Lord your God is he that goeth with you, to fight for you against your enemies, to save you." Deut. 20:3-4

JOSHUA

JOSHUA 1

"Be strong and of a good courage." Joshua 1:6

And Joshua's like, Roger that. That's a copy. He and Caleb take over after Moses has died.

JOSHUA 4

Joshua pulls a Moses, crossing the Jordan River on dry land. That guy never gets any press for that. And why all this water parting and crossing? *"That all the people of the earth might know the hand of the Lord, that it is mighty."* Joshua 4:24

JOSHUA 9

Tsk tsk. The good guys would not have to deal with those pesky Gibeonites except Joshua's men *"asked not the counsel at the mouth of the Lord."* Joshua 9:14

JOSHUA 10

"Then spoke Joshua to the Lord in the day when the Lord delivered up the Amorites before the children of Israel, and he said in the sight of Israel, 'Sun, stand thou still upon Gibeon; and thou Moon, in the valley of Ajalon.' And the sun stood still, and the moon stayed, until the people had avenged themselves upon their enemies. Is this not written in the book of Jasher? So the sun stood still in the midst of heaven, and hasted not to go down about a whole day. And there was no day like that before it or after it, that the Lord hearkened unto the voice of a man: for the Lord fought for Israel." Josh 10:12-14

Ever think prayer is a waste of time and that God isn't going to listen? He made the earth stop spinning for Joshua.

JOSHUA 14

When Caleb was 85 years old he said, *"As yet I am as strong this day as I was in the day that Moses sent me: as my strength was then, even so is my strength now."* Josh 14:11

Dang. I want to be that fly myself when I'm 85.

JOSHUA 22

Pretty simple. It works like this. If ye rebel against the Lord, then He's fixing to be wroth. Joshua 22:18. Sister we can't be hanging out with people who *"have no part in the Lord."* Joshua 22:25

JOSHUA 23

"For the Lord your God is he that hath fought for you." Joshua 23:3

That verse makes me feel very courageous. Oh hey, that must have been God's point because check this out:

"Be ye therefore very courageous to keep and to do all that is written in the book of the law of Moses, that ye turn not aside there from to the right hand or to the left...but cleave unto the Lord your God, as ye have done unto this day. Take good heed therefore unto yourselves, that ye love the Lord your God." Josh 23:6, 8, 11

It's nice to know this: *"And ye know in all your hearts and in all your souls, that not one thing hath failed of all the good things concerning you; all are come to pass unto you, and not one thing hath failed thereof."* Joshua 23:14

JOSHUA 24
"Choose this day whom ye will serve; whether the gods which your fathers served that were on the other side of the flood, or the gods of the Amorites, in whose land ye dwell: but as for me and my house, we will serve the Lord." Joshua 24:15

1 SAMUEL

1 SAMUEL 3
Now God has chosen the prophet Samuel to lead His people. The priest Eli taught and trained Samuel from when he was a young boy. You know it's about to hit when God says, *"both the ears of everyone that heareth it shall tingle."* 1 Sam 3:11

Everything Samuel said was so great that the Lord *"let none of his words fall to the ground."* 1 Sam 3:19

1 SAMUEL 7
May I say here that the *Raiders of the Lost Ark* movie people were not exaggerating that whole sacredness of the ark thing. Smitings and slaughterings for

real. Well, the war plan isn't that complicated folks: *"Prepare your hearts unto the Lord, and serve him only, and he will deliver you out of the hand of the Philistines."* 1 Sam 7:3

That's right Philistines. You'd better run to mama.

1 SAMUEL 8

The people beg and whine for a king. They want to be like all the other nay-shunnnns. God says okay but you won't like it. Saul is anointed by Samuel as Israel's first king. I would like to say Saul was awesome. However, when his kingship was announced, he went and hid. Saul was actually fairly faithful to God at first, if lacking in braveness, but then here comes young whipper snapper shepherd boy David and Saul starts bugging out.

This is how David manages to be such a boss: *"The Lord preserved David whithersoever he went."* 1 Sam 8:6

1 SAMUEL 12

"For the Lord will not forsake his people for his great name's sake, because it hath pleased the Lord to make you his people." 1 Sam 12:22

The good guys must have been weary and could use the pep talk.

"Only fear the Lord, and serve him in truth with all your heart; for consider how great things he hath done for you." 1 Sam 12:24

1 SAMUEL 14

This is what Saul's son Jonathan says before defeating a bunch of bad guys that everyone else was too chicken to fight:

"It may be that the Lord will work for us: for there is no restraint to the Lord." (another translation: *"nothing can hinder the Lord."*) 1 Samuel 14:6

1 SAMUEL 15

Samuel the prophet is rebuking king Saul for disobeying God, and Jesus alludes to this passage later in the New Testament:

"And Samuel said, Hath the Lord as great delight in burnt offerings and sacrifices, as in obeying the voice of the Lord? Behold, to obey is better than sacrifice, and to hearken than the fat of rams. For rebellion is as the sin of witchcraft, and stubbornness is as iniquity and idolatry. Because thou hast rejected the word of the Lord, he hath also rejected thee from being king." 1 Sam 15:22-23

1 SAMUEL 16
When anointing king David who was a young ruddy fellow, God said this to Samuel, who was confused thinking God would've planned for one of the older, buff sons of Jesse to be king:
"But the Lord said unto Samuel, Look not on his countenance, or on the height of his stature, because I have refused him; for the Lord seeth not as man seeth, for man looketh on the outward appearance, but the Lord looketh on the heart." 1 Sam 16:7

After that, the *"spirit of the Lord came upon David,"* but *"the Spirit of the Lord departed from Saul."* Now David's about to whoop up on the giant Philistine Goliath, who was nine feet tall and stood there shouting threats at the Israelites all day long, daring anyone to come and fight him.

"Then said David to the Philistine, 'Thou comest to me with a sword, and with a spear, and with a shield, but I come to thee in the name of the Lord of hosts; the God of the armies of Israel, whom thou has defied.'" 1 Sam 17:45

1 SAMUEL 17
And Goliath in his big ol' soldier metal outfit's like, *"Am I a dog?"* (He actually says that in the Bible.) Here you are coming at me with sticks and a couple little rocks (that's more of a paraphrase). And then David talks some other junk to him and is all: right now today I'm fixing to kill you man, me this little dude and you think you're all bad with your big armor outfit, so that after I do this, everyone will know about God. And more talk of carcasses. Then David says:

"And all this assembly shall know that the Lord saveth not with sword and spear: for the battle is the Lord's." 1 Sam 17:47

After David killed Goliath, all the fair maidens danced and said, "Ooooo David has slain his ten thousands," and Saul's like: Wait now, hold up. Saul is consumed with jealousy and fears that David will take over as king. Which pretty much he actually does. Saul fails to see it is not David grabbing the kingdom away, but rather it is God giving it to David.

Saul is not having that and wants David to die so he says, hey David all you have to do to marry my daughter is slay 100 Philistines and David's like, "cool." He goes and does it.

King David says, *"As for God, his way is perfect."* 2 Sam 22:31. Triumphant women say: True that.

1 SAMUEL 25
David's constantly running away from Saul, who keeps doing crazy stuff like throwing javelins at him. He and his people set up camp at a guy named Nabal's territory, and they are shepherds. David's like, What up, Nabal shepherd homies! I used to do a lil shepherding myself back in the day. 1 Sam 25:7

Abigail's husband Nabal did David and his men really wrong and was so grumpy, *"such a son of Belial, that a man cannot speak to him."* 1 Sam 25:17

But Abigail was wise and cool, and came out to meet David to make up for Nabal's offenses: *"And David said to Abigail, blessed be the Lord God of Israel, which sent thee this day to meet me."* 1 Sam 25:32

I do have one question. Is it weird that Laban spelled backward is Nabal?

1 SAMUEL 30
Then when the bad guys (the Amalekites, whoever they are) had burned David's city and taken their wives and children captive while David and the army were away, *"David was greatly distressed, for the people spake of stoning him,*

*because the soul of all the people was grieved, every man for his sons and for his daugh-
ters: but David encouraged himself in the Lord his God."* 1 Sam 30:6

It's like the Roadrunner and the Coyote. David is still running from Saul. I'm
liking the covert strategy, David. Go hide among the Philistines because that's
the last place Saul would think to look.

———✺———

2 SAMUEL

2 SAMUEL 1
After a fierce battle where Saul is severely injured, he takes his own life. David's so
classy to be mourning the death of Saul. I might be singing: ding dong the witch is
dead.

2 SAMUEL 4
King David groupies: Once and for all, he is not impressed when you go slay-
ing the Lord's anointed. 2 Sam 4:12. Some fellows had run up to David taking
credit for Saul's death. David was not amused.

However, now that Saul is gone, let's be honest, David rejoices and who can
blame him. In 2 Samuel 4 David says, *"As the Lord liveth, who hath redeemed my soul
out of all adversity."* And *"David danced before the Lord with all his might."*

2 SAMUEL 6
Saul's daughter Michal doesn't like seeing David dance explosively in public and
wants him to simmer down. Michal's all, Who's the fancy pants David dancer? Way
to prance a fool. David says get over yourself, *"it was before The Lord."* 2 Sam 6:21

2 SAMUEL 22
Here is a lovely sentence in 2 Samuel 22: *"As for God, his way is perfect."*

2 Samuel 24

When David was in trouble he said, *"I am in a great strait, let us fall now into the hand of the Lord: for his mercies are great, and let me not fall into the hand of man."* 2 Samuel 24

———∞∞∞———

1 Kings

1 Kings 3

David has now died and his son Solomon is king. In 1 Kings God tells king Solomon that He will give him anything he wants and Solomon says:

"Give therefore thy servant an understanding heart." 1 Kings 3:9

I'm respecting the guy for that. God did give Solomon such an understanding heart that he wrote much of the book of Proverbs.

1 Kings 6

"And the word of the Lord came to Solomon saying, 'Concerning this house which thou art building, if thou wilt walk in my statutes, and execute my judgments, and keep all my commandments to walk in them, then will I perform my word with thee, which I spake unto David thy father.'" 1 Kings 6:11-12

1 Kings 12

I painted the following passage on my bathroom wall, to remind me to be gentle and tenderhearted toward my children. But then I got tired of the red walls – the ceiling is vaulted and my daughter said one day "Mommy your bathroom looks like a barn," and actually she was right – so we painted it a lovely soft green but I never painted those Bible verses back and here they are in a moment. The background story is Solomon's son Rehoboam took over and asked everyone how he should rule. The old men said what was painted on my bathroom wall, but he didn't take their advice and rather took the advice of his young friends who said to go all big tough guy on the people and rule them with an iron fist. Here's what the wise men said:

"If thou wilt be a servant unto this people this day, and wilt serve them, and answer them, and speak good words to them, then they will be thy servants forever."

"And the king answered the people roughly, and forsook the old men's counsel that they gave him." 1 Kings 12:7 and 13

1 KINGS 17

Okay so that Rehoboam guy who was Solomon's son totally lost the kingdom, ignoring the wise men's advice. Young adults take note: Old people know stuff. Now Elijah the prophet is on the scene and God has come down hard on the people for their rebellion and said: No food or water for a while. But He took care of Elijah who was faithful: *"'And it shall be that thou shalt drink of the brook; and I have commanded the ravens to feed thee there.' So he went and did according unto the word of the Lord; for he went and dwelt by the book Cherith that is before Jordan. And the ravens brought him bread and flesh in the morning, and bread and flesh in the evening; and he drank of the brook."* 1 Kings 17:6

Amazing right? God sent birds to bring Elijah food.

1 KINGS 18

One time when Elijah was rebuking the people he said, *"How long halt ye between two opinions? If the Lord is God, follow him, but if Baal, then follow him."* 1 Kings 18:21. That's the KJV but the translation from the Bible from my childhood church cracks me up, it says, *"How long will you go on limping?"* (RSV). I suppose *"how long halt ye"* is hard to beat in eloquence. So that helps us stay dedicated to the Lord by asking ourselves, girl how long will you go on limping? When will you be devoted fully to God?

1 KINGS 19

Later Elijah's having a rough time (those prophets, ouch) and God talks to him in *"a still small voice,"* or another translation says a *"delicate whispering."* 1 Kings 19:12

1 Chronicles

1 Chronicles 10

This book reviews Saul's and David's stories. King Saul disobeyed God and didn't wait for what God had said to do, but went ahead and did his thing and consulted some witchcraft lady for advice rather than God. Was God cool with that? Nope. *"So Saul died for his transgression which he committed against the Lord, even against the word of the Lord, which he kept not, and also for asking counsel of one that had a familiar spirit, to enquire of it; and enquired not of the Lord; therefore he slew him, and turned the kingdom unto David the son of Jesse."* 1 Chronicles 10:13-14

1 Chronicles 16

Here is David and this is the same thing he wrote in Psalm 105: *"Seek the Lord and his strength, seek his face continually. Remember his marvelous works that he hath done, his wonders, and the judgments of his mouth."* 1 Chron 16:11-12

"For the gods of the people are idols; but the Lord made the heavens." 1 Chron 16:26

1 Chronicles 22

David says to Solomon his son: *"Only the Lord give thee wisdom and understanding."* 1 Chron 22:12
Which as we know He did, and then he was so wise that he could write all those kickin' Proverbs.

1 Chronicles 28

"And thou, Solomon my son, know thou the God of thy father, and serve him with a perfect heart and with a willing mind: for the Lord searcheth all hearts, and understandeth all the imaginations of the thoughts; if thou seek him, he will be found of thee; but if thou forsake him, he will cast thee off forever." 1 Chron 28:9

1 Chronicles 29

David is an ancestor of Jesus Christ, who was born in Bethlehem, which is the city of David. Before he dies David prays the following prayer, which sounds very much like the Lord's Prayer from Jesus, a foreshadowing:

"Wherefore David blessed the Lord before all the congregation: and David said 'Blessed be thou Lord God of Israel our father, for ever and ever. Thine O Lord is the greatness, and the power, and the glory, and the victory, and the majesty: for all that is in the heaven and in the earth is thine; thine is the kingdom, O Lord, and thou art exalted as head above all.'" 1 Chron 29:10-11

These Old Testament books repeat the same stuff, kind of like the gospels tell about Jesus four different ways. Personally, I appreciate the review because sometimes when I read my Bible, I totally space out and read eight pages and then I'm like huh?

---

2 Chronicles

2 Chronicles 10
That foolish King Rehoboam should have hearkened to the wise old guys rather than to *"the young men that were brought up with him."* 2 Chron 10

2 Chronicles 26
"As long as he sought the Lord, God made him to prosper." 2 Chron 26:5
Kind of makes one want to seek the Lord doesn't it.

2 Chronicles 30
"Now be ye not stiffnecked, as your fathers were, but yield yourselves unto the Lord... for the Lord your God is gracious and merciful, and will not turn away his face from you, if ye return unto him." 2 Chron 30:8, 9
Unstiff that neck honeychild.

2 Chronicles 32
Hezekiah was so cool for a while there till he let me down and had to go lifting his heart up, which put God's *"wrath upon him."* 2 Chron 32

"Be strong and courageous, be not afraid nor dismayed for the king of Assyria, nor for all the multitude that is with him: for there be more with us than with him: with him is an arm of flesh; but with us is the Lord our God to help us, and to fight our battles. And the people rested themselves upon the words of Hezekiah king of Judah." 2 Chron 32:7-8
God's word makes me feel so courageous about whatever battles I'm facing.

And finally: Rebellious, self-serving child award goes to Absalom for trying to move in on David's king action. Softy, delusional parent award goes to King David when it comes to Absalom.

Ezra

Ezra 7
"For Ezra had prepared his heart to seek the law of the Lord, and to do it, and to teach Israel statutes and judgments." Ezra 7:10

We need to prepare our hearts in the same way. This passage from Ezra says that he prepared his heart to seek the law of the Lord, and that's what you're doing right now girlfriend, rather than watching TV or checking your phone. Look at you, already like Ezra. Then it says Ezra prepared his heart to do the law. That means we can't just sit around and read about it, we have to implement it into our lives. Ask God how He wants this to look in your life? Then it says Ezra prepared his heart to teach the nation the law.

"Whatsoever is commanded by the God of heaven, let it be diligently done for the house of the God of heaven." Ezra 7:23
Go Ezra. You de man. We don't mind at all that you have a sissy name.

NEHEMIAH

NEHEMIAH 6

Nehemiah was that guy we like because he left his sweet cupbearer to the king job to help God's people rebuild the wall around Jerusalem after they were in captivity. Uh, which they haven't done yet chronologically but we'll come back to that. The prophets kept warning them about turning to God but they didn't listen.

So Nehemiah is helping to rebuild the wall around the city of Jerusalem, and the enemies of God's people are all, "We thought y'all were broken down and defeated, don't be building that wall back." So this one guy in particular starts trying to sabotage Nehemiah by sending all these threatening messages and *"thought to do me mischief,"* Nehemiah says. But the smooth part is, how Nehemiah responds: he says, *"And I sent messengers unto them saying, 'I am doing a great work, so that I cannot come down: why should the work cease, whilst I leave it, and come down to you?'"* Nehemiah 6:3

My beloved Sunday School teacher, Mary Jane, pointed out that God is instructing us here through this passage – and this is written in the margin of my Bible – that we can refuse to engage with someone who accuses us wrongly. Nehemiah stayed focused on his work for the Lord and did not stop working to ying and yang with this bully who came back with more threats and even saying he's going to report Nehemiah to the king, who gave Nehemiah permission to leave his job as his cupbearer to come and do this work for Jerusalem. Again Nehemiah says:

"Then I sent unto him, saying, there are no such things done as thou sayest, but thou feignest them out of thine own heart. For they all made us afraid, saying, Their hands shall be weakened from the work, that it be not done. Now therefore O God, strengthen my hands." Nehemiah 6:8-9. So he basically tells this guy, not even in person but writes him back and says in another translation, *"you have created these things in your own mind."*

You made all this up, sir. You're just trying to scare us, and you did, but God's going to keep us strong so just back off.

NEHEMIAH 8
Our man Ezra had dusted off the book of the law of God and read it to all the people, after they had ignored it for so long, *"So they read in the book in the law of God distinctly, and gave the sense, and caused them to understand the reading."* And Nehemiah and Ezra said to the people, *"This day is holy unto the Lord your God, mourn not, nor weep. For all the people wept, when they heard the words of the law."*

They realized how far they had strayed from God's teaching and were like: Dude we were supposed to be honoring God all this time and we weren't. *"Then he said unto them…This day is holy unto our Lord, neither be ye sorry;* (some translations say 'grieved') *for the joy of the Lord is your strength."* Nehemiah 8:8-10

NEHEMIAH 9
So the Nehemiah people *"read the book of The Lord their God one fourth part of the day."* Nehemiah 9:3
Liking that percentage. I think I'm really something if I read the Bible maybe 1/24 of the day.

ESTHER

ESTHER 4
O Esther, how we love thee. Here is a cool passage in the book of Esther where the Jewish people are about to get wiped out. Again. Somebody is All The Time Trying To Kill The Jews, God's chosen people, see Hitler. Clearly, this never works. Mordecai, Esther's uncle, says this to her after she had become queen and he's imploring her to go to the king to get help for the Jews:

"And who knoweth whether thou art come to the kingdom for such a time as this?" Esther 4:14

When everything's going wrong, hey who knows whether God placed me in this situation for such a time as this, and prepared me all along for this or that purpose. Or to do a great work on His behalf.

Next we go to Job which puzzlingly is in the middle of the Bible when it is one of the very first events chronologically and happened somewhere around the first few chapters of Genesis. But hey if that's where God wanted it to end up, then okay.

—————⦿⦿⦿—————

JOB

They say that women can do some talking but wow. Job (we say that "Jobe," like "choir robe") and his friends have some serious banter. Especially Elihu. Enough with the dramatic introductions bro. Just spit it out already. Guy takes like a hundred verses to say: Everyone listen to my insightful remarks. Remember, Job was in total anguish, has lost everything and is afflicted in every way.

JOB 15

Job's mocking buddy gets rhetorically sarcastic: *"Art thou the first man that was born?"* Job 15:7

JOB 37

"Stand still, and consider the wondrous works of God." Job 37:14

JOB 42

When God finally does appear to Job at the end of this book of the Bible, Job says *"I have heard of thee by the hearing of the ear: but now mine eye seeth thee. Wherefore I abhor myself, and repent in dust and ashes."* Job 42:5-6

Then God restored all his wealth and possessions after Job prayed, *"the Lord gave Job twice as much as he had before...So the Lord blessed the latter end of Job more than his beginning: for he had fourteen thousand sheep, and six thousand camels, and a thousand yoke of oxen, and a thousand donkeys."* Job 42:10, 12

I thought it was interesting that God also told Job to pray for his obnoxious friends. That's how merciful God wants us to be. And we are fond of our happy ending for Job.

———— ∞ ————

PSALMS

King David wrote many of the Psalms, an outpouring of his agony, fears and love to his God. People who seem to have it all together have most likely spent a lot of time on their knees weeping to God in the same way that David did.

PSALM 4

"Stand in awe, and sin not: commune with your own heart upon your bed, and be still." Psalm 4:4

PSALM 7

Pronoun "he" here is referring to wickedness (insert whoever's done you wrong, girlfriend). *"Behold, he travaileth with iniquity, and hath conceived mischief, and brought forth falsehood. He made a pit, and digged it, and is fallen into the ditch which he made. His mischief shall return upon his own head, and his violent dealing shall come down upon his own pate. I will praise the Lord according to his righteousness, and will sing praise to the name of the Lord most high."* Psalm 7:14. "Pate" means "head." Ouch. And before that it says, *"Oh let the wickedness of the wicked come to an end; but establish the just ... My defence is of God, which saveth the upright in heart."*

PSALM 14

Sorry atheists but hoop there it is: *"The fool hath said in his heart, there is no God."* Psalm 14:1

"The Lord looked down from heaven upon the children of men, to see if there were any that did understand, and seek God." Psalm 14:2
It makes you want to raise your hand as if in a classroom and say, "Me, me, I seek you Lord."

PSALM 16

"I have set the Lord always before me...in thy presence is fullness of joy." Psalm 16:11
Here is a helpful mathematical statement for us. Set the Lord before you = joy.

PSALM 22

Ever feel like a nerd for Christ? David feels you: *"All they that see me laugh me to scorn."* Psalm 22:7. He gets the last laugh though.

These words from David sound suspiciously exactly like what Jesus says when He is crucified. So it is a prophetic passage. Either way it tells us that God understands our despair and desperation and anguish:

"My God, my God, why hast thou forsaken me?"
"All they that see me laugh me to scorn."
"They pierced my hands and my feet." Psalms 22:1, 7, 16

PSALM 23

And of course the entire Psalm 23 is always refreshing when you apply it to yourself and speak these words as if they are true and are just for you.

"The Lord is my shepherd. I shall not want. (Meaning I shall not be in want of anything, or lacking anything.)
He maketh me to lie down in green pastures: he leadeth me beside the still waters. (The Hebrew is more something like 'waters of rest.')
He restoreth my soul: he leadeth me in the paths of righteousness for his name's sake. (I look at that like, check it, God's reputation is at stake, when we are afflicted: He won't forsake His faithful believers so that when we come out of the crisis, He will be glorified. I'll stop chiming in now and let you read the thing already.)
Yea, though I walk through the valley of the shadow of death, I will fear no evil: for thou art with me; thy rod and thy staff they comfort me.

Thou preparest a table before me in the presence of mine enemies: thou anointest my head with oil; my cup runneth over.
Surely goodness and mercy shall follow me all the days of my life, and I will dwell in the house of the Lord forever."

PSALM 39
Not trying to take the Bible out of context or anything but I thought I would mention Psalm 39 does actually say, *"O spare me."*

PSALM 55
"Cast thy burden upon the Lord, and he shall sustain thee; he shall never suffer (allow) the righteous to be moved" (shaken.) Psalm 55.
And this whole chapter is one that is a comfort when facing betrayal. Somebody betrays you? Read Psalm 55, which we talked about regarding painful relationships. I'm telling you, you'll be like oh wow, no way, God gets me. Here it is:

"For it was not an enemy that reproached me; then I could have borne it: neither was it he that hated me that did magnify himself against me; then I would have hid myself from him: But it was thou, a man mine equal, my guide, and mine acquaintance. We took sweet counsel together, and walked unto the house of God in company ... The words of his mouth were smoother than butter, but war was in his heart; his words were softer than oil, yet were they drawn swords. Cast thy burden upon the Lord, and he shall sustain thee: he shall never suffer the righteous to be moved ... bloody and deceitful men shall not live out half their days: but I will trust in thee."

PSALM 86
"I cry unto thee daily." Psalm 86:3

PSALM 106
Pick your friends carefully, girls. The people are forgetting God and provoking Him to anger, did not obey Him but instead *"were mingled among the heathen, and learned their works."* Psalm 106:35

PSALM 119

"Turn away mine eyes from beholding vanity (another translation: "worthless things"), *and quicken thou me in thy way. And I will delight myself in thy commandments, which I have loved."* Psalm 119:37, 47

Feeling feisty and highly offended? Something ain't right: *"Great peace have they which love thy law: and nothing shall offend them."* Psalm 119:165, also translated *"nothing shall make them stumble."*

PSALM 139

"Whither shall I go from thy spirit?" Psalm 139:7
I can run but I can't hide.

PROVERBS

"The fear of the Lord is the beginning of knowledge: but fools despise wisdom and instruction. My son, hear the instruction of thy father, and forsake not the law of thy mother, for they shall be an ornament of grace unto thy head, and chains about thy neck."
It means a lovely necklace, rather than, um, mean chains. Proverb 1:7-9

"But whoso hearkeneth unto me shall dwell safely, and shall be quiet (or, "be at ease") *from fear of evil."* Proverb 1:33

"Trust in the Lord with all thine heart; and lean not unto thine own understanding. In all thy ways acknowledge him, and he shall direct thy paths." Proverb 3:5

"A virtuous woman is a crown to her husband." Proverb 12:4

"He that spareth his rod hateth his son, but he that loveth him chasteneth him betimes." Proverb 13:24

So we've heard "spare the rod, spoil the child," and that is not from scripture. But what it does say in scripture, is "spare the rod, hateth his son."

"A soft answer turneth away wrath, but grievous words stir up anger." Proverb 15:1
Dealing with a grump? Try replying with a soft answer and see what happens.

"Pleasant words are as an honeycomb, sweet to the soul, and health to the bones." Proverb 16:24
Want to breathe life and joy into other people's hearts? Speak pleasant words to them. God really means it:
"Death and life are in the power of the tongue." Proverb 18:21

"Who can find a virtuous woman? (I can, it's you.) *For her price is far above rubies ... Strength and honor are her clothing: and she shall rejoice in time to come. She openeth her mouth with wisdom: and in her tongue is the law of kindness."* Proverb 31:10, 25-26

ECCLESIASTES

"A threefold cord is not quickly broken." Ecclesiastes 4:12
Wise and famous sayings such as these come from the ... Bible. Well what do you know, our favorite book.

"Yet surely I know that it shall be well with them that fear God." Eccl 8:12

"Whatsoever thy hand findeth to do, do it with thy might." Eccl 9:10

And of course the famous hippie song about a time to live, a time to die, a time to laugh, and time to mourn, is from Ecclesiastes.

ISAIAH

The book of Isaiah is startingly scathing yet surprisingly reassuring, depending on whose team you're on. We are on God's team and Isaiah reminds us why. The first half of the book of Isaiah could be summed up in these five words: It's fixing to go down.

ISAIAH 3

"Woe unto the wicked! As for my people, children are their oppressors, and women rule over them." Isaiah 3:11, 12

ISAIAH 6

Isaiah says: *"Here am I: send me."* Isaiah 6:8

ISAIAH 9

"For unto us a child is born, unto us a son is given: and the government shall be upon his shoulder: and his name shall be called Wonderful, Counsellor, The mighty God, The everlasting Father, the Prince of Peace." Isaiah 9:6. This is talking about Jesus Christ. That beautiful chorus The Messiah is belted out singing these words from the Bible. I love that He's my counselor. We ladies like to talk about stuff, and figure things out. He's the counselor. Nothing is too intense, tedious, emotional, or stressful to share with our Papa.

ISAIAH 11

We see that, all throughout the Bible, God is pointing us to our Lord and Savior Jesus Christ. Isaiah is talking of the righteous Branch that will grow out of Jesse. He was David's father, and they are ancestors of Jesus Christ, who will not come shooting two guns at once like the people in some futuristic movie. This is how Christ wages war: *"With righteousness shall he judge the poor, and reprove with equity for the meek of the earth: and he shall smite the earth with the rod of his mouth, and with the breath of his lips shall he slay the wicked."* Isaiah 11:4
And that is so true when you hear the brilliant things Jesus says in the New Testament, especially to the pesky Pharisees.

ISAIAH 14

Description of Satan is next, and also a description of us when we start thinking we're all that: *"How art thou fallen from heaven, O Lucifer, son of the morning! How art thou cut down to the ground, which didst weaken the nations! For thou hast said in thine heart, I will ascend into heaven, I will exalt my throne above the stars of God: I will sit also upon the mount of the congregation, in the sides of the north: I will ascend above the heights of the clouds; I will be like the most High."* Isaiah 14:12-14

ISAIAH 19 AND 26

God is getting fed up with sinful nations and here are His plans to smite them: *"In that day shall Egypt be like unto women: and it shall be afraid and fear because of the shaking of the hand of the Lord of hosts, which he shaketh over it."* Isaiah 19:16
There it is girls, we are the weaker sex if the cut-down insult here is that the fighters will be as women. Weaker doesn't mean bad or terrible or we are worthless. It just means men are stronger and we are to be cared for and cherished. I'm good with that.

"Thou wilt keep him in perfect peace, whose mind is stayed on thee: because he trusteth in thee." Isaiah 26:3
The "stayed on" part can be translated "steadfast" or "fixed." Right there is most of the wisdom we ever need for the rest of our lives. Everyone is searching for how to be at peace. It says right there that anyone whose mind is fixed on the Lord will be kept in perfect peace. That doesn't mean nothing bad is going to happen. We are circumstance-dependent too often. Whatever swarms about to engulf us, keeping our minds stayed on the Lord allows Him to keep us from despair.

ISAIAH 28

God is rebuking the stubborn people whom He tried to tell *"this is the rest wherewith ye may cause the weary to rest; and this is the refreshing, yet they would not hear."* Or translated simply, *"they would not listen."* Isaiah 28:12

"Wherefore hear the word of the Lord." Isaiah 28:14
And, yay you, that's what you're doing right now.

ISAIAH 31

So Isaiah tells us today that God *"will be very gracious unto thee at the voice of thy cry; when he shall hear it, he will answer thee. And though the Lord give you the bread of adversity, and the water of affliction, yet shall not thy teachers be removed into a corner any more, but thine eyes shall see thy teachers: and thine ears shall hear a word behind thee, saying, This is the way, walk ye in it, when ye turn to the right hand, and when ye turn to the left."* Isaiah 31:19-21

ISAIAH 40

"He shall feed his flock like a shepherd: he shall gather the lambs with his arms and carry them in his bosom, and shall gently lead those that are with young." Isaiah 40:11

ISAIAH 41

Here is a very sweet verse from Isaiah:
"For I the Lord thy God will hold thy right hand, saying unto thee, Fear not; I will help thee." Isaiah 41:13

ISAIAH 44

"I am the first, and I am the last." That alpha omega thingy. Isaiah 44:6

ISAIAH 48

"O that thou hadst hearkened to my commandments! Then had thy peace been as a river, and thy righteousness as the waves of the sea." Isaiah 48:18

ISAIAH 49

Okay if we ever start to feel like God has forgotten us, here is a reminder that He never will.

"But Zion said, The Lord hath forsaken me. Can a woman forget her nursing child? That she should not have compassion on the son of her womb?" Isaiah 49:14-15
Ha. God makes me laugh. Of course a mother can't forget her hungry baby.

ISAIAH 53

Jesus wasn't buff as not to threaten anyone; He's very approachable:
"For he shall grow up before him as a tender plant, and as a root out of a dry ground; he hath no form nor comeliness; and when we shall see him there is no beauty that we should desire him." Isaiah 53:2
Those descriptions can also be translated no "stately form" or no "splendor."

ISAIAH 55

"Hear, and your soul shall live." Isaiah 55:3

ISAIAH 64

"For since the beginning of the world men have not heard, nor perceived by the ear, neither hath the eye seen, O God, beside thee, what he hath prepared for him that waiteth for him." Isaiah 64:4
This is the y'all just wait, heaven's going to be amazing passage.

ISAIAH 66

"For all those things hath mine hand made, and all those things have been, saith the Lord; but to this man will I look, even to him that is poor and of a contrite spirit, and trembleth at my word." Isaiah 66:2
My husband wrote in the margin for contrite spirit = "crushed in heart."

JEREMIAH

Now we cruise into Jeremiah, whose name means "sent forth by the Lord." I would say the book of Jeremiah could be summed up in these four words: *"But they hearkened not."* Jeremiah 44:5.

Talking about what's going to go down if the people don't stop their rebellion to God:

"And their houses shall be turned unto others, with their fields and wives together, for I will stretch out my hand upon the inhabitants of the land, saith the Lord. For from the least of them every one is given to covetousness: and from the prophet even unto the priest every one dealeth falsely. They have healed also the hurt of the daughter of my people slightly, saying Peace, Peace: when there is no peace. Were they ashamed when they had committed abomination? Nay, they were not at all ashamed, neither could they blush: therefore they shall fall among them that fall: at the time that I visit them they shall be cast down, saith the Lord. Thus saith the Lord, Stand ye in the ways, and see, and ask for the old paths, where is the good way, and walk therein and ye shall find rest for your souls. But they said, 'We will not walk therein.'" Jeremiah 6:12-16

More spankin's from Jeremiah for us:
"Yet they hearkened not unto me, nor inclined their ear. . ." as in, they would not listen. Jeremiah 7:26

"But thou shalt say unto them, this is a nation that obeyeth not the voice of the Lord their God, nor receiveth correction, truth is perished, and is cut off from their mouth." Jeremiah 7:28

Can't really take this two ways: *"But if they will not obey, I will utterly pluck up and destroy that nation, saith The Lord."* Jeremiah 12

"This evil people, which refuse to hear my words, which walk in the imagination of their heart. . .they would not hear," meaning they would not listen. Jeremiah 13:10, 11

"Every one walketh after the imagination of his own heart . . . they shall return to me with their whole heart." Jeremiah 23:17, 24:7

"Yet ye have not hearkened unto me, saith the Lord . . . Ye have not heard my words." Jeremiah 25:7, 8
Have ye?

Our man Jeremiah speaks the truth and gets imprisoned and dumped in miry wells. Got to hate it for the guy.

Ezekiel

Now we are on to Ezekiel who has a chilling description of Satan, which is kind of a downer but the reason I like this passage is that it demonstrates that God rules over the enemy. The forces of evil are not stronger than God. It's long but we are up for plowing through this because if we don't know our enemy, we're in trubb-uhhhhhl. By the way, we are amazed by our prophet buddy Zeekie. He had to lie on his left side for 390 days to make a point. God's like, don't worry Zeekie if the people don't listen to you, *"for they will not hearken unto me"* either (Ezekiel 2:7). God also says, *"Thou art wiser than Daniel."* Ezekiel 28:3. I knew it! I knew it all along. Oh wait, He's talking to Ezekiel, not to me. Anyway, here's that thing about Satan, not that we care about him or anything:

Ezekiel 28

"Thou hast been in Eden the garden of God; every precious stone was thy covering, the sardius, topaz and the diamond, the beryl, the onyx, and the jasper, the sapphire, the emerald, and the carbuncle, and gold: the workmanship of thy tabrets and of thy pipes was prepared in thee in the day that thou wast created. Thou art the anointed cherub that covereth: and I have set thee so, thou wast upon the holy mountain of God; thou hast walked up and down in the midst of the stones of fire. Thou wast perfect in thy ways from the day that thou wast created, till iniquity was found in thee. By the multitude of thy merchandise they have filled the midst of thee with violence, and thou hast sinned; therefore I will cast thee as profane out of the mountain of God: and I will destroy thee, O covering cherub, from the midst of the stones of fire. Thine heart was lifted up because of thy beauty, thou hast corrupted thy wisdom by reason of thy brightness: I will cast thee to the ground, I will lay thee before kings, that they may behold thee. Thou hast defiled thy sanctuaries by the multitude of thine iniquities, by the iniquity of thy traffick; therefore will I bring forth a fire from the midst of thee, it shall devour thee, and I will bring thee to ashes upon the earth in the sight of all them that behold thee. All they that know thee among the people shall be astonished at thee, thou shalt be a terror, and never shalt thou be any more." Ezekiel 28:13-19

EZEKIEL 34

In these next three passages, God tells us how much He loves us:

"For thus saith the Lord God: Behold I, even I, will both search my sheep and seek them out ... And will deliver them out of all places where they have been scattered in the cloudy and dark day." Ezekiel 34:11, 12

EZEKIEL 36

"And I will put my spirit within you, and cause you to walk in my statutes, and ye shall keep my judgments, and do them." Ezekiel 36:27

EZEKIEL 38

"Neither will I hide my face any more from them: for I have poured out my spirit upon the house of Israel, saith the Lord God." Ezekiel 38:29

———⚍⚍⚍———

DANIEL

Now Daniel's not just some goober who sits back and lets thing happen. No. He and his buddies are taken away into captivity into Babylon but Daniel *"purposed in his heart"* that he would remain faithful to the true God. (Daniel 1:18) And by the way God knows all about astrology. Daniel 1:20 says that the king in Babylon found Daniel and his buds to be *"ten times better than all the magicians and astrologers."*

DANIEL 6

After Daniel survived getting thrown into the lions' den for praying to God, the Bible says it was *"because he believed in his God."*

"For he is the living God ... he delivereth and rescueth." Daniel 6:23, 26, 27

DANIEL 7

Talking about the "Ancient of days:"

"And there was given him dominion, and glory, and a kingdom, that all people, nations, and languages, should serve him: his dominion is an everlasting dominion, which shall not pass away, and his kingdom that which shall not be destroyed." Daniel 7:14

These kings in the book of Daniel though. They have no long term memory. It's like, "Oh. Wow there's this guy named Daniel who knows stuff." Another example: Help me out here. Nebuchadnezzar has this way ominous dream about a statue. Next thing he does is build a gold statue of himself. Not that bright.

Now I lovvvvve the first half of the book of Daniel. But when he starts explaining all these dreams with rams and goats I'm like what?

DANIEL 10
"Then said he unto me, fear not Daniel, for from the first day that thou didst set thine heart to understand, and to chasten thyself before thy God, thy words were heard, and I am come for thy words." Daniel 10:12

Like Daniel, we need to purpose in our hearts to follow God's ways. It won't happen by accident.

———— ∞ ————

HOSEA AND JOEL
Less TV, more Bible: *"My people are destroyed for lack of knowledge; because thou hast rejected knowledge, I will also reject thee."* Hosea 4

Jesus quotes this later, and says Yo, go find out what this means: *"For I desired mercy, and not sacrifice."* Hosea 6:6

"Therefore turn thou to thy God, keep mercy and judgment, and wait on thy God continually." Hosea 12:6.

That's all I've got. Now Joel. Not as in Billy.

"Therefore also now, saith the Lord, turn ye even unto me with all your heart … turn unto the Lord your God: for he is gracious and merciful, slow to anger, and of great kindness, and repenteth him of the evil." Joel 2:12, 13

This passage is huge, it has helped me when a crisis has hit, and I feel robbed of happiness during that phase of my life:
"And I will restore to you the years that the locust hath eaten." Joel 2:25

"Let the weak say, I am strong." Joel 3:10

MICAH AND SOME OTHER DUDES

"Even of late my people is risen up as an enemy: ye pull off the robe with the garment from them that pass by securely as men averse from war." *"But truly I am full of power by the spirit of the Lord, and of judgment, and of might."* Micah 2:8 and 3:8

"He hath shewed me, O man, what is good; and what doth the Lord require of thee, but to do justly, and to love mercy, and to walk humbly with thy God?" Micah 6:8

Somebody trying to sabotage your world? No biggee: *"Rejoice not against me O mine enemy; when I fall I shall arise."* Micah 7:8

"Why dost thou show me iniquity, and cause me to behold sorrow? for spoiling, and violence are before me: and there are that raise up strife and contention." Habbakuk 1:3. Don't be stirring up strife, no ma'am.

"My spirit remaineth among you: fear ye not." Haggai 2:5

Now that's cold: *"I smote you with blasting and with mildew and with hail … yet ye turned not to me, saith The Lord."* Haggai 2:17

"They are the eyes of the Lord, which run to and fro through the whole earth." Zech 4:10 He sees you when you're sleeping. He knows when you're awake. Not Santa, the Lord.

We've got to gravitate toward other Bible chicks: *"We will go with you, for we have heard that God is with you."* Zech 8:23

CHAPTER 23

NEW TESTAMENT TALK

⁃⁃⁃

We now come to the major turning point in the Bible where Jesus Christ is born. Scripture has convinced me that Jesus is God's son, but that is merely His manifestation.[44] What I mean is that Jesus is God, in the form of a man, much like ice is water, only frozen. The Holy Spirit is God too, the way steam is water too, only steamy. And so Jesus' birth was not the beginning of Jesus' life, but rather was the beginning of His time on Earth as the savior. Jesus has always been, just as God the Father always has. The four gospels, Matthew, Mark, Luke and John, tell us about His time here on Earth from slightly different viewpoints. The book of Acts comes next, and it is the exciting account of how the new Christian apostles spread Christianity after Jesus was crucified and resurrected. Paul's letters and other writings are much of the remainder of the New Testament.

⁃⁃⁃

MATTHEW

MATTHEW 4

Here is Satan tempting Jesus (does that guy ever give up?), Matthew 4:9: *"And saith unto him, All these things will I give thee, if thou wilt fall down and worship me. Then saith Jesus unto him, 'Get thee hence, Satan.'"*

Step back. I wrote in my margin here: what we worship takes control of our lives. And it's really annoying and funny how Satan quotes scripture to Jesus, trying to use the Bible against Him. Which so doesn't work. Quotes it right back at him.

Jesus to the disciples: *"And he saith unto them, 'Follow me, and I will make you fishers of men.'"* Matthew 4:19. The difference between catching fish and men is when you catch fish, they are alive and die, but when we catch men for Him, they were dead and brought to life. I got that idea from a speaker at the Fellowship of Christian Airline Personnel.

MATTHEW 5
One of Jesus' "beatitudes:" *"Blessed are the poor in spirit...blessed are ye, when men shall revile you, and persecute you, and shall say all manner of evil against you falsely, for my sake. Rejoice, and be exceeding glad; for great is your reward in heaven, for so persecuted they the prophets that were before you."* Matthew 5:3,11,12

MATTHEW 6
Three times in chapter 6 Jesus says, *"take no thought for your life,"* also translated *"do not be anxious."*

MATTHEW 7
Not everyone shall enter heaven. Why? Because they weren't nice enough? Nope. Jesus will say, *"I never knew you."* Matthew 7:23. That's it. We really could have pretty much slapped that verse on the first page of this book and been done.

MATTHEW 10
"Think not that I am come to send peace on earth, I came not to send peace, but a sword." Matthew 10:34. The purpose of this passage is to convict people they need Him. He's not coming to tell us everything is awesome, keep up the great work.

MATTHEW 11
"Come unto me, all ye that labour and are heavy laden, and I will give you rest. Take my yoke upon you, and learn of me: for I am meek and lowly in heart: and ye shall find rest unto your souls. For my yoke is easy, and my burden is light." Matthew 11:28-30

Jesus Christ is ready and waiting. He said this wonderful thing right there, and yet, it is slightly insane how offended our society is by Christ. He saw it coming: *"Blessed is he, who shall not be offended in me."* Matthew 11:6

MATTHEW 12
"He that is not with me is against me, and he that gathereth not with me scattereth abroad." Matthew 12:30. We cannot be religiously neutral. Everyone has a belief system, a faith system, whether or not he realizes it.

MATTHEW 16
"For whosoever will save his life shall lose it: and whosoever will lose his life for my sake shall find it. For what is a man profited, if he shall gain the whole world, and lose his own soul? Or what shall a man give in exchange for his soul?" Matthew 16:25, 26

MATTHEW 20
"Whosoever will be great among you, let him be your minister: And whosoever will be chief among you, let him be your servant." Matthew 20:26, 27
Ladies, when we make ourselves the greatest servant in our home, we are obeying the Lord Jesus Christ.

MATTHEW 22
"Jesus said unto him, 'Thou shalt love the Lord thy God with all thy heart, and with all thy soul, and with all thy mind. This is the first and great commandment. And the second is like unto it, Thou shalt love thy neighbour as thyself. On these two commandments hang all the law and the prophets." Matthew 22:37-40
Yes this is the golden rule. For some reason folks like to focus on the second part. Notice the first part is to love God with all your heart.

MATTHEW 24
Talking of the second coming here:
"For as the lightning cometh out of the east, and shineth even unto the west; so shall also the coming of the Son of man be ... and they shall see the Son of man coming in the clouds of heaven with power and great glory." Matthew 24:27, 30

I like this answer Jesus gives, for the next time my child keeps asking about dessert: *"Behold, I have told you before."* Matthew 24:25

MATTHEW 25
"Well done, thou good and faithful servant; thou hast been faithful over a few things, I will make thee ruler over many things; enter thou into the joy of thy lord." Matthew 25:21

"Inasmuch as ye have done it unto one of the least of these my brethren, ye have done it unto me." Matthew 25:40

———

MARK

MARK 3
Talking about Jesus here: *"... he had looked round about on them with anger, being grieved for the hardness of their hearts..."* Mark 3:5

"How can Satan cast out Satan? And if a house be divided against itself, that house cannot stand." Jesus said in Mark 3:23 and 25. So we don't need to waste our lives fussing and fighting with our husbands. This is rebellion to God sistah.

MARK 4
"And he said unto them, 'Why are ye so fearful? how is it that ye have no faith?'" Mark 4:40. That was when Jesus calmed the storm out on the sea and His disciple buddies be like: Jesus calmin' even the sea, ain't never seen that befo. Child?

MARK 5
Loving this part when this sweet suffering lady knew if she could just touch Jesus' cloak in a crowd of people, perhaps she would be made well. Which He did, and afterward He said to her, *"Daughter, thy faith hath made thee whole; go in peace, and be whole of thy plague."* Mark 5:34

Mark 9

The father of a sick child goes to Jesus for help. *"Jesus said unto him, 'If thou canst believe, all things are possible to him that believeth.' And straightway the father of the child cried out, and said with tears, 'Lord I believe; help my unbelief.'"* Mark 9:23-24

That can be our prayer when our faith is weak.

Mark 11

"What things soever ye desire, when ye pray, believe that ye receive them, and ye shall have them." Mark 11:24. There's ye olde Ask And Ye Shall Receive plaque, it really is in the Bible.

Mark 13

When under attack, Jesus says Yo, no worries, *"for it is not ye that speak, but the Holy Ghost."* Mark 13:11

Mark 14

Before Jesus is crucified, willingly by the way, He could've totally run away or had God send hundreds of angels to rescue Him, it was agonizingly terrible and He says, *"My soul is exceeding sorrowful unto death,"* Mark 14:34 and I wrote in my Bible: "so he prayed."

Luke

Luke 1

An angel is talking of John the Baptist here to his parents: *"he shall be filled with the Holy Ghost,"* Luke 1:15.

This chapter of Luke mentions the Holy Ghost several more times including talking about Mary. Which is cool. One question is, Mary was visiting her cousin Elizabeth who was expecting to give birth to John, but why did Mary not stay for Elizabeth's childbirth? I thought that was like a chick thing back in the day and midwives came, you were surrounded by the ladies in your family. I dunno. I totally would've stayed.

LUKE 3
John says, *"Be content with your wages,"* Luke 3:14.

LUKE 4
More talk of the Holy Ghost and how Jesus was filled with it, in chapter 4.

Jesus buh-lows everybody away with all this wise talk. They look at one another like Say What? *"Is not this Joseph's son?"* Luke 4:22

LUKE 6
The Pharisees are picking on Jesus and of course He totally takes care of that and they go away scratching their heads in amazement but what I love here specifically is when He asks them, *"Have you not read ...?"* Luke 6:3. He's referring to King David here and we can wonder when clueless people get combative toward Christians, most likely they haven't read. Don't you people know? Haven't you read? Aren't you familiar with God's word? We cannot have an intelligent conversation with you people unless you've read the thing.

Before Jesus made the big move to recruit his 12 disciple guys, He *"continued all night in prayer."* Luke 6:12. That motivates me to pray five minutes for my decisions, if even the Lord Himself prayed all night.

"If ye lend to them of whom ye hope to receive, what thank have ye? for sinners also lend to sinners, to receive as much again. But love your enemies, and do good, and lend, hoping for nothing again; and your reward shall be great, and ye shall be the children of the Highest, for he is kind unto the unthankful and to the evil. Be ye therefore merciful, as your Father also is merciful." Luke 6:34-36

LUKE 7
Jesus is speaking of the lady who washed His feet with her hair: *"Wherefore I say unto thee, Her sins, which are many, are forgiven, for she loved much: but to whom little is forgiven, the same loveth little."* Luke 7:47. And then after that He says to her, *"Thy faith hath saved thee, go in peace."* Luke 7:50

LUKE 8

"...*having heard the word, keep it.*" Luke 8:15. Some other translations of this passage are "cling to it" and "hold it fast."

"*Take heed therefore how ye hear* ..." Luke 8:18
Pay attention to what you are hearing. What is persuading you? Whom are you listening to? What ideas are you believing? Take heed.

LUKE 11

"*Lord teach us to pray,*" Luke 11:1 and then Jesus tells them the Lord's prayer.

"*If ye then, being evil, know how to give good gifts unto your children, how much more shall your Father give the Holy Spirit to them that ask him?*" Luke 11:13

LUKE 12

"*The Holy Ghost shall teach you in the same hour what ye ought to say.*" Luke 12:12. No need to fret about responding to adversaries because the Holy Spirit will tell us what to say. That's a comfort.

LUKE 15

Lost sheep parable explains how happy the Lord is when one of His peeps returns to Him in his heart: "*And when he hath found it, he layeth it on his shoulders, rejoicing.*" Luke 15:5

LUKE 18

Most arrogant prayer award goes to this Pharisee who said, ahem, fix the hair, sniff: "*God I thank thee, that I am not as other men are.*" Luke 18:11

LUKE 23

After Jesus died, the people who crucified Him said, "*Certainly this was a righteous man.*" Luke 23:47
Yeah, you dummy.

———∞∞∞———

JOHN

JOHN 1

"He it is, who coming after me is preferred before me, whose shoe's latchet I am not worthy to unloose." John 1:27.

John the Baptist is saying, Look I should not even untie this guy's shoelace, I'm so nothing compared to our Lord.

JOHN 3

Talking to Nicodemus, who asked how can someone get to go to heaven? *"Jesus answered and said unto him, 'Verily, verily I say unto thee, Except a man be born again, he cannot see the kingdom of God.'"* John 3:3

"For God so loved the world, that he gave his only begotten Son, that whosoever believeth in him should not perish, but have everlasting life." John 3:16

My husband wrote "receive" by "believeth." I mean even Satan believes in Jesus. This passage doesn't mean we merely believe He existed but rather receive Him as our savior. Big difference.

JOHN 8

I don't get why Jesus didn't clear up that whole being born in Bethlehem thing. I guess He would not have been crucified. *"Shall Christ come out of Galilee?"* people said. John 8:41

Jesus says we can't go all God this God that without also meaning Jesus Christ too. *"If God were your father, you would love me."* John 8:42

JOHN 10

"...and he calleth his own sheep by name, and leadeth them out." John 10:3

In the margin of my Bible I wrote, "Jesus is the shepherd and the door."

JOHN 11

The Pharisees weren't bullying Jesus just for fun; they were skeert. *"The Romans shall come and take away … our nation."* John 11:48

Now that's cold when Caiaphas that high priest dude says to the Jesus haters: *"Ye know nothing at all."* John 11:49

JOHN 14

"Let not your heart be troubled, neither let it be afraid." John 14:27

JOHN 18

Jump back. Bad guys came to capture Jesus, He said *"I am he,"* and they *"went backward, and fell to the ground."* John 18:6
I heard that.

JOHN 20

John 20: *"Peace be unto you,"* vs 19, *"Receive ye the Holy Ghost,"* vs 23, *"be not faithless, but believing,"* vs 27 and *"blessed are they that have not seen, and yet have believed."*
I was windexing the kitchen windows the other night, after dark, and because it was dark I couldn't see the windows getting clean. But I've done it so many times that I knew they were getting clean. I thought about faith and believing even when we can't see. We have to trust that the results are going to be what they always are: that my windows are sparkly and that God is faithful. Who knew windexing could be so profound?

———— ❧ ————

ROMANS

ROMANS 1

"For I am not ashamed of the gospel of Christ: for it is the power of God unto salvation to every one that believeth: to the Jew first, and also to the Greek." Romans 1:16

"For the invisible things of him from the creation of the world are clearly seen ... so they are without excuse." Romans 1:20

People have no excuse but to acknowledge the Almighty as we are surrounded by His creation.

ROMANS 4

As a mother, I'm tough on my children. My rules are not arbitrary strictness just for fun, they are the things of God that we value and want to instill in our children. We sometimes have rebellion or resistance from our children because of this. We deal with that and call it out for what it is. If we never have resistance from our children, maybe there is something wrong; maybe there is nothing against which to rebel? *"...for where no law is, there is no transgression."* Romans 4:15

ROMANS 6

"Let not sin therefore reign in your mortal body, that ye should obey it in the lusts thereof." Romans 6:12 Paul says that whatever we obey, that's what we're servants to. *"Know ye not, that to whom ye yield yourselves servants to obey, his servants ye are to whom ye obey..."* Romans 6:16

ROMANS 7

O wretched chick that I am! Romans 7:24

ROMANS 8

"And we know that all things work together for good to them that love God, to them who are the called according to his purpose." Romans 8:28.

Bad news is, unbelievers (let's call them pre-believers) sometimes are heard mistakenly saying that everything happens for a reason, everything works out, everything is for their good. Mm, no. The scriptures tell us everything works for good for those who love God, and who have been called to act for His purposes.

ROMANS 9

"O man, who art thou that repliest against God?" Romans 9:20

Now see? This is why we love the King James Version. You just can't beat that way of putting it. Who am I to question? Who am I to reply against God?

ROMANS 14

"Let us therefore follow after the things which make for peace, and things wherewith one may edify another." Romans 14:19

What percentage of our time is spent following trends, celebrities, our favorite TV series, or what's going on with Facebook? And what percentage of our time is spent on the things that will edify ourselves and others? Don't make me draw you a pie graph now.

---

1 CORINTHIANS

1 CORINTHIANS 1

"God is faithful, by whom ye were called unto the fellowship of his Son Jesus Christ our Lord." 1 Corinthians 1:9

You know being a grammar nerd, I like to play around with sentence diagrams in my head (isn't everyone else doing that?) and I wonder if we could do a little switcharoo on that "faithful" word there and change the way we think about it. If we thought about it as less of an adjective and more as a predicate nominative, then it would be something like this: God equals faithful. God *is* faithful(ness.) Faithfulness *is* God. God defines faithfulness.

Lose you? Sorry about that. My quirkiness aside, I'm just saying God's faithful. I love that we can count on that. So much is not reliable in this world, so much will let us down, but He never will. That doesn't mean we always get our way, it just means He won't let us down.

God can do great things when we obey: *"But God hath chosen the foolish things of the world to confound the wise, and God hath chosen the weak things of the world to confound the things which are mighty."* 1 Corinthians 1:27

Triumphant Womanhood

1 CORINTHIANS 2

"But God hath revealed them unto us by his Spirit, for the Spirit searcheth all things, yea, the deep things of God." 1 Corinthians 2:10

Christians recognize and appreciate the great depth contained in the scriptures and found in a relationship led by the Holy Spirit. Condescending secular discussions begin to sound like a bunch of whatever, compared to the deep things of God found in the Bible and revealed to us by the Holy Spirit.

1 CORINTHIANS 3

"Know ye not that ye are the temple of God, and that the Spirit of God dwelleth in you?" 1 Corinthians 3:16

Our bodies are the temple of the Holy Spirit, so we kind of need to take care of them because of that (one reason.) This is the passage that helps us articulate why it matters how we look.

1 CORINTHIANS 7

"Let not the wife depart from her husband, but and if she depart, let her remain unmarried, or be reconciled to her husband; and let not the husband put away his wife." 1 Corinthians 7:10-11

Not my doctrine on divorce, it's the Bible. And why argue with it? Why be scared of it? We should be grabbing hold of it like a life preserver as we're drowning. What's scarier: staying with a difficult marriage or defying God's word? We're supposed to fear Him and Him alone. God's word is our umbrella of protection.

"And the woman which hath an husband that believeth not, and if he be pleased to dwell with her, let her not leave him. For the unbelieving husband is sanctified by the wife, and the unbelieving wife is sanctified by the husband; else were your children unclean, but now are they holy." 1 Corinthians 7:13-14

Well that just fixes all the problems Christians might agonize over if one of them is a believer and the other is not. Paul goes on to say:

"For what knowest thou, O wife, whether thou shalt save thy husband? or how knowest thou, O man, whether thou shalt save thy wife?" 1 Corinthians 7:16

That is such a ray of hope for a wife who is in a painful marriage with an unbeliever.

1 CORINTHIANS 9
Okay Paul cuh-racks me up in this next passage. I can relate: he says he is fighting the good Christian fight, *"not as one that beateth the air."* 1 Corinthians 9:26 Sometimes I feel like I am just punching the air and no good comes from my efforts. Everything I do is futile. That thought is not from God but rather from Satan. Who seriously needs to get a life.

1 CORINTHIANS 10
"Whether therefore ye eat, or drink, or whatsoever ye do, do all to the glory of God." 1 Corinthians 10:31
Everything we're about needs to be about God's glory, if we want to live a triumphant life. I've had to do some evaluating of our family's activities, and make sure that they are glorifying God, and not just conforming to the world. Or at least not de-glorifying Him.

Glorifying Him is the whole reason we are alive. It's the place where we find true joy. If He's our focus then glorifying Him is what spills out of us. If it's not spilling, we might want to evaluate where our loyalty lies. Whom are we worshipping? That's whom we glorify. (Generally if it's not Christ it's our own self.)

1 CORINTHIANS 11
"... the head of every man is Christ, and the head of the woman is the man, and the head of Christ is God." 1 Corinthians 11:3
This is God's order of things. This is where I got the concept for those helpful marriage charts, with Christ as the head, husband next, then wife. This does not mean that women are ditzy and men have this No Girls Allowed sign on their treehouse. We might think outsmarting or avoiding any authority or leadership is freeing but it's actually the opposite: it's bondage. We're only outsmarting ourselves. And that's not very smart.

1 CORINTHIANS 13

We've got to include that famous passage everyone reads out loud at their wedding, and the King James has it "charity" rather than "love." I like the word charity because it implies that the person doesn't really deserve it. And you know it is easy to say these pretty words at a wedding but much harder actually to do in marriage. Once the honeymoon is over. Literally. A strong marriage is not always built upon feelings – no one can sustain good feelings – but is rather based on charitable actions. I love my husband. But there are always going to be ups and downs in marriage, "vexations and grief" as Jane Austen says.

I don't get why we think marriage should be based on feelings every single day forever and ever. Are jobs based on feelings? Do people get up and go to work because they feel like it? I shudder to think what I'd be like if I based my actions on my feelings. Especially in traffic. Do you even know how slowly people drive in the South? That green light is not getting any greener. Here is that wedding ceremony passage: *"Charity suffereth long, and is kind, charity envieth not, charity vaunteth not itself, is not puffed up, Doth not behave itself unseemly, seeketh not her own, is not easily provoked, thinketh no evil, Rejoiceth not in iniquity, but rejoiceth in the truth: Beareth all things, believeth all things, hopeth all things, endureth all things."* 1 Corinthians 13:4-8

1 CORINTHIANS 14

For this next passage, we are going to have a dialogue with Paul. I promise you 100 percent that I am not changing anything he says. It is completely intact from the King James Version. I'm only responding the way we ladies might respond when we first hear what he says. Here we go.

"Let your women keep silence in the churches," 1 Corinthians 14:34

I'm frowning. I wonder if I trust this whole Bible situation at all and Paul hasn't even finished his sentence.

"for it is not permitted unto them to speak, but they are commanded to be under obedience, as also saith the law." 1 Corinthians 14:34

I might even have some smug neck action going at this point, and a disapproving grunt. But we keep listening anyway:

"And if they will learn anything let them ask their own husbands at home: for it is a shame for women to speak in the church." 1 Corinthians 14:35

Now hold up. Who you tryin' ta tell not to speak. Boy you trippin.

"What?" 1 Corinthians 14:36

I'll tell you what. After I pop you upside the head with this book.

"Came the word of God out from you?" 1 Corinthians 14:36

I didn't say I wrote no Bible, I'm just saying don't be telling me to be silent. Shoot.

"Or came it unto you only?" 1 Corinthians 14:36

Well all right then. I know it didn't come just to me. I hear what you're saying. Maybe.

1 CORINTHIANS 15

Having forgiven Paul for all that in Chapter 14: Prepare yourself, here is one of my all time favorite scriptures, are you ready?

"I die daily." 1 Corinthians 15:31

My Bible I had when I was growing up says, *"I die every day."* (RSV) Don't we all totally get that, in the sense that we choose every day to die to self, and not live for ourselves but rather for the Lord? Giving our life to Him (once we've received our salvation) is a daily, ongoing thing. The baffling part is, when we die to self, that's when we really begin living. "I die daily" sounds terrible from our culture's way of looking at things. Why would anybody sign up for this Christianity thing? Here's the ad campaign: "Christianity for you, free of charge, all you have to do is die daily." Sounds kind of bleak. But Godly girls like us are thinking eternally. So we realize it's actually the secret to joy.

Talking of Christ's return: *"Behold, I shew you a mystery, We shall not all sleep, but we shall all be changed, in a moment, in the twinkling of an eye, at the last trump, for the trumpet shall sound, and the dead shall be raised incorruptible, and we shall be changed."* 1 Corinthians 15:51-52.

He's coming back baby. Do a dance, He's coming back. Bust a move, He's coming back.

———— ✐ ————

2 CORINTHIANS

2 CORINTHIANS 1
*"... we were pressed out of measure, above strength, insomuch that we despaired even of life: But we had the sentence of death in ourselves, that we should not trust in ourselves, but in God which raiseth the dead." *2 Corinthians 1:8-9
You know we could read that scripture right there and explain so much. It answers the question "why" in so many different circumstances. God is telling us He allows things to press us beyond our strength, so that we would not trust in ourselves but rather trust in Him. That's the reason. Snap.

God *"hath also sealed us, and given the earnest of the Spirit in our hearts."* 2 Corinthians 1:22
There's that earnest thing we're going to hear about again in chapter 5. Paul is saying: Yo, here's our earnest, here's our guarantee that all this stuff I'm saying to you is not just crazy talk.

2 CORINTHIANS 2
*"For we are unto God a sweet savour of Christ, in them that are saved, and in them that perish: to the one we are the savour of death unto death, and to the other the savour of life unto life." *2 Corinthians 2:15-16
It's nice to know that if someone is repelled by Christians, and perhaps finds that we "stinketh," just shake the dust baby, shake the dust.

2 CORINTHIANS 3
*"... our sufficiency is of God." *2 Corinthians 3:5
Par-tay! There's no emptiness or searching, when we look to Him for every little thing and that's sufficient.

If our nation really values liberty then we will value the Lord Jesus Christ: *"…when it shall turn to the Lord, the vail shall be taken away. Now the Lord is that Spirit: and where the Spirit of the Lord is, there is liberty."* 2 Corinthians 3:16-17

We as believers reflect His glory: *"But we all, with open face beholding as in a glass the glory of the Lord, are changed into the same image from glory to glory."* 2 Corinthians 3:18

"… Christ, who is the image of God." 2 Corinthians 4:4
Can't separate the Father from the Son. If you're not referring to Jesus, then you're not referring to God.

"We are troubled on every side, yet not distressed, we are perplexed, but not in despair: persecuted, but not forsaken, cast down, but not destroyed…" 2 Corinthians 3:8-9
Paul is encouraging us toward hope when he says that when troubles come, God's not going to let those destroy us. We will triumph.

2 Corinthians 5
God *"hath given unto us the earnest of the Spirit."* 2 Corinthians 5:5
That's our guarantee that all this Jesus talk is for real. It's the difference between Christianity and every other religion. In the Old Testament when Elijah said to the Baal worshipers in the time of king Ahab: okay let's see who can make fire come from heaven. Elijah prayed to God, some serious fire came down. The Baal guys shouted and flipped out for hours trying to get their little pitiful make believe Baal to send some fire, but there's not going to be any fire. We have the real God and the Holy Spirit is our earnest that proves that.

God *"… who hath reconciled us to himself by Jesus Christ, and hath given to us the ministry of reconciliation."* 2 Corinthians 5:18
Normally the What Would Jesus Do concept irritates the fire out of me. One, I like to be difficult. But two, if you think about it, we can't and shouldn't try to be like Christ in the full sense because, um, we can't save the world. We can't be a deity. We can't be perfect. Trying is spooky. And Jesus didn't have a family as God desires other men to, because that would've muddled up everything.

One, a good husband does not gallivant all over the place ignoring his own wife, like Jesus would've had to do. And two, or is that three, somebody figure that out for me, Jesus could not have had children or we'd have this bizarre race of Jesus children running around who were part-deity.

That grumpiness aside, this scripture (if you even remember what it said at this point, bonus points for you) is telling us that we must do our part to reconcile to others the way Christ reconciled us to Himself. This means we have to have some mercy action going on in our hearts, eh? Mercy is not giving people what they deserve. For example, a quote in my son's Instagram said this: "You deserve a high five. In the face. With a chair."

So yeah, not doing that is merciful.

2 CORINTHIANS 11
Now Paul warns us against crazies, who try to pose as somebody but really they're false, deceitful people, and the like. Women especially can be taken by these sorts of fakes. Nice sweet ladies like you and I love everybody, we're tenderhearted, everybody's just so sweet and good, we were created to follow (our husbands) and if we ourselves are trustworthy it's easy to think everyone else is. So we ladies need to be aware that these kind of liars are out there: *"And no marvel, for Satan himself is transformed into an angel of light."* 2 Corinthians 11:14

I love "no marvel." Paul's all: No marvel, no biggee. Don't be surprised, folks. People are trying to deceive us, it's going to happen, just don't let it fool you. Wink.

GALATIANS

GALATIANS 1
"For do I now persuade men, or God? or do I seek to please men? for if I yet pleased men, I should not be the servant of Christ." Galatians 1:10

I have to remind myself often that the moment anything I am doing becomes about what other people think, it has started to be about me and stopped being about God. I have stopped being about God. And that scares me. As it ought.

"I lie not," Galatians 1:20
Paul it's okay, we believe you.

GALATIANS 2
"I live by the faith of the Son of God ..." Galatians 2:20
Every religion places its faith in something. Ours is in the real deal, the true Son of God. Without the Son of God, we could just say, Oh I have faith in cucumbers, or I place my faith in zebras. Faith in humanitarian issues, faith in environmental efforts, faith in unBiblical progressive ideas. Fill in your brilliant blank. We can do that, but we won't have any Holy Spirit action going on and so any other religion ultimately gets us nowhere. Roger that? Bravo tango. Charlie foxtrot. That's a copy, over. Sometimes people who are married to pilots think they know like three things about airplanes? And then start talking that way. Just for fun.

GALATIANS 3
"O foolish Galatians, who hath bewitched you, that ye should not obey the truth?" Galatians 3:1
Might need to be asking myself if I get off track in my faith: O less than triumphant woman, who hath bewitched you? And then let their bewitching bewitch no more.

GALATIANS 4
"God hath sent forth the Spirit of his Son into your hearts, crying Abba, Father." Galatians 4:6
So, did the funky rock group ABBA know they were naming themselves after the Father? One has to wonder, as one spins around to the song Dancing Queen with Atlanta journalist Jennifer Brett, who by the way says the following: "Haters gone hate and Galatians gone Galate."

"Am I therefore become your enemy, because I tell you the truth?" Galatians 4:16
Preach it, Paul. We can handle some truth.

GALATIANS 5
"Stand fast," Galatians 5:1. Yes sir Paul, we are standing fast, *"therefore in the liberty wherewith Christ hath made us free, and be not entangled again with the yoke of bondage."* He is imploring us to stay strong and not slip back into our old ways. I love the way he puts it: *"be not entangled."* There's this constant struggle, this constant war between our Spirit and our flesh. We have to keep our eyes on God, else we are vulnerable to get all tangled up in a yoke of bondage.

"Ye did run well: who did hinder you that ye should not obey the truth?" Galatians 5:7
Who's been hindering you girlfriend? Probably those same people who were be-witching you before.

"But the fruit of the Spirit is love, joy, peace, longsuffering, gentleness, goodness, faith, meek-ness, temperance: against such there is no law." Galatians 5:22-23
Can't arrest me for doing any of that. There's no law against these attributes. There can be no objection against any of these attributes. They are not something to work for and strive for and pride oneself in, however. It's the other way around. All of these traits are about to flow out of us when we are tight with the Lord on a daily basis. And the only way to be tight with Him is to spend time with Him.

GALATIANS 6
"And let us not be weary in well doing, for in due season we shall reap, if we faint not." Galatians 6:9
I'm fainting not.

EPHESIANS

EPHESIANS 1
"... the earnest of our inheritance..." Ephesians 1:14

This passage, like 2 Corinthians, tells us that the Holy Spirit is our earnest, our guarantee that this whole salvation through Christ thing is the real deal.

EPHESIANS 2

"For by grace are ye saved through faith, and that not of yourselves, it is the gift of God: not of works, lest any man should boast." Ephesians 2:8-9

We can easily slip into thinking we're so great and forget that nothing we do or have is boast worthy. Rather, every bit of it comes from God as a gift to us. I adore author and columnist Thomas Sowell's writing. But I was really disappointed when I read on his website that he denied that he has been given any sort of gift with his writing. He had the chance to give all the glory to his Creator, or even a little bit of glory to his Creator. Instead, he took the glory for himself and said there is no gift at all, and that he'd worked very hard to become a skillful writer.

Sorry dude but if that were true, it would mean that the only reason the rest of us don't have syndicated newspaper columns is because we're just not working as hard as he is. We could all compete as Olympic runners if we'd only work hard enough, the erroneous thinking goes. Hard work is extremely necessary, because we are developing our God-given gifts. We have to meet the Lord half way. But ultimately, no matter how hard I work, I'm not getting signed as a Rockette.

"For through him we both have access by one Spirit unto the Father." Ephesians 2:18

I like that Paul puts it this way, that the Holy Spirit gives us access to God the Father. The Holy Spirit is our Twitter account to God, it puts us on His Facebook page, it gives us his cell phone number. If we ignore that, we're thtupid.

"In whom ye also are builded together for an habitation of God through the Spirit." Ephesians 2:22

The Spirit dwells in us. It's kind of amazing to realize this about ourselves. And a relief, because we don't have to conjure up greatness in our own strength. We rely on the working of the Holy Spirit.

EPHESIANS 3

"For this cause I bow my knees ..." Ephesians 3:14

It makes me cry every single time I hear a good singer belt out the part that says "fall on your knees" in O Holy Night. It might make you cry to hear me sing it but for a different reason.

"Now unto him that is able to do exceeding abundantly above all that we ask or think, according to the power that worketh in us, unto him be the glory ..." Ephesians 3:20

When we get discouraged, we can remember that God has not forgotten us believers; and He can do exceedingly abundantly more than we ever ask or think. Wow. This passage is the: Child, anything beyond your wildest imagination passage, multiply that by about a billion, that's what God is able to do for us. Do we care, or do we watch reality TV?

EPHESIANS 4

"I therefore, the prisoner of the Lord, beseech you that ye walk worthy of the vocation wherewith ye are called, With all lowliness and meekness, with longsuffering, forbearing one another in love." Ephesians 4:1-2

This whole talk of being a prisoner for Christ was not a literary allegory thing. Paul is actually in jail y'all. We love Paul, our boy's in jail and he's writing letters to glorify God and encourage entire cities throughout the Roman Empire to love and regard His ways.

"Let all bitterness, and wrath, and anger, and clamour, and evil speaking, be put away from you, with all malice: and be ye kind one to another, tenderhearted, forgiving one another, even as God for Christ's sake hath forgiven you." Ephesians 4:31-32

Now this is a very important scripture to commit to memory. We women can get our feathers ruffled, can't we. It's so easy to get fired up in our relationships. We have to guard against this tendency to be pugnacious by being forgiving in our relationships. Even if no one asked us to forgive them. And they probably won't. But I am so over that because I already forgave.

"Wives, submit yourselves unto your own husbands, as unto the Lord. For the husband is the head of the wife, even as Christ is the head of the church: and he is the savior of the body." Ephesians 4:22-23

Hoop, there it is.

EPHESIANS 5

"... the wife see that she reverence her husband." Ephesians 5:33

We can get a little comfortable and familiar with our hubbies and forget that God would have us reverence them.

EPHESIANS 6

"Finally, my brethren, be strong in the Lord, and in the power of his might. Put on the whole armor of God, that ye may be able to stand against the wiles of the devil. For we wrestle not against flesh and blood, but against principalities, against powers, against the rulers of the darkness of this world, against spiritual wickedness in high places. Wherefore take unto you the whole armour of God, that ye may be able to withstand in the evil day, and having done all, to stand. Stand therefore, having your loins girt about with truth, and having on the breastplate of righteousness, and your feet shod with the preparation of the gospel of peace: faith, wherewith ye shall be able to quench all the fiery darts of the wicked. And take the helmet of salvation, and the sword of the Spirit, which is the word of God: Praying always ..." Ephesians 6:10-18

One of my purposes in writing to you is spiritual warfare. Our spiritual enemy hates families, he hates marriage, he hates the truth. If we ladies will all just keep being feisty, selfish, and oblivious to Biblical counsel, then Satan can kick back, curl up on a chaise lounge on the front porch and take a nap. Drink a smoothie. But I would add that I'm not actually about Satan because he's just a whatever. I'm ultimately about the things of God. Spiritual warfare cup's half full. If you will. Oh and we will.

PHILIPPIANS

PHILIPPIANS 1

"But I would ye should understand, brethren, that the things which happened unto me have fallen out rather unto the furtherance of the gospel ..." Philippians 1:12
Well I look at that passage this way, for me personally: I can trust God that my past mistakes and suffering help me to proclaim the gospel. This verse tells us to view the junk in life that has "fallen out" in a hopeful way. No wallowing, just triumphing. I really do not think I could have written this book without the many times of "falling out" God allowed in my life as times of painful learning. Could I maybe be done with adversity now? Probably not.

"Only let your conversation be as it becometh the gospel of Christ ..." Philippians 1:27
When you read the King James Version of the Bible, do you ever feel like you have a lisp? *"As it becometh."* Lisp or not, we ladies seriously need to dwell on this passage and take it as a command because we are sometimes guilty of not having very nice conversation about other people. Otherwise known as, "gossip." And gothip doth not becometh the gothpel of Chrithst. Tho thtop it.

PHILIPPIANS 2

"Let nothing be done through strife or vainglory; but in lowliness of mind let each esteem others better than themselves." Philippians 2:3
The Bible is telling us to chill on the strife. God desires for us not to bask in our own vanity, which stirs up strife with people. It's handy that He tells us what He does want us to do after He tells us what He doesn't want us to do: Esteem others as better than ourselves. That'll take care of that right there. It's famous Christians in the public eye who ignore passages like that and have no humility, who end up making us all look goofy. Speaking of humble:

I'm his: *"... he humbled himself, and became obedient unto death ..."* Philippians 2:8
Kind of makes you want to be obedient to God's word. If Christ could willingly die for my sins, I'm up for doing what He asks of me. Whatever it ends up being, isn't going to be quite as bad as getting nailed to a cross most likely.

"For it is God which worketh in you ..." Philippians 2:13
Sometimes as a Mom I feel extremely incapable and inadequate. Then I remember this whole parenting situation is God working in me. He can handle it.

"Do all things without murmurings and disputings," Philippians 2:14
Also translated: "grumbling or questioning."

"Yea, and if I be offered upon the sacrifice and serve of your faith, I joy, and rejoice with you all." Philippians 2:17
Am I that committed to do whatever it takes to serve someone else's faith? Yea. Hoping so. We love big, dramatic sacrifices. Ones that make headlines. Well that's not much of a sacrifice now is it. A real sacrifice would be something that is done quietly and no one ever knows about it but God. Mothers are doing that every day.

PHILIPPIANS 3
"That I may know him, and the power of his resurrection, and the fellowship of his sufferings ..." Philippians 3:10
Paul wants to know God above all. So should we. And there's that fellowship of suffering action there, which comes with the territory in being a born-again Christian.

PHILIPPIANS 4
"Rejoice in the Lord alway: and again I say, Rejoice. Let your moderation be known unto all men. The Lord is at hand. Be careful for nothing; but in every thing by prayer and supplication which thanksgiving let your requests be made known unto God. And the peace of God, which passeth all understanding, shall keep your hearts and minds through Christ Jesus. Finally, brethren, whatsoever things are true, whatsoever things are honest, whatsoever things are just, whatsoever things are pure, whatsoever things are lovely, whatsoever things are of good report, if there be any virtue, and if there be any praise, think on these things." Philippians 4:8
I have made my children write this puppy down on paper when they get all negatah-crazy. I love how the Bible tells us exactly how to have a joyful life. It's

right there. The Bible is bursting at the seams with wisdom. God telling us how to give Him control of our minds and hearts, rather than our thoughts controlling us. And that's a good thing too because if my thoughts were in control, there would be a whole lot of Oreo cookie eating going on in my world.

"... *for I have learned, in whatsoever state I am, therewith to be content.*" Philippians 4:11

O those who readeth, if we would only pay attention to that bit of wisdom on a regular basis, we would all avoid a lot of heartache and drama. I try to look at it like resisting my circumstances is rebellion to God. Here is my life, here is what God has for me, it's time to be content and stop waiting for everything to be the way we want it. It's hard to do, it can take a lifetime to reach the point where, whatever's dragging us down or not going our way, we are in the habit of releasing right away and saying: Not controlling me sistah.

COLOSSIANS

COLOSSIANS 1
We need to seek "*the knowledge of his will,*" Colossians 1:9 so that "*ye might walk worthy of the Lord ...*" Colossians 1:10
And how can we know His will? By reading His book. By praying and then listening.

We are appreciating our Heavenly Father "*who hath delivered us from the power of darkness, and hath translated us into the kingdom of his dear Son ...*" Colossians 1:13

This next passage basically tells us why we exist. That's nice information to have isn't it. People go through life seeking a fulfilling existence but they're just going to keep right on searching unless they get this: We were created for Him and our purpose is to glorify the Son, "*Who is the image of the invisible God, the firstborn of every creature: for by him were all things created, that are in heaven, and that are in earth, visible and invisible, whether they be thrones, or dominions, or principalities, or powers: all things were created by him, and for him."* Colossians 1:15-16

COLOSSIANS 2

All the answers come from God. We are seeking a deep, intimate knowledge of Him, *"In whom are hid all the treasures of wisdom and knowledge."* Colossians 2:3

COLOSSIANS 3

"Set your affection on things above, not on things on the earth." Colossians 3:2
I'm taking that one as an order, ladies. I love and enjoy my marriage, which is a blessing from God, and I love and enjoy my children, but we are told not to set our hearts on the things of this Earth. That includes people who are precious to us. And certainly we can't set our hearts on worldly things such as riches. We have to keep our focus upward.

Anything that meets your needs besides Christ is going to be idolatry. *"Mortify therefore your members which are upon the earth: fornication, uncleanness, inordinate af-fection, evil concupiscence* (desire), *and covetousness, which is idolatry."* Colossians 3:5

"But now ye also put off all these: anger, wrath, malice, blasphemy, filthy communication out of your mouth. Lie not one to another ..." Colossians 3:8-9
Your clothes have changed once you are a born again Christian. So you put off the old clothes, which is that ugly stuff Paul talked about before, and replace it with behavior that is of God's character. This is one way we can tell if we're dealing with a believer or not. Everybody slips up, but are we seeing a consis-tent lifestyle of anger and even wrath in someone? Are we seeing a consistent lifestyle based on malice and blasphemy, of lying and filthy communication? I'm thinking run away girlfriend. I'm right behind you.

"Let the word of Christ dwell in you richly in all wisdom." Colossians 3:16
That's what we're doing right now.

"And whatsoever ye do, do it heartily, as to the Lord, and not unto men ..." Colossians 3:23

I'm writing for the Lord, I'm working for Him, He's my boss man. If people like it too then hey that's a bonus, and it's exciting when God brings people to my writing. All both of y'all. But I'm doing it heartily for Him. It has taken me a while to understand that. It's so opposite of the world's way, to yield our work fully to God. It comes so naturally to strive, try, seek, gain, accomplish for our own purposes. We can do this, but scripture tells us it won't satisfy.

COLOSSIANS 4

We need to devote ourselves to prayer: *"Continue in prayer ..."* Colossians 4:2
And all of this "need to do this, and need to do that" we are hearing in Colossians is not a list of tedious stuff we have to do, it's not supposed to be burdensome or hard. It's not the way to gain God's favor. It's not like that. All of this rather is what we can do if we want to be joyful. It helps us live a victorious life.

"Let your speech always be gracious." Colossians 4:6
Yeah so this verse is why I really try to keep it clean and not let any profanity fly. Not only that, but sarcasm, irritated tone of voice, making fun of people, whew so many things I ask God to help me with. How am I doing? Ask my children.

———— ⚬⚬⚬ ————

THESSALONIANS

"For God hath not called us unto uncleanness, but unto holiness." 1 Thessalonians 4:7
There you go. Squeaky clean on the inside.

"Edify one another." 1 Thessalonians 5:11
Do you have a Lego builder or Minecraft fanatic in your family? Well all right then. You understand edifying. To edify others is to:

- Build people up
- Improve them
- Teach knowledge

"Quench not the Spirit." 1 Thessalonians 5:19
I think this means don't let the Holy Spirit run out. Keep thirsting for it and see your need for it. We don't ever get to think: "Okay I'm good on that Holy Spirit thing. I've had my fill." Instead, it's a lifelong, ongoing thirst.

"But the Lord is faithful, who shall stablish you, and keep you from evil." 2 Thessalonians 3:3
Anything starting with the word "but" generally means the Bible is saying, Child don't you worry, I know you've got stuff dragging you down, but the Lord is faithful. He will establish you. He will keep you from evil.

Now I did not write this, did not make this up, and I'm thinking we all need to hear this sometimes: *"For we hear that there are some which walk among you disorderly, working not at all, but are busybodies."* 2 Thessalonians 3:11
No he didn't. The Bible actually says "busybodies." Does anyone else find that amusing? It's not okay to be gossiping and in people's business, instead of being productive and hard working.

"But ye, brethren, be not weary in well doing." 2 Thessalonians 3:13
Paul calls us brethren here which is quite possibly the King James Version of, "Hay bro." Those of us devoting ourselves to God cannot weary in well doing. We just can't, it's not an option people, we must persevere. We have to think of "weary" as a verb in order to roll with this scripture. It is a choice after all, to allow ourselves to get weary and down-trodden. We fight it by continually turning every day over to God and tapping into His endless strength.

1 TIMOTHY

1 TIMOTHY 2

God our savior *"who will have all men to be saved, and to come unto the knowledge of the truth."* 1 Timothy 2:4

This verse is like the time my daughter got a Polly shoe stuck in her nose. It gets me asking "why?" a little bit. It says that God does desire for every single person to come to salvation and the knowledge of the truth. Not everyone does come to this knowledge. If He really wanted us all to come to truth, then He would have made it impossible for us not to come to the truth. But He didn't do that. So He must have thought something else (free will with a splash of predestination) was more important.

It's so handy to be a mother when you see passages like this in the Bible because you understand that you always want your child to obey, be respectful, have integrity, and eventually to come to a surrendered life to Christ. So we nudge our children toward the truth of the Bible, we expose them to it, we reveal it to them in every way we possibly can in the 18 years that we have them.

But we realize that, ultimately, a life fully yielded to God's truth is that child's choice. We cannot make him choose it. God must be very grieved sometimes as a papa, at how His own children insist on rejecting His truth after He has revealed it to us so clearly in His word and so beautifully in His creation. If we have a stubborn and rebellious child who refuses to accept the truth, then God understands: "I tried."

"Let the women learn in silence with all subjection. But I suffer not a woman to teach, nor to usurp authority over the man, but to be in silence. For Adam was first formed, then Eve. And Adam was not deceived, but the woman being deceived was in the transgression. Notwithstanding she shall be saved in childbearing, if they continue in faith and charity and holiness with sobriety." 1 Timothy 2:13-15

Now ladies, this is why my book is called *Triumphant Womanhood* rather than *Triumphant Personhood*. I take seriously this situation here, that God is telling me as a female that I'm not supposed to be teaching the general population. Elsewhere in the Bible we are told that the older women are to teach the younger women so that's my heart in my writing. I'm not teaching men, just women. Does this insult me, does this deeply offend me, cut me to my core essence and threaten to strip away my very being while causing ripples of outrage throughout my powerful femininity? Nah, I'm good with it. If it's in the Bible, that's good enough for me. We can ask why when we get to heaven. If we even care by then because wow? Heaven is going to rock.

1 TIMOTHY 6
"But godliness with contentment is great gain." 1 Timothy 6:6
Fist bump, Timothy. Put it right here.

"For the love of money is the root of all evil; which while some coveted after, they have erred from the faith, and pierced themselves through with many sorrows." 1 Timothy 6:10
So if we read this carefully it is saying the love of money is the problem, not the existence of money. I don't think I like the sound of getting pierced through with many sorrows? So I'm fixing to try not to love money over here. I love God instead. Yes sirree Bob.

TITUS AND PHILEMON

TITUS 1
"God, that cannot lie," Titus 1:2
I'm asking you sugar would I lie-ie-ie-ie to you? Sorry, retro throwback musical lyrics. God is not able to lie. If He decided He wanted to then He could. But He has decided that He won't. It's contrary to His nature. And lying should be contrary to ours as we allow ourselves to be molded into His image.

TITUS 2

"The aged women likewise, that they be in behaviour as becometh holiness, not false accusers, not given to much wine, teachers of good things; that they may teach the young women to be sober, to love their husbands, to love their children, to be discreet, chaste, keepers at home, good, obedient to their own husbands, that the word of God be not blasphemed." Titus 2:3-5

I'm feeling rather triumphant reading that passage, how about you? We are totally doing that, girls. It's what we triumphant women are all about.

PHILEMON 1
We can say to the book of Philemon: "Philemon? You are my one and only." It's only got one chapter. Philemon was a wealthy slave owner and Paul is writing to him in this short little book of the Bible.

"I thank my God, making mention of thee always in my prayers, hearing of thy love and faith, which thou hast toward the Lord Jesus and toward all the saints." Philemon 1:4-5
Wow, Paul was kind of gushy for a guy.

"I beseech thee for my son Onesimus, whom I have begotten in my bonds ..." Philemon 1:10
Paul mentored Philemon's slave Onesimus in Christ. Good job, Paul, way to witness.

HEBREWS

HEBREWS 2
We ought to *"heed to the things which we have heard, lest at any time we should let them slip."* Hebrews 2:1

HEBREWS 5
This is what Jesus did in His affliction and it is what we should do in ours: *"Who in the days of his flesh, when he had offered up prayers and supplications with strong crying and tears unto him that was able to save him from death, and was heard in that he*

feared: though he were a Son, yet learned he obedience by the things which he suffered." Hebrews 5:7-8
We can learn obedience through the things that we suffer, in turning to God.

Our culture today says that anything goes if it makes you happy and isn't hurting anyone. That's a very humanistic, unBiblical view and we cool God fearing ladies are not to espouse this view. Rather, God would like for us to discern good and evil. He basically calls us big babies until we can see the difference, in the following passage:

We do not want to be those who *"have need of milk, and not of strong meat. For every one that useth milk is unskilful in the word of righteousness: for he is a babe. But strong meat belongeth to them that are of full age, even those who by reason of use have their senses exercised to discern both good and evil."* Hebrews 5:12-14

HEBREWS 10
Well we have an argument for going to church here, or at least having some sort of fellowship with other believers: *"And let us consider one another to provoke unto love and to good works: not forsaking the assembling of ourselves together, as the manner of some is; but exhorting one another; and so much the more as ye see the day approaching."* Hebrews 10:24-25

HEBREWS 11
"Now faith is the substance of things hoped for, the evidence of things not seen." Hebrews 11:1

"...the worlds were framed by the word of God." Putting the entire universe in a picture frame with His words, wow. Paul is saying all the heavens and planets were created when God spoke. He said it, and it happened. I wish that would happen when I need to make dinner. Speak and the tacos appeareth.

Paul says, *"without faith it is impossible to please Him."* Hebrews 11:6. This whole chapter is pretty cool with Paul taking us through all the dudes in the Old

Testament who were faith personified. All the heavy hitters: Noah, Abraham, Joseph, Moses, all those guys.

HEBREWS 12

"Now no chastening for the present seemeth to be joyous, but grievous, nevertheless afterward it yieldeth the peaceable fruit of righteousness unto them which are exercised thereby. Wherefore lift up the hands which hang down, and the feeble knees..." Hebrews 12:11-12
The Bible is so descriptive, talking about lifting up our hands that hang down and strengthening our feeble knees. We're stronger than that, we can do this thing even when God allows chastening in our life.

HEBREWS 13

"Let your conversation be without covetousness, and be content with such things as ye have: for he hath said, I will never leave thee, nor forsake thee. So that we may boldly say, the Lord is my helper, and I will not fear what man shall do unto me." Hebrews 13:5-6
Huge passage for ladies right there. We are so bad about wanting what other girls have. We have to be content and I'm taking that passage right there as an order, not a suggestion. God's saying, no worries, I've got you.

———— ∞ ————

JAMES

JAMES 1

"My brethren, count it all joy when ye fall into divers temptations: knowing this, that the trying of your faith worketh patience." That patience can also be thought of as "endurance" or "steadfastness." James 1:3
The rough junk that God allows in our life is actually the good stuff. It's what makes us patient.

"If any of you lack wisdom, let him ask of God, that giveth to all men liberally, and upbraideth not, and it shall be given him." James 1:5

Sometimes we think we have to figure out challenging situations. God just told us that He will give us wisdom whenever we ask Him.

"Let every man be swift to hear, slow to speak, slow to wrath." James 1:19

"But be ye doers of the word, and not hearers only, deceiving your own selves." James 1:22

"If any man among you seem to be religious, and bridleth not his tongue, but deceiveth his own heart, this man's religion is vain." James 1:26
As in worthless.

JAMES 2
"...so faith without works is dead also." James 2:26
It's kind of like, if you watch a cooking show, and then say, "Oh man that was awesome. What's for dinner?" We can't have only the belief in our hearts, we have to get up off our you-know-whats and ask God how He wants us to put that faith into action. Raising children and being supportive of a husband are tremendously valuable examples of works.

JAMES 4
Before we go praying for a beach house and a personal chef after seeing that "ask and ye shall receive" thing earlier, check this out: *"Ye ask, and receive not, because ye ask amiss, that ye may consume it upon your lusts."* James 4:3

"God resisteth the proud." James 4:6
Oh dear, I'd better check on a regular basis and make sure that is not me.

JAMES 5
"Elias was a man subject to like passions as we are, and he prayed earnestly that it might not rain: and it rained not on the earth by the space of three years and six months. And he prayed again, and the heaven gave rain, and the earth brought forth her fruit." James 5:17-18.

This is telling me two things. At least two. Prayer works. And also, James knew the scriptures. He's quoting the Old Testament.

———— ∞∞ ————

1 AND 2 PETER

1 PETER 2

"Endure grief, suffering wrongfully. For what glory is it, when ye be buffeted for your faults, ye shall take it patiently? But if, when ye do well, and suffer for it, ye take it patiently, this is acceptable with God. For even hereunto were ye called." 1 Peter 2:19-21

1 PETER 3

"Likewise, ye wives, be in subjection to your own husbands; that, if any obey not the word, they also may without the word be won by the conversation of the wives, while they behold your chaste conversation coupled with fear." 1 Peter 3:1-2

God can inspire the men through their wives.

"For the eyes of the Lord are over the righteous, and his ears are open unto their prayers, but the face of the Lord is against them that do evil." 1 Peter 3:12

Peter is quoting some Psalms here, really good ones I might add, and I didn't spend six years learning Hebrew to tell you that, I don't know Hebrew, it's all Greek to me, and you know I had to stick that joke in here at least one time. I'm just saying I'm no theologian (really?) and anyone can figure stuff like that out by staring at the footnotes in her Bible.

"Be ready always to give an answer to every man that asketh you a reason of the hope that is in you with meekness and fear." 1 Peter 3:15

1 PETER 5

"Casting all your care on Him, for He careth for you." 1 Peter 5:8

I like that. Cheer up. He careth.

———— ∞ ————

1 AND 3 JOHN

1 JOHN 1

"If we say that we have fellowship with him, and walk in darkness, we lie, and do not the truth. But if we walk in the light, as he is in the light, we have fellowship one with another, and the blood of Jesus Christ his Son cleanseth us from all sin." 1 John 1:6-7

"If we confess our sins, he is faithful and just to forgive us our sins, and to cleanse us from all unrighteousness." 1 John 1:9

There's that grace thing where if we've messed up in life, and we all have, He cleanses all our yuck once we confess it to Him.

1 JOHN 2

"And hereby we do know that we know him, if we keep his commandments." 1 John 2:3

If I ever start to wonder, now do I really know the Lord? Yep I pretty much do because I honor Him with my life. When we say commandments here we don't just mean the Ten Commandments, although we like those. We mean all of God's ways.

Here are some powerfully inspiring words just for you: *"...ye are strong, and the word of God abideth in you, and ye have overcome the wicked one."* 1 John 2:14

1 JOHN 3

"Marvel not, my brethren, if the world hate you." 1 John 3:13

I'm not marveling. Head's up, marvel not, the world will hate you. And I'm good with that. I'd rather be hated by the world and approved of by God than ... the other way around. Chill up my spine just then.

1 JOHN 4

"If a man say, I love God, and hateth his brother, he is a liar; for he that loveth not his brother whom he hath seen, how can he love God whom he hath not seen?" 1 John 4:20

Rather makes you want to evaluate your relationships and make sure you're not harboring any hatred toward anyone.

1 JOHN 5
"*...but he that is begotten of God keepeth himself, and that wicked one toucheth him not.*" 1 John 5:18
He just said: Satan you can't touch us!

3 JOHN
"*...thy soul prospereth.*" 3 John 1:2. It is well with your soul.

"*Beloved, follow not that which is evil, but that which is good.*" 3 John 1:11
Whenever the Bible says that "beloved," it's like, "sweety?" Beloved? Don't be following evil. Kay?

JUDE
You know? The book of Jude is great, because it rhymes with "dude."

This Jude dude talks of evil people and says, "*Woe unto them! For they have gone in the way of Cain.*" Jude 1:11
They went all Cain on us. They Cain'd out. There was some Cain-ing going on with these people. They were completely Cain-i-fied. It was just Cain-uh-licious. This is not a compliment. Cain was that guy in Genesis who was consumed with hatred and killed his brother Abel. This is where we get the expression "raising Cain," but, frankly, I like all of mine better.

"*Now unto him that is able to keep you from falling, and to present you faultless before the presence of his glory with exceeding joy...*" Jude 1:24

REVELATION

Let's revel in Revelation for a while, shall we? Now the root of that word Revelation is going to be "reveal," as in what God is trying to reveal to us will happen in the future, in the very last book of the Bible. It is prophetic.

REVELATION 1

"Behold, he cometh with the clouds, and every eye shall see him..." Revelation 1:7. Jesus is going to come again, only not in a manger this time around.

REVELATION 2

Jesus talking here: *"I know thy works, and thy labour, and thy patience, and how thou canst not bear them which are evil, and thou has tried them which say they are apostles, and are not, and hast found them liars."* Revelation 2:2

Theology without intimacy with God doesn't please Him. On the other hand, intimacy without theology is just as scary because we could be very easily led astray. Theology + Intimacy = Get down get funky we are right on.

"Nevertheless I have somewhat against thee, because thou has left thy first love. Remember therefore from whence thou art fallen..." Revelation 2:4-5

REVELATION 3

"I know thy works, that thou art neither cold nor hot: I would thou wert cold or hot. So then because thou art lukewarm, and neither cold nor hot, I will spue thee out of my mouth." Revelation 3:15

Are you checking to make sure I didn't make that up? These are the sorts of scriptures that never make it onto Christian stationery and calendars. Yes Jesus just said He would spue us out of his mouth if we keep being lukewarm in our faith.

"As many as I love, I rebuke and chasten; be zealous therefore, and repent. Behold, I stand at the door, and knock: if any man hear my voice, and open the door, I will come in to him, and will sup with him, and he with me." Revelation 3:19-20

Was sup? He's going to sup with us. Righteous.

REVELATION 7

"*Therefore are they before the throne of God, and serve him day and night in his temple: and he that sitteth on the throne shall dwell among them. They shall hunger no more, neither thirst any more, neither shall the sun light on them, nor any heat. For the Lamb which is in the midst of the throne shall feed them, and shall lead them unto living fountains of waters: and God shall wipe away all tears from their eyes.*" Revelation 7:15-17

REVELATION 11

"*And when they shall have finished their testimony...*" Revelation 11:7
God is still building your testimony and mine. It's a lifelong process.

REVELATION 12

Now we are speaking of "*that old serpent, called the Devil, and Satan, which deceiveth the whole world...for the accuser of our brethren is cast down, which accused them before our God day and night.*" Revelation 12:9-10
Satan can't change our salvation, so he tries to make us insecure through unbelief. Nice try.

"*...for the devil is come down unto you having great wrath, because he knoweth that he hath but a short time.*" Revelation 12:12
Poor ol' Satan's time is short and he is furious about this. It's like a toddler when he knows it's almost time to leave the toy store and he starts pitching a fit. His fun is almost over and it didn't quite go his way. That's our loser man Satan. I really hate it for him. Actually not.

REVELATION 19

Speaking here of Jesus' second coming: "*Behold a white horse, and he that sat upon him was called Faithful and True, and in righteousness he doth judge and make war.*" Revelation 19:11

"*And his name is called The Word of God.*" Revelation 19:13

"...*a name written KING OF KINGS AND LORD OF LORDS.*" Revelation 19:16
I didn't add the all-caps. It's written exactly that way in the Bible. This is what is going to be written on Jesus when He returns.

REVELATION 22
In Revelation 22:20, Jesus is speaking, and I believe that you and I are very pleased to hear this: *"Surely I come quickly."*

Sources

---

1. Adams, John Quincy. *Bible Lessons of John Quincy Adams for His Son.* 1811. Printed 2007 by Vision Forum.

2. Aristotle. *Nicomachean Ethics,* Book II, Chapter 1. 350 BC. From *Introduction to Aristotle* edited by Richard McKeon. 1947.

3. Augustine. *Confessions.* Translated 1961 by R S. Pine-Coffin.

4. Austen, Jane. *Pride and Prejudice.* 1813.

5. Barrow, John. *A Better Way.* 2013.

6. *Biblica Sacra Vulgata.* 400 AD. Translated 2007 by Institute for NT Textual Resea.

7. Botkin and Botkin. *It's (Not That) Complicated.* 2011.

8. Cothran, Martin. *Traditional Logic.* 2000.

9. Coulter, Ann. *Guilty: Liberal Victims and Their Assault on America.* 2009.

10. Cox, Carol. *The Way Back Home.* 2014.

11. *Creation Magazine.* Creation.com. 2013.

12. Dillow and Pintus. *Intimate Issues.* 2000.

13. Fourman, Brian. *Luke1428.com.* 2014.

14. Fugate, Richard. *What the Bible Says About Child Training.* 1996.

The Pond House
Bloomington, MN

15. *The Geneva Bible.* 1599.
16. Godawa, Brian. *Hollywood Worldviews: Watching Films with Wisdom and Discernment.* 2009.
17. Graves, Dan. *Scientists of Faith: 48 Biographies of Historic Scientists and Their Christian Faith.* 1996.
18. Ham, Ken. *The Answers Book.* 1990.
19. Harris, Joshua. *I Kissed Dating Goodbye.* 1997.
20. Homer. *Odyssey of Homer.* 700 BC. Translated 2007 by Richmond Lattimore.
21. Hopkins, Diane. *Best Homeschool Secrets.* 2005.
22. Hoth, Iva. *The Picture Bible.* 1998.
23. *The King James Bible.* 1611. Thomas Nelson Publishers. 1989.
24. *The Koran.* 630 AD. Translated 2004 by John Medows Rodwell.
25. Landis, Annie. *God Made a Way.* 2013.
26. Lewis, C.S. *Mere Christianity.* 1955.
27. Lowe, Cheryl. *First Form Latin series.* 2010.
28. Martin, Judith. *Miss Manners' Guide to Excruciatingly Correct Behavior.* 1982.
29. *McGuffey Readers,* 1830s.
30. Moore, Beth. *Daniel.* 2006.
31. *The New-England Primer,* Boston 1690.
32. Nickel, James. *Mathematics: Is God Silent?* 2001.
33. Orwell, George. *1984.* 1948.
34. Pearl, Debi. *Created to Be His Help Meet.* 2004.
35. Phillips, Doug. *George Washington: America's Joshua.* 2007.
36. Plato. *Republic.* 380 BC. Translated 1993 by Robin Waterfield.
37. Prabhupada. *Bhagavad-gita As It Is.* 1970.
38. Price, Weston. *Nutrition and Physical Degeneration.* 1939.
39. Ramsey, Dave. *Financial Peace.* 1997.
40. Reed, Anna. *Life of Washington.* 1842. Reprinted 2009 by Attic Books.
41. Schlessinger, Laura. *The Proper Care & Feeding of Husbands.* 2004.
42. Spielvogel, Jackson J. *Western Civilization.* 2009.
43. Strunk & White, *The Elements of Style.* 1918.

44. Turner, Wayne. *BibleTrack.org.* 2014.

45. *The Wall Street Journal Magazine.* December 2014/January 2015.

46. *The Wall Street Journal.* 2014 and 2015.

47. Webster, Noah. *American Dictionary of the English Language.* 1828. Reprinted 1995 by Rosalie J. Slater.

48. Wilson, Douglas. *Omnibus: Biblical and Classical Civilizations.* 2005.

ADDITIONAL SOURCES

49. Coleman, Joshua. *The Lazy Husband: How to Get Men to Do More Parenting and Housework,* 2005.

50. Mohler, Albert. *The Subtle Body — Should Christians Practice Yoga?* AlbertMohler.com. 2010.

51. *The Chicago Manual of Style.* 1993.

52. Cru.org. *How to Know God Personally.* 2015.

53. Hoover.archives.gov. *Pioneering Journeys of the Ingalls Family.* 2015.

54. Bluedorn, Nathaniel. *The Thinking Toolbox.* 2005.

55. OurHerbGarden.com. *History of Basil.* 2015.

56. Riley, Jason L. *Race Relations and Law Enforcement.* Hillsdale College's *Imprimis.* January 2015.

Acknowledgements

—⁓⁓⁓—

Highest thanks go to my Lord and Savior Jesus Christ, who takes me from tragic to triumphant on a daily basis. Thank you Father for not letting my jar of oil run out. Deep appreciation goes to my loving husband and precious children for their support, enthusiasm, strength and patience. I would have hardly known how to put a subject and verb together without the upbringing and education from my devoted parents, Mr. and Mrs. Ralph Cox.

Heartfelt thanks to Leigh Wagner, my sister in Christ, for her love and prayers. Warm thanks to Pam Davis and her ladies' group for believing in me. Thank you to the ladies at my church and all the wise women of God who have had an impact on my life. Special thanks to Jennifer Brett, Ann Severance and Chris Snell for giving me confidence and hope. Many thanks to Mr. and Mrs. Avery Cox, III for sharing their story and giving all the glory to God.

Thank you to Patrick Fisher for the use of his Pond House drawing. Original charcoal drawing of dog by Carol Cox. Back cover photo by René Victor Bidez Photography. Hair by Jaylee Williams of Kelli Paul Salon. About the Author family photo by Nathan Gehman Photography.

I am so grateful to every reader for allowing me to speak into her life. Without you, I would be talking to myself.

ABOUT THE AUTHOR

—⚬⚬⚬—

Jennifer Cox Houlihan, 43, is a homemaker who has been married for 19 years to her military pilot husband, Lt. Colonel Philip "Woody" Houlihan, who flies C-130s for the Air National Guard and the MD-88 for Delta Air Lines. They live in Georgia with their five homeschooled children: Rebecca, 2; Maggie, 6; Claire, 13; Elizabeth, 15; and Patrick, 17. Columns from Mrs. Houlihan have been published in *National Guard Magazine, The Atlanta Journal-Constitution* newspaper and *The Classical Teacher.* She has a degree in journalism from the University of North Carolina at Chapel Hill, where she was a member of the UNC Loreleis, the a capella singing group. Find her at TriumphantChicks.com.

The Houlihan family

25111382R00177

Made in the USA
San Bernardino, CA
18 October 2015